MARXISM AND THE QUESTION OF THE ASIATIC MODE OF PRODUCTION

STUDIES IN SOCIAL HISTORY

issued by the

INTERNATIONAL INSTITUTE OF SOCIAL HISTORY
AMSTERDAM

MARXISM AND THE QUESTION OF THE ASIATIC MODE OF PRODUCTION

by

MARIAN SAWER

MARTINUS NIJHOFF / THE HAGUE / 1977

The publishing of this volume has been made possible by the financial support of the University of Adelaide and the International Institute of Social History.

ISBN 90 247 2027 3

PRINTED IN THE NETHERLANDS

CONTENTS

PREFACE

Wherever possible in this monograph I have referred to English translations of works originally appearing in other languages. Where this has not been possible, for example with Russian material, I have followed the Library of Congress system of transliteration, but omitted the diacritics. I have also retained the conventional use of 'y' for the ending of certain Russian proper names (e.g., Trotsky not Trotskii). In accordance with the policy of using existing English translations, I have referred to the Martin Nicolaus translation of Marx's *Grundrisse*, which is relatively faithful to the text. (The *Grundrisse*, although the Dead Sea Scroll of Marxism, bear all the characteristics of a rough draft, characteristics which are preserved in the Nicolaus translation.) The term 'Marxian' has been employed in the conventional way in this book, to distinguish the views of Marx and Engels from those of their 'Marxist' followers.

In preparing this work I have received bibliographical assistance from Professor Israel Getzler, now of the Hebrew University, and critical assistance from Mr Bruce McFarlane of the University of Adelaide and especially from Professor Eugene Kamenka of the Australian National University. Professor Jean Chesneaux of the Sorbonne, as one of the leading participants in the more recent debates discussed here, provided me with some further insight into the issues, and Professor K.A. Wittfogel of Columbia also supplied some valuable information.

My thanks to Professor Shlomo Avineri of the Hebrew University, Professor Graeme Duncan of East Anglia, Dr T.H. Rigby of the Australian National University and Professor Maximilien Rubel of Paris for their comments on an earlier version. Finally, I am indebted to Mr Charles B. Timmer of the International Institute of Social History for his expert editorial guidance in the final stages. Remaining infelicities are all my own work.

ABBREVIATIONS

MEGA	Marx and Engels, *Historisch-kritische Gesamtausgabe*, ed. D. Rjazanov/V. Adoratskij, Frankfurt/Berlin, Marx-Engels-Archiv Verlagsgesellschaft/Marx-Engels, Verlag, 1927–1932.
Werke	Marx and Engels, *Werke*, 39 vols., 2 supplementary vols., Berlin, Dietz, 1956–68.
MESC	Marx and Engels, *Selected Correspondence*, 2nd edn, Moscow, Progress, 1965.
MESW	Marx and Engels, *Selected Works*, 2 vols., Moscow, Foreign Languages Publishing House, 1951–55.
Capital	Marx, *Capital: A Critique of Political Economy*, 3 vols., N.Y., International Publishers, 1967.
EPM	Economic and Philosophical Manuscripts, 1844.
Grundrisse	Marx, *Grundrisse. Foundations of the Critique of Political Economy (Rough Draft)*, tr. Martin Nicolaus, Harmondsworth, Penguin, 1973.
Karl Marx on Colonialism and Modernization	*Karl Marx on Colonialism and Modernization*, ed. Shlomo Avineri, N.Y., Anchor Books, 1969.
The Russian Menace to Europe	Marx and Engels, *The Russian Menace to Europe*, ed. Paul W. Blackstock and Bert F. Hoselitz, London, Allen and Unwin, 1953.
N.Y.D.T.	*New York Daily Tribune.*
Ex Libris	*Ex Libris Marx und Engels; Schicksal und Verzeichnis einer Bibliothek*, ed. B. Kaiser, Berlin, Dietz, 1967.
Rubel	M. Rubel, *Bibliographie des Oeuvres de Karl Marx*, Paris, Marcel Rivière, 1956; Supplément, 1960.
Collected Works	V.I. Lenin, *Collected Works*, London, Lawrence and Wishart, 1960– (Vol. 40 appeared in 1968).
Selected Works	V.I. Lenin, *Selected Works*, 2 vols., Moscow, Foreign Languages Publishing House, 1950–52.
Sochineniia	G.V. Plekhanov, *Sochineniia*, 2nd edn, 24 vols., ed. D. Riazanov, Moscow, 1923–27.
History	G.V. Plekhanov, *Istoriia russkoi obshchestvennoi mysli*, Parts One and Two, *Sochineniia*, Vol. XX.
IISG	*Internationaal Instituut voor Sociale Geschiedenis*, Amsterdam.
AMP	*Asiatic Mode of Production.*
C.E.R.M.	Centre d'Etudes et de Recherches Marxistes.

INTRODUCTION

The past decade has seen a dramatic revival of the concept of the
Asiatic mode of production within Marxism. This has been one aspect
of the emergence of polycentrism, and of the accompanying attempt to
break down the 'theoretical sclerosis' induced by Stalinism. It has had
far-reaching implications for Marxist theory and practice – implications
that give the subject of this monograph contemporary relevance as
well as historical interest.

The present work attempts to explore in some detail the origin,
development, and consequences for Marxist historiography, of the
concept of the Asiatic mode of production as found in the work of
Marx and Engels and in subsequent Marxist writings. In doing so it has
to take into account the political dimensions of the concept which have
led to the controversies surrounding it both in the past and in the
present.

The idea of the particularistic nature of Asiatic society, already
present in Aristotle, was developed in political terms by Montesquieu,
and in politico-economic terms by the Physiocrats and the British
political economists; and the idea was taken over by Marx in the concept of an Asiatic mode of production. The present work begins by
tracing that development, and the development of an associated idea,
namely the idea of European superiority and of the universal character
of European civilisation. I attempt to show that Marx also took over
the latter idea, in the form of the belief that Western capitalism was
destined to universalise itself both conceptually and concretely, and to
'overcome' non-Western forms of historical development.

Because the place and functions of these ideas in the thought of Marx
and Engels have been, and are, a matter of debate, the account of the
origins of the concept of the Asiatic mode of production is followed by
an analysis of precisely how Marx and Engels used the concept and

what role it played in their work. The analysis includes an account of the manner in which the concept came to be dropped, for political reasons internal and external to the socialist movement, and in the interests of simplifying Marxism into a single universal account of human social development.

From there we move on to a study of one of the issues which the 'Asiatic' concept raises for historical materialism, namely the issue of the role of geographical factors in historical development. This problem is inherent in Marx's concept of the Asiatic mode of production, which is the only mode of production he explicitly states as being geographically circumscribed. The discussion leads on to the conception of alternative forms of historical development, determined by specific geographical, historical and ethnographic circumstances. Such an approach to Marxist historiography, associated with the concept of the Asiatic mode of production, is exemplified in a comparatively unknown work by the 'father of Russian Marxism', G.V. Plekhanov, *The History of Russian Social Thought*. Hence I analyse in some detail this work, which raises many of the problems involved in reconciling Marxism with the idea of the coexistence of different lines of historical development. One of those problems concerns the role of non-economic factors in the appropriation of surplus value in pre-capitalist production, and in providing the general dynamic of society. Plekhanov, like Marx, however, saw the coexistence of different forms of historical development as being brought to an end by the universalising impact of Western capitalism. Trotsky, on the other hand, at least in his earlier writings, was to foreshadow more recent Marxist theorising allowing for, and even welcoming, non-Western and non-capitalist forms of industrialisation. He also foreshadowed recent theories that such forms of industrialisation tend to lead to non-Western forms of socialism, based on non-Western historical experience combined with modern industrial technology.

Thus we come to the crux of the argument presented here: the fact that human history, on Marx's own account of it, cannot be presented as a single sequence of successive stages, each the necessary outcome of its predecessor, in accordance with the immanent logic of the development of productive forces. As I show, Marx believed that at least three alternative forms of historical development from the primitive community were possible, and only one of these, at first sight, contains within it a necessary set of subsequent stages. This eliminates, or at least conflicts with, the quasi-teleological view of world history often attributed to Marx, that world history consisted in a unitary process of development leading inevitably to socialism – and to socialism in a form which was the culmination of Western European civilisation (reconciling individualism with ideals of community, etc.), and also universal in both scope and content.

The new approach to Marxist historiography, which has been stimulated by the revival of the concept of the Asiatic mode of production, suggests the historical existence of various alternative forms of social production. These include forms identified by Marx, such as the classical, feudal and Asiatic, but also some not identified by Marx but which appear to incorporate sufficient distinctive features to warrant being described as separate modes of production – e.g., the tentative models of African and Central Asian modes of production.

Furthermore, the new approach to Marxist historiography implies the belief that the historical differences which it identifies will not be submerged in either universal capitalism or universal socialism, but rather, are likely to be preserved both as different roads to socialism and in different forms of socialism. This belief is linked with a second element in the new Marxist historiography, the abandoning of the rather dubious asset of 'historical necessity' and the stress on the role of social choice (or revolutionary consciousness) and social struggle in bringing socialism into being. The role of revolutionary consciousness is not part of the theme of the present monograph, but it is mentioned here because, together with the concept of alternative lines of historical development, it adds up to the post-Stalinist emphasis in Marxism on the openness of history. And it is the compatibility of Marxism with the idea of the openness of history which this monograph seeks to establish.

CHAPTER I

THE PREHISTORY OF THE MARXIAN CONCEPT OF THE ASIATIC MODE OF PRODUCTION

When the Greeks began to categorise political systems more than three thousand years ago, they introduced the idea, since recurrent in European political thought, of a political system specific to Asia[1] – that of Oriental despotism. Despotism has been traditionally considered a principle of political organisation foreign to Europe, although European rulers have frequently been attacked for attempting to transplant it there artificially. The dominance of this type of political organisation in Asia, on the other hand, has been explained by European theorists in terms of various ethnographic, geographic and historical factors held to be specific to the East.

The idea of a typically Eastern politico-economic system fundamentally distinct from European forms of social and political development has been seriously undermined by twentieth century intellectual developments, by the vast increase in the range and complexity of specialised knowledge of the countries concerned, and by the search for new categories of social organisation which cut across the distinction between East and West.

Nevertheless, one influential form of this idea, that contained in the Marxian concept of the Asiatic mode of production has, if anything, gone through a remarkable revival in recent years. This situation may at first sight seem anomalous, in that Marxism has often been taken to establish a universal pattern of development common to all societies, and, indeed, in many respects lends itself to such an interpretation. It is necessary to look at the reasons that led Marx to incorporate the idea of Asiatic particularism into his theory of history, at the way he did so, and at the impact of such an incorporation on Marxist historiography in general.

[1] With the usual exception of Japan, once Europe had become acquainted with that country.

The following account is intended to bring out the sources of Marx's analysis of non-Western society, rather than to be an exhaustive description of the cumulative body of belief about Asia on which Marx was drawing. In general the account is restricted to those writers who also contributed to the development of a *systematic model* of Oriental society, although it includes some description of the political functions the concept has served in the past – without which it is impossible to understand the emotional overtones which still surround the concept.

THE LEGACY OF ARISTOTLE

The concept of Oriental despotism as Marx encountered it in the mid-nineteenth century had its original source in Aristotle. It was Aristotle who systematised the distinction between Western and non-Western forms of political organisation as observed and polemicised by the Greeks during the preceding centuries of conflict with the Persians. In the *Politics* the distinction is presented as follows:

> There is another sort of monarchy not uncommon among the barbarians, which nearly resembles tyranny. But this is both legal and hereditary. For barbarians being more servile in character than Hellenes, and Asiatics than Europeans, do not rebel against a despotic government. Such royalties have the nature of tyrannies because the people are by nature slaves; but there is no danger of their being overthrown, for they are hereditary and legal. Wherefore also their guards are such as a king and not such as a tyrant would employ, that is to say, they are composed of citizens, whereas the guards of tyrants are mercenaries.[2]

According to Aristotle, the form of political organisation found among the barbarians (i.e. non-Greek speakers) or Asiatics was notable for the fact that the citizens had no rights *vis à vis* their sovereign, but rather were a 'community of slaves'.[3] Such a form of government differed from the tyrannies known among the Greeks, in that it was the rule rather than the exception: it was endowed with legitimacy, enjoyed the acquiescence of its subjects, and therefore had a stability unknown to the tyrannies of the Greeks.

Aristotle's concept of Asiatic government was reintroduced into European political thought with the translation of the *Politics* into Latin in the thirteenth century. New translations and commentaries

---

[2] Aristotle, *Politica*, tr. Benjamin Jowett in Vol. X of *The Works of Aristotle*, Oxford, Clarendon Press, 1921, reprinted 1946, Book III, Ch. 14, § 1285a.
[3] *Ibid.*, Book I, Ch. 2, § 1252b. Cf. Hegel's 'general slavery'.

were to appear at an increasing rate throughout the subsequent four centuries, during which time the *Politics* remained a focal point for study of the principles and forms of government.

In the thirteenth and fourteenth centuries the concept of despotic government was rendered by various forms of the Greek word 'despotes'.[4] With the rise of humanism, however, in the fifteenth and sixteenth centuries, such terms were temporarily banished from use as they were deemed incompatible with scholarly Latin.[5] Attempts were made to represent the concept by a more familiar terminology based on the Latin 'dominus' or the French 'seigneur'. These attempts were relatively short-lived, the terms 'seigneur' and 'dominus' having the disadvantage of being closely associated with Western political forms and indeed with contemporary European feudal institutions.[6] If there was one thing that all writers on despotism were agreed upon, it was that despotism was not a political system native to Europe.

In the fourteenth century the concept of Oriental despotism was already playing a role in the political controversies current in Europe. Marsilius of Padua and William of Occam, for example, took pains to explicate the concept in the course of their attacks on the power of papacy.[7] Thus the *Defensor Pacis* follows Aristotle in attributing the despotic system of government to Asia and then uses the term, and its associations, to criticise the attempts of the Popes to exercise unlimited power.[8]

It is in this period that the concept of (Asiatic) despotism becomes more precisely linked with the absence of private-property rights. This idea had been implicit in Western thinking about the Asiatic system of government since classical Greece, for example, in the Greeks' description of the claims of the Persian kings to absolute lordship over land and water. However the conceptualisation of the despot presented in the words 'despotes potest uti sibi subiectis & *bonis eorum* ad

---

[4] Richard Koebner's article, 'Despot and Despotism: Vicissitudes of a Political Term', *Journal of the Warburg and Courtauld Institutes*, Vol. XIV (1951), pp. 275–302, contains an excellent account of the fortunes of the term.

[5] By the seventeenth century they had made a come-back. See, for example, the use by Hobbes of derivatives such as 'despotical'.

[6] Whereas 'dominus' was one of the titles of the Roman emperors, 'despotes' was one of the titles of the Byzantine emperors, whose political system was already seen as more 'Eastern' in tone.

[7] William of Occam, *Dialogus de imperio et pontificia potestate* (facsimile of the 1495–1496 edition of Occam's works), London, Gregg Press, 1962, Pars III, Tract. I, Lib. II, Cap. 6; Marsilius of Padua, *Defensor Pacis*, Discourse I, Ch. IX, § 4, 5; Ch. XII, § 6; Ch. XIV § 3, Ch. XVI, § 16.

[8] Marsilius of Padua, *Defensor Pacis*, ed. C.W. Previté-Orton, Cambridge U.P., 1928, Discourse I, Ch. XVI, § 16.

propriam utilitatem'[9] does not seem to appear before the fourteenth century.

From this time onward the absence of private-property rights, or the weakly developed nature of these, becomes a standard component of the concept of Oriental despotism drawn from Aristotle; the despot is able to treat 'des biens des subiects comme des siens' (Bodin). The idea of the absence of private-property rights in Asiatic or non-Western society was soon to be further reinforced by the Western perception of Islamic law. According to Western observers, in Islamic countries the title to all land was vested in the ruler, or conqueror, and there existed no real private property in land.

By the beginning of the sixteenth century the figure of the Turkish sultan was beginning to appear as the epitome of the 'Asiatic' despot as known from Aristotle.[10] Niccolò Machiavelli, for example, did not make any direct comments on Aristotle's concept of Asiatic despotism, but he did draw up an interesting distinction between principalities in which there existed a hereditary nobility and principalities in which there existed only a service nobility. The latter category he felt was illustrated by the Persian kingdom of Darius, and in Machiavelli's own times by the Turkish empire. Machiavelli described the two types of kingship as follows:

... all principalities known to history are governed in one of two ways, either by a prince to whom everyone is subservient and whose ministers, with his favour and permission, help govern, or by a prince and by nobles whose rank is established not by favour of the prince but by their ancient lineage. Such nobles have states and subjects of their own, and these acknowledge them as their lords and bear a natural affection towards them. In states governed by a prince and his servants, the prince has greater authority. For throughout the whole country he alone is recognized as being entitled to allegiance; anyone else is obeyed as a minister and an official for whom no special love is felt.[11]

Machiavelli's distinction between a function-based elite and a hered-

[9] William of Occam, *Dialogus de imperio et pontificia potestate, op.cit.,* Pars III, Tract. I, Lib. II, Cap. 6, p. CXCIII.
[10] The figure of the Persian king had lingered anachronistically up to the sixteenth century as the paradigm of the despot, thanks to Aristotle.
[11] Niccolò Machiavelli, *The Prince,* tr. George Bull, Harmondsworth, Penguin, 1971, Ch. IV, pp. 44–45. While praising Machiavelli's structural distinction, Hume was to have some reservations about its application to Persia: 'The more ancient Persians, whose manners are described by Xenophon, were a free people and had nobility.' Even under Darius, when the government was conducted in many respects after the Eastern manner, this 'was not carried so far as to extirpate all nobility, and confound all ranks and orders. It left men, who were still great, by themselves or their family, independent of their office and commission.' (David Hume, 'That Politics may be reduced to a Science', *Essays, Moral, Political and Literary,* ed. T.H. Green and T.H. Grose, Vol. 1, London, Longmans, 1889, p. 104, fn. added to 1753–4 edition.

itary elite was to become an accepted component of the concept of Asiatic despotism as received from Aristotle. The feudal opponents of encroaching absolutism were to depict the existence of a hereditary nobility as the major bulwark against the introduction of an Asiatic type of political system, a system that was identified with the barbarian and infidel menace to Europe – the Turk.

Other sixteenth-century writers who helped to popularise the identification of the Sultan of Turkey with Aristotle's Asiatic despot were Loys le Roy and Jean Bodin. In the *Six Books of the Republic* Bodin used not only the Turkish empire, but also Muscovy, Tartary, and Ethiopia, as contemporary illustrations of Aristotle's concept.[12]

Bodin divides kingship into three main types, largely derived from Aristotle, namely royal, tyrannical and 'seigneurial' (despotic). The royal monarch or king is one who respects the laws of nature and hence respects the liberty and property of his subjects.[13] The seigneurial monarch, on the other hand, is master of both the persons and the property of his subjects.

In his discussion of seigneurial monarchy Bodin describes it as the first form of government known to man, and comments on the longevity of this form of political rule. He moves definitely beyond Aristotle in providing a reason for the development of this form of government which is more than the flat assertion of the servile character of Asiatics (although Bodin also indulges in the latter). He wrote that in this type of monarchy, 'the prince is lord and master of both the possessions and persons of his subjects by right of conquest in a just war'.[14] It was its origin in just war that differentiated seigneurial monarchy from tyranny, and gave it a legitimacy that pure tyranny could not enjoy. Bodin's derivation of despotism from the right of conquest was to become a standard explanation of the origin of Eastern forms of government in later centuries (cf. Richard Jones, *infra* p. 38).

Another interesting aspect of Bodin's work is his *ambivalence* towards the concept of Oriental despotism, an ambivalence reflecting his role as the first major theorist of the movement towards absolutism in Europe.

---

[12] Jean Bodin, *Les six Livres de la République* (facsimile of Paris, 1583 edition), Aalen, Scientia, 1961, Book II, Ch. II, 'De la Monarchie Seigneuriale', pp. 270–279. Bodin believed the despotic system to exist commonly in Asia and Africa, but in Europe only in Muscovy and the Turkish empire. See *ibid.*, p. 274.

[13] *Ibid.*, Book II, Ch. III, 'De la Monarchie Royale', p. 279.

[14] M.J. Tooley's translation, in his abridged edition entitled *Six Books of the Commonwealth*, Oxford, Blackwell, n.d., Book II, Ch. II, pp. 56–57 (*Les six Livres de la République, op.cit.*, p. 273).

In some later protagonists of absolutism this ambivalence was replaced by direct admiration for the system of Asiatic despotism.[15]

Thus Bodin praises the Turkish system of providing non-heritable service-lands and privileges for the class of military servitors.[16] He uses the Turkish system as a counter-example to the contemporary system of feudal privilege in Europe, though he presents his argument in the form of the necessity to return fiefs and feudal lands to their original purpose, rather than in the form of the necessity to copy a foreign paradigm. Although Bodin approved of the Turkish timariot system, as a French provincial lawyer and a good 'bourgeois' possessive individualist he could not countenance the further invasion of private property rights which for him the Eastern system represented.

TRAVELLERS' TALES

While Aristotle's ideas on Asiatic government were still being discussed and annotated, the European 'discovery' of the Far East had been taking place. By the end of the sixteenth century, the so-called 'Century of Discovery', a considerable amount of evidence had been accumulated by merchants and missionaries concerning these previously semi-fabulous regions. The burden of the reports reaching home was that Asia was dominated by absolute monarchies. Of these, the kingdoms of Burma, Siam and Cambodia were deemed the most absolute, 'the land being entirely the royal domain and the tillers of the soil being royal chattels'.[17] In Siam, for example, no grants of land were given in perpetuity, so there was no basis for a landed aristocracy of the Western sort.

China was seen as the most powerful and influential state in the region, though not as the most absolute. The Chinese emperor was regarded as sharing his power with a meritocracy, a meritocracy which was recruited through a system of state-supported schools which supplied candidates for the national system of civil-service examinations. Western observers saw the Chinese bureaucracy, thus recruited,

[15] Bodin's contemporary, the Muscovite, S. Peresvetov, already far exceeded Bodin in his admiration for all aspects of the despotic system as exemplified in the Turkish empire. This might perhaps have been expected if one accepted Bodin's account which included Muscovy itself among the despotic monarchies. For more discussion on this subject see Ch. IV.

[16] Jean Bodin, Les six Livres de la République, op.cit., Book V, Ch. V, p. 780.

[17] From the composite picture drawn up by Donald Lach in Asia in the Making of Europe, Vol. 1 (The Century of Discovery), Book Two, University of Chicago Press, 1965, p. 828. The next two paragraphs follow Lach.

as the organising force in the country, and they noted that there existed an elaborate system of public welfare services.

In general, the literature of the period observes that it is an Eastern practice for the state to control key economic activities by means of state monopolies, as well as retaining a controlling interest in all landed property. A quite different aspect of Eastern society which also struck Western observers at this time, in the sixteenth century, was the prevalence of religious toleration. While the Asiatic state appeared to be more deeply involved in the economic life of its subjects than its Western equivalent, it appeared less concerned to regulate minutely their religious beliefs.

In the seventeenth century there was a still greater boom in Eastern travel-literature. Produced in popular form, it provided further corroborative evidence for the concept of Oriental despotism nurtured in the West. The two travellers of most significance in promoting the further development of the concept were Jean Baptiste Tavernier and François Bernier. They were to elaborate and provide concrete illustrations of already existing notions concerning the absence of private property in land in Asia, and of the related notion of the existence of a service-based elite as contrasted with a landed hereditary nobility. In the nineteenth century, when the absence of private property in land came to be viewed as the key to understanding the Oriental system, Tavernier and Bernier were cited copiously.

Bernier was a French physician who lived and practised for some years at the court of the Great Mogul. His writings included an eloquent letter to the French finance minister, Colbert, in which he attributed the decline of Asian states to the absence in the East of private property and its incentives.[18] He argued Colbert to preserve France from a similar decline – a reference to the contemporary rumours that Louis XIV and his minister were planning to proclaim all land in France royal property.

Bernier was convinced of the special (i.e. non-Western) character of the Oriental land-tenure system with its absence of 'strong' property rights, and he distinguished it carefully from Western feudalism. The Oriental system was illustrated by the case of Hindostan, where the sovereign made conditional grants of land to governors and tax farm-

[18] François Bernier, *Travels in the Mogul Empire, A.D. 1656–1668*, London, Constable, 1891, pp. 200–238.

ers, and of service-land (jaghir) to military men, without surrendering his title to it.[19]

One aspect of Bernier's work, which was to be developed more 'scientifically' two centuries later by the British political economists, in particular by Richard Jones, was his account of the barriers the Oriental system posed to the development of manufacture. He provided a vivid picture of the 'moving cities of Hindostan' made up of artisans who perforce had to follow the prince, on whose arbitrary will they were dependent for a living.[20] Artisans suffered from this complete dependence on the revenue centrally distributed by the sovereign and his servants. The security which would have been provided by a middle-class market was completely lacking in the East, Bernier reported.[21] Richard Jones, as we will see was to build on Bernier's observations in order to draw a more general theoretical comparison between the categories of wages paid from revenue and the category of wages paid from capital. Jones was also to employ Bernier's description of the Oriental city to illustrate the differences in development between the Eastern and Western city, and the consequences of this difference for the growth of industry.

Tavernier's travel books likewise enjoyed great popularity, both in the seventeenth century and later. With Bernier's work, they helped to reinforce the belief that absence of private property in land was an integral feature of 'Oriental despotism'. Tavernier wrote:

In the territories of this Prince [the Great Mogul], the nobles are but Royal Receivers, who render account of the revenues to the Governors of Provinces, and they to the Treasurers General and Ministers of Finance, so that this grand King of India, whose territories are so rich, fertile and populous has no power near him equal to his own.[22]

This passage also brings out the structural characteristic noted by Machiavelli and which had since become a generally accepted feature of the popular Western model of Oriental society – the absence of loci of power independent of the king himself.

Another popular work of the seventeenth century was Pierre Bergeron's 'Relation des Voyages en Tartarie ...' which applied the concept of Oriental despotism to Tartary. Bergeron echoes vividly Bodin's

---

[19] *Ibid.*, pp. 224–225. The jaghir was the equivalent of the Turkish timar, discussed by Bodin.

[20] *Ibid.*, p. 200.

[21] *Ibid.*, p. 256.

[22] Jean Baptiste Tavernier (Baron d'Aubonne), *Travels in India* (a translation from his *Les six voyages*, 1676), 2 vols., London, Macmillan, 1889, Vol. I, p. 324.

definition of the 'seigneurial monarch' (despot) in recording that in Tartary: 'Everything belongs to the Emperor to such an extent that there is nobody who can, or dares to, say that this or that is his, but everything is the Emperor's.'[23]

ORIENTAL DESPOTISM AND FRENCH POLITICS, THE FIRST PHASE: A NEGATIVE MODEL FOR EUROPE

It was in France in particular that the concept of Oriental despotism flourished at this time as a political slogan, nurtured on the one hand by the contemporary *Türkenfurcht*, and on the other hand by the continued strengthening of the central power. In this first phase it was employed by the feudal party to discredit the supporters of absolutism by identifying them with the infidel Turks and otherwise inferior Asiatics.

As the development of French absolutism reached its peak under Mazarin and Louis XIV a vigorous pamphlet literature appeared in which the French monarchy was likened to the despotic kingdoms of the East or to the Turkish sultanate – as the prime example of a monarchy not tempered by aristocracy. The allusions made by his critics were strengthened by Louis the Fourteenth's own claims that as representative of the state he was master of both his subjects and all their goods, and that the state was sole proprietor of the land.[24] He could hardly have fitted himself more neatly into the classical definition of the Asiatic despot.

In order to describe adequately the policies of Mazarin and Louis XIV, various forms of the Greek term 'despotes' came to be revived in France, after their temporary eclipse by forms of the term 'seigneur', which had been used to denote the same concept. A neologism which made its first appearance at the very end of the seventeenth century was the word 'despotism' itself. Etymologically 'despotism' was the first of the great political 'isms' that have besieged modern language.

---

[23] 'Tout appartient tellement à cet Empereur, qu'il n'y a personne qui puisse ou ose dire cecy ou cela estre à soy, mais tout est à l'Empereur.' Pierre Bergeron, *Relation des Voyages en Tartarie*, plus un traicté des Tartares ...', Paris, 1634, p. 356, quoted in Geoffroy Atkinson, *The Extraordinary Voyage in French Literature*, 2 vols., N.Y., Burt Franklin, 1965, Vol. 1 "Before 1700", p. 121.

[24] See Sven Stelling-Michaud, 'Le mythe du despotisme oriental', *Schweizer Beiträge zur allgemeinen Geschichte*, 1960–1961, pp. 332–336. For Louis the Fourteenth's claim to dispose freely and fully over the property of his subjects see Louis *XIV, Memoires ... pour l'instruction du Dauphin*, ed. C. Dreyss, Paris, 1860, Vol. II, pp. 120–121. This claim was more than simply the *dominium* over property and land traditionally exercised by Western kings.

(Religious 'isms', on the other hand, had long been accommodated into both Latin and vernacular.)

The first important political work in which the actual word 'despotism' (i.e. the French 'despotisme') appears is Pierre Bayle's *Réponse aux Questions d'un Provincial* of 1703.[25] In his two chapters entitled 'Du Despotisme' Bayle was replying to a French disciple of Hobbes, named Sorbière, who had written in favour of absolute or despotic monarchy.[26] Sorbière had put forward as examples of good government the absolute empires of Asia, in particular the Ottoman Empire. He had contrasted the peace and prosperity of these empires with the turbulence and insecurity arising in the West from the existence of political liberty, or counterpoises to sovereign power. Bayle, in his reply, defended the 'Western' system, which for him meant the existence of traditional liberties and institutionalised checks on the crown.

The greatest of those political writers who employed the concept of Oriental despotism as a weapon against absolutism in France was undoubtedly Montesquieu. All subsequent writers on the subject of Oriental despotism were to relate themselves to Montesquieu, whether to affirm or deny his general propositions. Inspired by his dislike of the development towards absolutism in his time, Montesquieu drew up a vast critique of despotism, as the illustration of what must occur when a system of checks and balances to central power is lacking. The form of government which Montesquieu personally favoured was the monarchy, but a monarchy in which sovereignty was tempered by the existence of intermediary bodies. He wished to see in France the retention of the feudal monarchy, in which the central power was held in check by the independent power of the nobility. Should the power of the feudal nobility continue to be whittled away, Montesquieu believed that one would arrive at despotism – a system which thrived where the political scenery consisted only in the king on the one hand, and an atomised mass of social nothings on the other.

In *De l'esprit des lois*, Montesquieu's model of despotism became, as in the writing of previous European political theorists, the form of government empirically existing in Asia, 'that part of the world where

---

[25] See Pierre Bayle, *Réponse aux Questions d'un Provincial*, Chapters LXIV and LXV, in *Oeuvres Diverses*, Vol. 3, Hildesheim, Georg Olms, 1966, pp. 620–628.

[26] Hobbes himself did not contribute to the development of the concept of *Oriental despotism*, though the idea of the 'Dominion Despotical' is central to his work. What Hobbes did was to universalise the idea, and also give it a contract basis, so that it had no particular reference to an Asian system of government.

absolute power is to some measure naturalized ...'[27] Montesquieu's picture of Asiatic government was put together somewhat imaginatively from the contemporary travel and missionary literature available to him. His model of Oriental despotism was intended as a negative example for home consumption, rather than as a systematic explanation of the principles of Asiatic government. Nonetheless the broad sweep of his comparative political theory was powerful enough to guarantee his lasting influence in this area. (See, for example, Wittfogel's *Oriental Despotism*, which was to depend heavily on the polarity between the multicentred 'free' societies of the West, and the unicentred, potentially totalitarian societies of the East.)

The method of Montesquieu's analysis, in particular his use of geographical environment as a major explanatory variable, was also to exercise lasting influence. The geographical factor which Montesquieu regarded as having the most impact on the character of political systems was extensiveness of the natural unit of territory. Despotism was the political correlate of large land empires. These, in turn, were native to Asia because of the lack of natural barriers in the shape of mountains and seas.[28]

On the correlation between despotism and extensiveness of territory Montesquieu wrote as follows:

A large empire supposes a despotic authority in the person who governs. It is necessary that the quickness of the prince's resolutions should supply the distance of the places they are sent to; that fear should prevent the remissness of the distant governor or magistrate; that the law should be derived from a single person, and should shift continually, according to the accidents which incessantly multiply in a state in proportion to its extent.[29]

This argument appealed to Catherine the Great so much that she reproduced it exactly in her own *Instructions to the Commissioners for Composing a New Code of Laws*. Having described the magnitude of Russian territorial possessions, she wrote that:

The Extent of the Dominion requires an absolute Power to be vested in that Person who rules over it. It is expedient so to be, that the quick Dispatch of

---

[27] Charles Louis de Secondat, Baron de la Brède et de Montesquieu, *The Spirit of Laws*, tr. Thomas Nugent, 2 vols., London, Colonial Press, 1900, Vol. 1, Book V, Ch. 14, p. 61.

[28] *Ibid.*, Book XVII, Ch. 6, p. 269.

[29] *Ibid.*, Book VIII, Ch. 19, p. 122. This argument had appeared in the popular work by Sir Paul Rycaut, entitled *The Present State of the Ottoman Empire*, which is used extensively by Montesquieu. This work had survived the Great Fire of London (in which according to Pepys most of the first edition was lost) to go into many editions, including French, German and Italian.

Affairs, sent from distant Parts, might make ample Amends for the Delay occasioned by the great Distance of the Places.[30]

To emphasise her point she added:

Every other Form of Government whatsoever would not only have been prejudicial to Russia, but would even have proved its entire Ruin.[31]

A second geographical factor which Montesquieu considered as having an important impact on political systems was that of climate. Asia was divided into extremes of heat and cold, and lacked a temperate zone such as found in Europe. The cold regions gave rise to strong nations which easily conquered the enervated nations of the South and reduced them to political slavery.[32]

As we have mentioned, Montesquieu's ideas concerning the relationship between Asiatic geography and Asiatic despotism were to exercise great influence in succeeding centuries, particularly in Germany. The correlation of physical geography and social institutions was however to receive its most direct statement in the widely-read work of Marx's contemporary, the English historian Henry Thomas Buckle. According to Buckle, the political destiny of Asia was determined by the fact that the lavishness of nature with regard to soil, climate and food led invariably to overpopulation, a depressed labour market, slavery and despotism.[33]

Non-geographical factors which Montesquieu regarded as also having an important impact on political systems were those of religion and laws. The Islamic religion, for example, greatly encouraged the veneration of the prince.[34] In India, the laws 'which give the lands to the prince, and destroy the spirit of property among the subjects, increase the bad effects of climate, that is, their natural indolence.'[35]

---

[30] Catherine the Great, *The Instructions to the Commissioners for Composing a New Code of Laws* (1767), in *Documents of Catherine the Great*, ed. W.F. Reddaway, Cambridge U.P., 1931, Ch. 11, § 10, p 216.

[31] *Ibid.*, Ch. 11, § 11, p. 216.

[32] Montesquieu, *The Spirit of Laws, op.cit.*, Vol. I, Book XVII, Ch. 3, p. 266. In Europe, on the contrary, nations of nearly equal strength contended with each other.

[33] Henry Thomas Buckle, *History of Civilisation in England*, Vol. I, 2nd edn, London, Parker, 1858, Ch. Two, pp. 36–137.

[34] Montesquieu, *The Spirit of Laws, op.cit.*, Vol. I, Book V, Ch. 14, p. 59.

[35] *Ibid.*, Book XIV, Ch. 6, p. 226. Montesquieu did not regard the absence of private property in land as one of the defining characteristics of despotism, but rather, as an optional extra. He wrote: 'Of all despotic governments there is none that labors more under its own weight than that wherein the prince declares himself proprietor of all the lands, and heir to all his subjects.' (*Ibid.*, Book V, Ch. 14, p. 59.) Montesquieu defined despotism in terms of its power structure, the existence of a single centre, operating with equal force on all parts of the organism.

Religion could, on the other hand, counteract the influence of geographical factors which would otherwise give rise to a despotic system:

It is the Christian religion that, in spite of the extent of the empire and the influence of the climate, has hindered despotic power from being established in Ethiopia, and has carried into the heart of Africa the manners and laws of Europe.[36]

In defending the continuance of feudal restraints on central power, Montesquieu was careful to deny the analogy drawn by some previous writers (such as Bodin) between the early period of French feudalism and the Eastern system of distributing property as service land. He wrote:

If at a time when the fiefs were precarious, all the lands of the kingdom had been fiefs, or dependencies of fiefs; and all the men in the kingdom vassals or bondmen subordinate to vassals; as the person that has property is ever possessed of power, the king, who would have continually disposed of the fiefs, that is, of the only property then existing, would have had a power as arbitrary as that of the Sultan is in Turkey; which is contradictory to all history.[37]

That is to say, the later system of feudal diffusion of power was in no way a distortion of the original system of central control of the fiefs.

Throughout the eighteenth century one important stream of writers was to follow Montesquieu in employing Oriental despotism as a negative model for Europe, the epitome of all that was to be avoided at home. One of the earliest of these was Helvétius, who agreed with Montesquieu's use of the concept as a means to attack native French absolutism, but disagreed with the alternatives to absolutism put forward by Montesquieu. Where Montesquieu wished to preserve aristocratic privilege as a counterbalance to the monarchy, Helvétius wished to initiate a limited and secular monarchy, uncluttered by such a multiplication of petty despotisms.[38] It is in Helvétius' *De l'esprit* (1758) that the phrase 'Oriental despotism' appears, probably for the first time.[39] Helvétius rejected Montesquieu's geographical determinism

[36] *Ibid.*, Vol. II, Book XXIV, Ch. 3, p. 29. Perhaps to some extent written with tongue in cheek, considering the satirical portrait of the form of Christianity assumed in Ethiopia which Montesquieu put into his *Spicilège*.

[37] *Ibid.*, Vol. II, Book XXX, Ch. 5, p. 174.

[38] See the letter written by Helvétius to Montesquieu in 1747, after reading the manuscript of *De l'esprit des lois*, quoted in Sven Stelling-Michaud, 'Le mythe du despotisme oriental', *loc.cit.*, p. 343.

[39] See, for example, Helvétius, *De l'esprit*, Discours Troisième, *Oeuvres*, Paris, Briand, 1794, Vol. II, Ch. XVII, p. 89; Ch. XXII, p. 121; Ch. XXIX, pp. 172, 174. Helvétius also used the term 'Asiatic despotism'. See, for example, his *A treatise on man*, tr. W. Hooper, N.Y., Burt Franklin, 1969, Vol. I, p. viii.

and argued instead that it was the progress of civilisation itself that led inevitably to a degeneration into despotism; as the nations of Asia were organised into society earlier than those of Europe they had also reached the despotic stage of development earlier.[40]

Although Helvétius employed the term 'Oriental despotism', it probably only came into general use with the publication in 1761 of a work by Nicolas Boulanger entitled *Recherches sur l'origine du despotisme oriental*.[41] This book was published after Boulanger's death by Holbach, who was himself influenced by its contents. John Wilkes published his own English translation in London, in 1764.

Boulanger also used the concept of Oriental despotism as a negative example for home consumption. His book is an interesting account of the 'irrational' sources of political power, and of the ways in which charisma comes to be institutionalised in political systems. He argued that the despotic systems of the East were a hangover from the period of human history when the rule of *theocracy* was general.[42] Theocracy had originally arisen out of the disappointed millenialism of the Hebrews. Men compensated for the non-arrival of the millennium by attributing to their wordly rulers supernatural powers. The fact that political power became surrounded by superstition led to all sorts of excesses, and to the general exploitation of the irrational by the rulers.

In the West men eventually began to assert their own (rational) nature, i.e., the autonomy of reason, and to a large extent abandoned this mystical political form. Boulanger was unclear as to just why this same development did not take place in the East. He acknowledged the relevance of Montesquieu's climatic argument but regarded it as insufficient explanation.

The purpose of Boulanger's account of Oriental despotism was to plead the cause of completely rational monarchy in Europe, based on the human and natural laws uncovered by the progress of reason. Republicanism was no longer suitable for modern states with their

[40] Helvétius, *De l'esprit*, Discours Troisième, *Oeuvres, op.cit.*, Vol. II, Ch. XXIX, p. 174.
[41] There does not appear to be any basis for Joseph Needham's remark that the phrase 'despotism', as applied to China, originates with Quesnay, whose work appeared much later. (See Needham's review of K.A. Wittfogel's *Oriental Despotism, Science and Society*, Vol. 23 (1959), p. 61.)
[42] Cf. Turgot, Condorcet, and Voltaire in his *The Philosophy of History*, (first published London, 1766), London, Vision Press, 1965. Voltaire, however, believed that the Chinese were the first to transcend this rule of theocracy, because although their histories extended further back in time than that of any other people, they 'do not refer to those savage times when it was necessary for men to be cheated in order to be guided'. (*Ibid.*, p. 83).

great size (an echo of Montesquieu), so the desirable antithesis to the Oriental despot was the philosophically instructed monarch.[43]

The type of argument put forward by Boulanger became much more popular in the nineteenth century, when India rather than China had become the prime reference point for the model of Oriental despotism.[44] The passivity and submissiveness towards the 'supernatural' (including temporal power) supposedly inculcated by eastern religions then became a popular explanation for Asiatic despotism. For example, Lieut.-Col. Wilks, one of Marx's sources on India, was also to raise Montesquieu's climatic explanation only to dismiss it,[45] and to write that: 'The shackles imposed on the human mind by the union of the divine and human code [including political, civil and criminal codes] have been stated as the efficient causes of despotism . . .'[46]

Meanwhile, the concept of Oriental despotism had been undergoing a metamorphosis, and in eighteenth-century France it emerged for the first time as a positive model, held up for the instruction of the West in rational government.

ORIENTAL DESPOTISM AND FRENCH POLITICS, THE SECOND PHASE: A POSITIVE MODEL FOR EUROPE

During the seventeenth and eighteenth centuries the Jesuit missionaries in China had done much to create a more flattering image of the Orient than that which had prevailed in Europe prior to the seventeenth century. It was largely owing to the information provided by the Jesuits and other missionaries that the concept of Oriental despotism came to be used by one faction of French political life in the eighteenth century as a positive, rather than a negative model for Europe.

---

[43] Nicolas Antoine Boulanger, *Recherches sur l'origine du despotisme oriental*, in *Oeuvres de Boullanger* (sic), 8 vols., Paris, Jean Servieres and Jean-François Bastien 1792–1793, Vol. IV, 1792, pp. 236–237. A similar attempt to use the Oriental example as a warning to the contemporary French monarchy to reform itself is to be found in the *Essai sur le despotisme* of Mirabeau (2nd edn, London, 1776). Mirabeau urged the monarch not to indulge in despotism, because this would bring on France the weakness it had brought on Turkey, Persia and Mogul India.

[44] Boulanger himself had been swimming against the tide of eighteenth-century thought in applying his concept of the politics of irrationalism to China. He conceded to the Jesuits that natural law might set the tone at the beginning of each dynasty in China. Thereafter, however, the hidden vices of the system were bound to re-emerge. (*Recherches sur l'origine du despotisme oriental*, loc.cit., p. 222).

[45] Lieut.-Col. Mark Wilks, *Historical Sketches of the South of India*, 3 vols., London, Longman, 1810–1817, Vol. I, p. 22.

[46] *Ibid.*, p. 29. Marx quotes from this work in *Capital*, Vol. I, pp. 357–358.

This faction, as we shall see, sought the strengthening and rationalisation of central government at the expense of feudal powers, and in the process of their propaganda campaign, fused models of enlightened despotism and of Oriental despotism.

One of the most influential examples of the Jesuit literature produced in this period, and one which in fact was utilised by both the proponents and opponents of despotism, was the *Description géographique, historique, chronologique, politique et physique de l'Empire de la Chine et de la Tartarie chinoise*, by Père Jean-Baptiste du Halde.[47] This work enjoyed the honour of being translated from the original French into English, German, and Russian; of being misquoted by Montesquieu;[48] and finally, of being acclaimed in the *Dictionnaire de Biographie Française* as having exercised on the history of ideas in the eighteenth century 'une influence dont on n'a pas fini de mesurer le retentissement'.[49]

The work itself consisted in a collation of a mass of material sent to Paris from members of the Order who were in the field. It included chapters on education, the examination system, and the system of government. Concerning the latter, du Halde wrote: 'There is no monarchy more absolute than that of *China*.'[50] The outcome of this was a happy one, however, as 'no People in the world have better [Laws of Government]'.[51] These laws were interpreted and administered by men of the highest merit; position in Chinese society and government being dependent not on birth but on ability.[52] The Emperor exercised ultimate control over property, through taxation, but this contributed to the general prosperity as the tax revenue was used to provide welfare services, public buildings, salaries for the mandarins, etc.[53]

Above all, du Halde saw in the Chinese political system that great eighteenth-century virtue of *stability*. He wrote:

China has this Advantage over all other Nations, that for 4,000 Years, and upwards, it has been governed almost without Interruption, by its own native Princes, and with little Deviation, either in Attire, Morals, Laws, Customs, or Manners, from the wise Institutions of its first Legislators.[54]

---

[47] First published in Paris, 1735, in four vols.
[48] Montesquieu quotes du Halde as saying 'It is the cudgel (bâton) that governs China.' (*The Spirit of Laws.*, *op.cit.*, Book VIII, Ch. 21, p. 123; see also Book XVII, Ch. 5, p. 268.) No such statement in fact appears in du Halde's book.
[49] Entry under Jean-Baptiste du Halde in the *Dictionnaire de Biographie Française*.
[50] J.-B. du Halde, *History of China*, London, Watts, 1841, Vol. II, p. 12.
[51] *Ibid.*, Vol. III, p. 60.
[52] *Ibid.*, Vol. II, pp. 99–108.
[53] *Ibid.*, p. 22.
[54] *Ibid.*, p. 1.

Works such as that of du Halde became the fuel for the eighteenth-century vogue of sinophilia, which in France became a veritable sinomania.[55] This vogue was more than just a demonstration of enlightenment cosmopolitanism. It was part of the intellectual campaign against feudal prejudice at home, in favour of a 'modern' state, administered by a rational bureaucracy.

The mandarinate and examination system, for example, were of particular interest to enlightenment figures in arms against the old forms of government based on ascriptive principles. This interest was finally transformed into practical policy in the nineteenth century, when the 'Chinese' system of recruitment to the civil service through examination was generally adopted in Europe. The system of state schools admired by Western observers of China in the eighteenth century was also eventually transplanted to Europe.

China was credited by missionary observers with having a political system that was both rational and based on natural law in spite of the absence of the Christian religion. Society was sustained through a practical morality that was inculcated through the legal system, without the benefit of revealed religion – a claim that in other hands became useful ammunition in the struggle for religious toleration.

French sinomania reached its height with figures such as Voltaire and the Philosophes (with the notable exceptions of Diderot and Rousseau). It was revived towards the last quarter of the century by the Physiocrats. The significance of the Physiocrats was that they saw in China a positive model for France, not only in its political aspects, but also in its economic aspect.

The Physiocrats were advocates of what they termed 'legal despotism' in France. What they meant by the term legal despotism was aptly defined by one of their number, Le Mercier de la Rivière. He decribed Euclid as the epitome of the legal despot; his laws rightly had absolute authority because they were backed by the irresistable force of the evidence, or, in other words, because of their obvious congruence with natural laws.[56] In the same way, governments should wield

---

[55] For the most comprehensive account of this aspect of French thought in the eighteenth century see Basil Guy, 'The French image of China before and after Voltaire', *Studies on Voltaire and the Eighteenth Century*, Vol. 21 (1963), pp. 1–468. Henri Cordier's *Bibliotheca Sinica* (2nd edn, Paris, Guilmoto, 5 vols., 1904–1924) is still indispensable for the bibliographical details of this period of Western writing on China.

[56] Le Mercier de la Rivière, *L'Ordre naturel et essentiel des sociétés politiques*, London & Paris, 1767, facsimile edn, Paris, P. Geuthner, 1910, Ch. 24. For further explanations of the concept see Dupont de Nemours in *Ephémérides du citoyen*, Vol. XII (1767), pp. 188–204, and in *de l'Origine et des progrès d'une science nouvelle*, London, 1768.

absolute power in order to uphold the laws of nature relating to society (i.e. economic laws).[57]

The major tenet of the Physiocrats was that the source of all value lay in agricultural production, or in land made fertile by labour. Hence they believed that taxation should be limited to a direct tax on agricultural production, payable by the proprietor to whom the surplus accrued in rent.[58] The revenue thus obtained should be used by the government to provide the general conditions for agriculture.

Where the government was co-proprietor of the 'net product' through its share of the agricultural surplus it would have a natural interest in encouraging productivity. *Per contra*, any other form of taxation, tolls, or internal barriers to trade served only to upset the natural laws of the economy, and was detrimental to the prosperity of the nation.

As was noted by Marx himself,[59] the intellectual position of the Physiocrats was complex: objectively they sought the removal of obstacles from the path of capitalist production, but they did this in the name of beliefs about land as the only source of value. 'The bourgeois glorify feudalism in theory [...] only in order to ruin it in actual practice.'[60] They were the 'fathers of modern economics',[61] in that they made value a function of labour rather than an intrinsic property, but they did *not* believe that value could be created in the labour of manufacture. The kind of taxation system advocated by the Physiocrats would have aided, and indeed partly assumed, the extension of capitalist production, but this advocacy was coupled with an admiration for political patriarchalism.

Furthermore, the Physiocrats used as a medium for their economico-political theory a model drawn from a country which could not be described as either capitalist or feudal in any Western sense. China was the illustration and proof of Physiocratic theories.[62] Thus Quesnay, the

[57] François Quesnay, *Despotism in China*, comprising Vol. 2 (bound together with Vol. 1) of Lewis A. Maverick, *China: A model for Europe*, San Antonio, Texas, P. Anderson, 1946, p. 225.

[58] The Physiocrats anticipated the 'iron law' of wages, whereby competition forces wages down to the minimum level necessary to maintain the existence of the labourer. For this reason, the Physiocrats argued, tax could not be deducted from the wages of farm-labourers without making them a burden on their employers.

[59] *Marx*, [Private Property and Labour], *Early Writings*, ed. T.B. Bottomore, London, Watts, 1963, pp. 149–150.

[60] *Grundrisse*, p. 329.

[61] *Ibid.*, p. 328.

[62] It is difficult to establish the precise role which Western accounts of China played in the formation of Physiocratic economic theory. Pierre le Poivre had given a recent address before the Academy at Paris on the flourishing state of agriculture in China resulting from the attentiveness of the government. Already in the seventeenth century Fernandez Navarrete

creator of the Physiocratic school, in his *Despotism in China* (published in 1767),[63] argued that China was a uniquely well-regulated and wealthy state, and that this was because the Chinese economy was soundly based on the single-tax system. The reason that the Chinese had been able to achieve such an exemplary economic system was that in China the study of natural law was the 'principal aim of the sovereign and of the scholars entrusted by him with the detailed administration of the government'.[64] Government, and the general supervision of the economy, was in the hands of those dedicated to the employment of reason (rather than a purely hereditary nobility) and hence China was blessed with a stability and prosperity unknown in France.

In one Physiocratic work, 'China' was specifically put forward as a model for Russia – the reverse of twentieth-century developments.[65] This work was intended as instruction in the essential principles of government including the participation of the sovereign in the economy, for the benefit of the Russian Grand Duke who later became Tsar Paul I.

The Physiocrats viewed the economic system long associated with Oriental despotism as exemplary, at least with regard to the intervention of the state in agriculture. Tnis attitude towards the Oriental system of land-tax was to be shared with other opponents of the outmoded forms of aristocratic land-tenure at home,[66] in contrast with aristocratic sympathisers, such as Montesquieu, who found this aspect of the Oriental system quite abhorrent.

One eighteenth-century writer whose attitude towards the economic aspect of Oriental despotism was even more radical than that of the Physiocrats was Simon Nicolas Linguet. Marx was later to prize Linguet's critique of Montesquieu, which was summed up in the epigram, 'l'esprit des lois, c'est la propriété'.[67]

Linguet praised the control exercised by Oriental governments over privilege and property, a control he saw as acting to the advantage of the poorer classes.[68] He discounted the so-called freedom which existed

and Père Louis le Comte had praised the Chinese system of taxation, and Navarrete had urged European governments to imitate the Chinese in their care for agriculture.

[63] Published serially in *Ephémérides du citoyen*, March, April, May and June 1767.

[64] François Quesnay, *Despotism in China*, loc.cit., p. 212.

[65] Nicolas-Gabriel Le Clerc, *Yu le Grand et Confucius*, four vols., Soissons, 1769.

[66] See, for example, James Mill in the nineteenth century.

[67] Marx, *Capital*, Vol. I, p. 615, fn. 2; p. 738, fn. 1. The epigram appears in Linguet, *Théorie des lois civiles, ou Principes fondamentaux de la société*, Vol. 1, London, 1767, p. 236.

[68] Marx made excerpts (via Villegardelle) from *Théorie des lois civiles* in Brussels, 1846, and later took notes directly from Linguet which are to be found in a notebook dating from about March-April 1859. See also the section on Linguet in Marx's *Theories of Surplus Value*, Part I,

in Europe – the freedom to die of hunger – and made the claim that even the serf or slave was better off than the contemporary working man. The slave, for example, was at least a valuable property for his owner, and was looked after accordingly.[69]

Bentham's editor, Dumont, was so incensed by Linguet's analysis of Western law as simply a device for maintaining an inequitable distribution of property that he described it as:

> ... the product of a disordered imagination in the service of an evil heart. Oriental despotism is the model to which he seeks to make all European governments conform, in order to cure them of the notions of liberty and humanity which seem to torment him like lugubrious spectres.[70]

In spite of his radicalism, Linguet was against revolution, fearing that it would entail the collapse of civilisation. His fears were vindicated, in so far as he was finally guillotined during the Terror for 'inciting the despots of London and Vienna'.

A quite different kind of critique of Montesquieu was provided by the Orientalist and pioneer of Persian studies, Anquetil-Duperron. Anquetil-Duperron was one of the few eighteenth-century writers on Oriental despotism who was more interested in the functions of the concept than in employing it for his own purposes, which is not to say that he did not have his own political purposes for exposing the hypocrisy of British intervention in India.

In his work *Législation orientale*, Anquetil-Duperron claimed that the idea of Oriental despotism elaborated by Montesquieu and others was simply a *rationalisation* for European intervention in the East. He was less interested in analysing the role the concept had served within Europe with regard to opposing, reforming or justifying absolute monarchy than in analysing its role in external politics.[71]

Anquetil-Duperron was utterly opposed to the motion that in the East, for example Persia, Turkey and India, the native system of government was a so-called despotism. He argued that the idea of the absence of the rights of private property in Asia was a fiction employed by colonialists who favoured the confiscation of native estates. Their

London, Lawrence Wishart, 1969, pp. 345–350. Marx did not share Linguet's enthusiasm for the Asiatic model, although he appreciated his critique of bourgeois liberalism. According to Marx, Linguet 'defends Asiatic despotism against the civilized European forms of despotism, thus he defends slavery against wage-labour.' (*Ibid.*, p. 345).

[69] S.N. Linguet, *Théorie des lois civiles ...*, *op.cit.*, p. 467.

[70] Jeremy Bentham, *Traités de législation civile et pénale*, ed. Et. Dumont, 3 vols., 2nd edn, Paris, 1820, Vol. 1, p. 138.

[71] See Franco Venturi, 'Oriental Despotism', *Journal of the History of Ideas*, Vol. 24 (Jan.-March 1963), p. 137.

reasoning was that in Asia conquest automatically bestowed ownership of all land on the conqueror.[72]

In his later life, Anquetil-Duperron appeared on the margin of the prolonged controversy over the nature of land-tenure in Bengal, which involved this very question of whether conquest bestowed a proprietory right to all the land in Asiatic countries. It was partly the use of the concept of Oriental despotism for such 'colonialist' purposes which led Marx to reconsider the notion of the absence of property in land at the time of the annexation of Bengal.[73]

Anquetil-Duperron can only be regarded as exceptional in his treatment of the concept of Oriental despotism. It was far more usual for eighteenth-century writers to adopt the model of Oriental despotism most suited to their political purposes at home, regardless of how little it might correspond to the reality of Asiatic society.

Thus, as seen in reference to du Halde, the eighteenth-century aspiration to political stability, under the shadow of revolution, found its expression in an exaggerated admiration for the *longevity* of the Chinese political order. This quality had long been associated with Oriental despotism, but had not received the same stress in the past. On this subject Quesnay wrote:

Does not this vast empire, subjected to the natural order, present an example of a stable, permanent and invariable government, proving that the inconstancy of transitory governments has no other basis or rule except the inconstancy of men themselves?[74]

For many eighteenth-century thinkers, as for Aristotle and Polybius, the ideal system of government and society was static in form, by its very unchangingness expressing its close conformity to unchanging natural law. For this reason the 'eternal standstill' (Ranke) of China could be viewed as wholly admirable, and proof that natural law formed the basis of Chinese society.

A change in this general attitude came about fairly rapidly at the end of the eighteenth century with the political and philosophical developments associated with the French Revolution and the economic development and conception of economic progress associated with the industrial 'revolution'. Nineteenth-century economists, such as Marx,

---

[72] *Ibid.*, p. 139.

[73] E.g. [Plans for English Colonization in India], *N.Y.D.T.*, 3 April 1858, *Karl Marx on Colonialism and Modernization*, p. 262. Other instances of the colonial exploitation of the concept with regard to land policy were noted by Marx and Engels in connection with the French in Algeria and the British in Ireland.

[74] François Quesnay, *Despotism in China, loc.cit.*, p. 304.

might agree with the Physiocrats that the notable stability of the Oriental system arose out of the particular organisation of the economy it represented. However in the nineteenth century this stability was regarded as stagnation.

EMPIRES BELONGING TO SPACE AND NOT TO TIME

The philosophical developments which culminated in the work of Hegel meant that popular concepts of natural law gradually gave way to the idea of history as the dynamic process of self-development of men and nations. The tendency to measure historical progress in terms of approximation to external and unchanging laws of reason was abandoned in favour of viewing history itself as the progressive revelation of reason.

In the light of these new ideas a more critical image of the East once more reigned in the West. Static systems were no longer regarded favourably, as reflecting truly the operation of universal and static natural laws – instead they were seen as unnatural hangovers from the past, that had simply not shared in the historical development of the Western nations.

The transition between these two sterotyped evaluations of Oriental despotism appears clearly in the work of Johann Gottfried von Herder. Already in 1784 Herder was outlining a theory of history which presaged in many ways the nineteenth-century approach to historical development.

What Herder in fact did was to up-date Montesquieu's theories of geographical determinism by introducing elements to account for dynamic progress and change in human society. Firstly, he depicted man's historical relationship with nature in terms of *mutual interaction*: men through their activity changed nature, which in turn, in its new aspect, influenced men.[75] Secondly, according to Herder, this interaction between man and nature was simultaneously influenced by the organic national traditions of the people concerned.

Herder wrote that 'The natural state of man is society',[76] and for him society was no longer the *polis* of Aristotle, but a *national* society. It was man, with the powers developed within the medium of particular

[75] Johann Gottfried von Herder, *Outlines of a Philosophy of the History of Man*, tr. T. Churchill, London, 1800, reprinted N.Y., Bergman, n.d. p. 176.
[76] *Ibid.*, p. 244.

national societies, who created history. However, although the nation was the vehicle of progress, not all nations in fact sustained progress.

For example, the form which man's interaction with nature assumed in the process of production might be detrimental to the progress of the nation. Herder had a particular distrust of the effects of agricultural production on man's social organisation. Agricultural production was liable to give rise to a 'frightful despotism' wherein the ground 'ceased to belong to man, but man became the appertenance of the ground'.[77] Such despotism was a characteristic feature of Asia, where the effects of the climate and of the mode of production were reinforced by national traditions.

Herder described 'Asiatic despotism'[78] as a non-developmental political form, which did not permit the restless pursuit of knowledge which was the driving force of Western nations. China, for example, 'stands as an old ruin on the verge of the World'.[79] Confucian traditions inhibited any further progress in education or politics, and despotism prevented any rival school of thought from competing with Confucianism.[80] Hence national traditions, combined with the effects of climate and a non-progressive mode of production, produced a completely static social system.

Once a despotism was instituted, the political and intellectual straitjacket it imposed doomed the system to perpetuate itself into eternity. The Chinese empire was in fact 'an embalmed mummy wrapped in silk, and painted in hieroglyphics: its internal circulation is that of a dormouse in its winter sleep'.[81]

The idea that Eastern nations lacked within themselves the conditions for further organic development was to become the dominant theme of nineteenth-century writing on Oriental despotism. As such, it was to be absorbed by Marx, and to form the basis of his analysis of the non-Western world. It was closely linked with the notion that Asia could only be restored to the path of progress through the intervention of the West.

[77] *Ibid.*, p. 207.
[78] *Ibid.*, p. 315.
[79] *Ibid.*, p. 297.
[80] *Ibid.*, p. 298.
[81] *Ibid.*, p. 296. Cf. Marx's description of China: 'Complete isolation was the prime condition of the preservation of Old China. That isolation having come to a violent end by the medium of England, dissolution must follow as surely as that of any mummy carefully preserved in a hermetically sealed coffin, whenever it is brought into contact with the open air.' 'Revolution in China and in Europe' (printed as leading article), *N.Y.D.T.*, 14 June 1853, *Karl Marx on Colonialism and Modernization*, p. 69.

Herder's concept of the stasis of the East was further systematised by Hegel. According to Hegel's historical schema the first phase of world history took place in the Orient, but subsequently the scene of the development of the world spirit had moved elsewhere. In the East empires persisted that belonged to space and not to time, thus perpetuating 'unhistorical history'.[82]

Hegel's philosophical analysis of the historical phase in which the Eastern nations had become suspended was as follows: the Eastern nations had been the first to attain the phase of 'substantial freedom',[83] embodied in the state. However, they had not progressed to the principle of subjectivity, and only the will of the despot was free. Morality existed only in the form of external demands imposed on the individual. In China, which Hegel took as the 'classic type' of the Oriental state,[84] even family relations were externalised and enforced by law. Moreover, in countries such as Egypt and India, man was still in the thrall of mystified nature.

Hegel presents a not unflattering picture of the Chinese educational system and bureaucracy – in line with contemporary German bureaucratic reformers. Hegel, however, dismisses these virtues of the Chinese system as necessities in a situation where all political decisions stemmed from one will, and the interests of the governed were not consulted.

The political conception of Oriental despotism that appears in Hegel stems directly from Montesquieu, and retains the bias of Montesquieu's model. The principal feature of Oriental despotism was the absence of any system of corporate or individual rights, *vis à vis* the state, and hence the absence of intermediary bodies. The absolute equality prevailing in the East (apart from the servants of the state with their conditional tenure of office) constituted the very foundation of despotism.[85]

Hegel also, like Herder, absorbed Montesquieu's methodology into his own system, while ridding it of its static quality. The way in which Hegel amalgamated Montesquieu's geographical determinism with his own 'idealist' view of history as the self-unfolding of the world spirit was as follows.

Firstly, the general movement of the world spirit through time was

[82] Georg Wilhelm Friedrich Hegel, *The Philosophy of History*, tr. J. Sibree, London, Bell, 1905, p. 112.
[83] I.e. the negation of the arbitrariness arising from the unreflecting and uncontrolled instinctual gratifications of 'natural man'.
[84] 'China is quite peculiarly Oriental.' Hegel, *The Philosophy of History*, op.cit., p. 119.
[85] Hegel, *The Philosophy of History*, op.cit., pp. 124–125.

from East to West.[86] Civilisation began where nature provided the optimal conditions for the development of agriculture – the river-plains of the East.[87] Agriculture necessarily gave rise to private-property rights and hence to the development of the state form to mediate these rights.[88] The development of the state form in itself represented a great advance in human civilisation, in man's creation of objective universals.

The limits of progress possible within the river-plain civilisations were, however, soon reached. Such civilisations were inward-looking and undifferentiated, affording a monotonous attachment to the soil. The next stage of human development could only take place in a completely different geographical context – i.e. the Mediterranean. It was the existence of geographic diversity in territories brought into communication with one another by convenient sea-lanes that gave rise to individualism and the growth of pluralistic forms of society.

Hegel's impressive attempt to incorporate universal history into a philosophical system, and to combine objective idealism with geo-graphical determinism, served him in one respect only to arrive at that nineteenth-century commonplace – that it was 'the necessary fate of Asiatic Empires to be subjected to Europeans'.[89] In no other way could the Asiatic nations rejoin the developing process of world history. The Slavs represented a half-way house between Asia and Europe. As a nation they had partaken in world history only very late, and even then had not completely broken free from their connections with Asia.[90]

The most immediate influence of Hegel's analysis of the non-Western world was, however, manifested among the internal critics of the Prussian government. The Young Germany movement in the 1830s and 1840s used Hegel's model of China as a negative example of the results

---

[86] This idea was of great antiquity, apparently stemming from the astrological belief that the course of civilisation followed the course of the sun. Hegel felt that the future unfolding of world history would take place in the Americas. (*Ibid.*, p. 90).

[87] *Ibid.*, p. 93.

[88] Marx's notion that the state form was indissolubly linked with the rise of private-property relations was foreshadowed by Hegel. Hegel also preceded Marx in the view that the development of the state form was correlated with the development of classes, and that where the latter were weakly developed, as in America, the state power with its unifying function was also weakly developed. (*Ibid.*, p. 89). On the former point see also Adam Smith, according to whom, 'Till there be property there can be no government, the very end of which is to secure wealth, and to defend the rich from the poor.' (Adam Smith, *Lectures on Justice, Police, Revenue and Arms*, ed. Edwin Cannan, first published 1896, reprinted N.Y., Kelley & Mill-man, 1956, p. 15).

[89] Hegel, *The Philosophy of History*, *op.cit.*, p. 149.

[90] *Ibid.*, p. 107.

(in terms of utter stagnation) of oppressive state power. 'China' functioned both as the symbol of pure conservatism and reaction, and as a popular metaphor for the Prussian government.[91]

In general, political romanticism and political liberalism coincided in the nineteenth century in their negative image of Asiatic society. In Asia, the free development of society (or the nation) had been brought to an artificial halt for thousands of years, thanks to Oriental despotism.

THE CONTRIBUTION OF POLITICAL ECONOMY:
THE RELATION OF PRIVATE PROPERTY TO PROGESS

It was the British political economists who were responsible for the first serious attempt to analyse 'Oriental despotism' as an economic system. The Physiocrats had pointed the way, but their theories were still, to a certain extent, shrouded in metaphysics. Adam Smith, on the other hand, in the *Wealth of Nations*, presented a model of Oriental despotism couched purely in economic terms.

According to Smith, there existed a distinctive Asiatic political economy, characterised by the fact that the sovereign derived the whole, or a considerable part, of his income from a variable land tax or land rent. A corollary of this was the particular attention Asiatic sovereigns paid to the interests of agriculture and to public works, in order to maximise the value of produce, and thence their own income.[92]

The involvement of the executive power in the public economy distinguished Asiatic countries from the agricultural countries of Europe, where the sovereign did not have such a direct interest in productivity, and hence did not engage in the same public works. In Egypt and Hindostan, according to Smith, the public works engaged in by the state included irrigation schemes, which directly increased productivity.[93] In Hindostan and China, they included public roads – and in China also navigable canals – which served to extend markets by providing cheap transport.[94]

---

[91] See E. Rose, 'China as a Symbol of Reaction in Germany 1830–1880', *Comparative Literature*, Vol. III (1951–1952), pp. 57–76. Heinrich Heine's 'Der Kaiser von China', published in the *Pariser Deutsche Zeitung*, 1842, is a good example of the use of the metaphor for political criticism.

[92] Adam Smith, *The Wealth of Nations*, London, Routledge, 1898, pp. 535–537; pp. 572–573.

[93] *Ibid.*, p. 535.

[94] *Ibid.*, pp. 572–573.

In the process of freeing economics from the grip of natural law, Smith was able to introduce a more genuinely *comparative* note into the economic analysis of the East. Even if Quesnay's idea of natural law was no more than the distinguishing of fundamental relations of production and exchange from the secondary phenomena of political forms and legislation,[95] the fact that the Physiocrats linked economics to natural law meant that ultimately they saw one set of economic relations as universally appropriate to man.

By contrast, Smith found the Asiatic system to be suited to the agrarian countries of the East, but unsuited to the countries of Europe, where there were greater local complexities which would render a central distribution of funds awkward to handle.[96] In fact Smith was opposed in principle to the performance of economic functions by a centralised executive at home, though he found it appropriate in parts of Asia.

Smith shared with the Physiocrats and other eighteenth-century writers a relatively favourable attitude towards the Asiatic form of society and economy. The later political economists were to provide a marked contrast in this respect. In an early essay (Essay on the History of Astronomy) Smith had raised the question of whether the despotic systems of Chaldea and Egypt might not have prevented the growth of philosophy in those countries, but had not answered it. In the nineteenth century, James Mill was to praise Smith for having raised this question, but censure him for leaving it open, thus compromising with 'popular opinion and his own imperfect views'[97] – i.e. by portraying Asiatic society too favourably.

Mill, in his *History of India*, pledged himself to remove those illusions about the East which had been propagated in particular by the 'Popish missionaries'.[98] He attempted to demonstrate that the Hindus, for example, had made 'but a few of the earliest steps in the progress to civilisation'. The point was that they should be governed accordingly, and not as though they were a 'quite civilised nation'.

Mill relied on the kind of model of Oriental despotism introduced by Herder. The Asiatic social system was one in which all progress had ceased thousands of years before.[99] Superficial movement had taken

---

[95] This was how Marx analysed Quesnay's idea of natural law (*MEGA* I/VI, pp. 612–613).
[96] Smith, *The Wealth of Nations, op.cit.*, p. 573.
[97] James Mill, *The History of British India*, nine vols., ed. and with commentaries by H.H. Wilson, London, J. Madden, 1840–48, Vol. II, 1840, pp. 231–32.
[98] *Ibid.*, Ch. X ('General Reflections'), pp. 152–233.
[99] *Ibid.*, pp. 213–215.

place in these systems, with conquest or dynastic change, but the texture of society, and its basic component, the *village*, had remained unchanged.[100] Here we are seeing the definite emergence of the village as an integral component of Asiatic despotism – the village which through its economic self-sufficiency inhibits the development of a more complex social division of labour and which is the linch-pin of the stability of the East.

Like the other nineteenth-century British political economists, Mill held that exogenous factors had to be introduced into the Asiatic system (i.e. by the British) for the sake of *Progress*. Unlike the other political economists, however, Mill believed that the basic economic structure of Oriental despotism should be retained – i.e. the government appropriation of the surplus. The reason for Mill's rather radical approach to this question was his fear that the creation of 'strong' private-property rights in India would lead to the creation of an un-productive and reactionary class of landed aristocrats. Marx's analysis of his motives was as follows: 'We understand such economists as Mill [...] demanding that rent should be handed over to the state to serve in place of taxes. That is a frank expression of the hatred the industrial capitalist bears towards the landed proprietor, who seems to him a useless thing, an excrescence upon the general body of bourgeois production.'[101]

The bias against the landed interest evident in Ricardo's theory of rent[102] and taken to extremes by Mill was indeed attacked by Malthus on the grounds that the Asiatic system was its logical consequence wherever the theory was applied. Malthus wrote that even if 'the government did not adopt the Eastern mode of considering itself as sole proprietor, it might at least take a hint from the Economists, and declare itself co-proprietor with the landlords ...'; and the ensuing despotism 'would certainly rest on very solid foundations.'[103]

The utilitarians in general, other than Mill, regarded private property as the prime desideratum for India. Private property would bring competition and incentive into the Indian economy. They argued that under the native system private property could not be said to exist,

[100] *Ibid.*, p. 164.
[101] Marx, *The Poverty of Philosophy*, N.Y., International Publishers, 1963, p. 161.
[102] See for example Ricardo's arguments in favour of a tax on rent in his *Principles of Political Economy and Taxation*, 3rd edn, London, Murray, 1821, pp. 201 ff.
[103] T.R. Malthus, *Principles of Political Economy*, London, Murray, 1820, pp. 434–435. Malthus provides a standard account of the Asiatic system of economy *ibid.*, pp. 155–160.

because the tax in kind had been so high as to make land unsaleable.[104] The individual was bound to the land by his obligation to contribute taxes. Marx was to write that it was difficult for the English mind to understand that '*fixity of tenure* may be considered a *pest* by the *cultivator* himself' (where the government appropriation of the surplus was particularly onerous).[105]

It was Mill's contention, however, that the government appropriation of the surplus need not retard the economy if the surplus was calculated scientifically, according to the utilitarian theory of rent. Should the *zemindars*, or tax collectors, be allowed to retain the surplus, like European gentry, they would be most unlikely to put it to productive purposes.[106] On the other hand it was unlikely that the ryots would put the surplus to profitable use either, if *they* were permitted to retain the major part of it. It was better, according to Mill, that the government should collect directly from the producers the whole 'rent' of the soil (that is the surplus after costs and an average profit had been calculated and deducted).

The expressed desire to preserve the economic basis of Oriental despotism (the 'nationalisation of the soil') is the most interesting aspect of Mill's work on the subject. Moreover, although the denial of the right to private rent-property was unacceptable to the colonial authorities, his theory of rent was an important influence on the British administration throughout the nineteenth century.

Mill aimed to rid colonialism of its role as an annexe of the obsolete land-owning class at home. This class needed to be prevented from extending its own lifespan and from reproducing itself overseas. Mill was particularly concerned to distinguish clearly between India's Asiatic system and Western feudalism in order to defeat those who argued that the foundations existed on which to build up a native land-owning aristocracy. He argued his case both in terms of land-tenure systems, and in terms of institutional complexity – he claimed that the Indians were not capable of the layered and articulated political and military organisation which had been present in Western feudalism.[107]

---

[104] For a good account of the utilitarian analysis of the Indian economic system see Eric Stokes, *The English Utilitarians and India*, Oxford University Press, 1959, esp. Ch. II (Political Economy and the Land Revenue), pp. 81–139.

[105] Marx, [Marginal note on Irwin's *The Garden of India*], *Ex Libris*, p. 103.

[106] Mill, *The History of British India*, *op.cit.*, Vol. V, 1840, Ch. V (Lord Cornwallis's Financial and Judicial Reforms), pp. 468–640.

[107] *Ibid.*, Vol. II, pp. 197–200, pp. 210–212; Vol. V, pp. 480–482.

John Stuart Mill, like the rest of the British political economists, saw the basic character of the Asiatic form of society as determined by the government appropriation of the surplus.[108] However this idea had been undergoing a metamorphosis. In the Physiocratic model, government appropriation was complementary to private property; in John Stuart Mill's model it prevented the necessary and proper development of private property.

J.S. Mill was influenced by his father's radicalism to the extent that he was prepared for landlord rights to be limited to some extent by government protection of the ryots. He also allowed that the surplus appropriated by the state from the direct producers in the Asiatic system had served certain functions of public utility. It was employed in irrigation works; in supporting government functionaries (and favourites); and in supporting a craftsman class.[109]

The gains from this system were, however, according to J.S. Mill, far outweighed by the debits; through it the state achieved an overweening power, which was detrimental to the rights of the individual. The burden of liberal doctrine, as represented by J.S. Mill, was that respect for the rights of the individual, particularly as embodied in the rights of private property, was essential for a healthy society. Hence Mill attributed the lack of progress in Oriental states to the endemic lack of personal rights and security (particularly of property) *vis à vis* the state.[110] He explained this as follows:

The only insecurity which is altogether paralysing to the active energies of producers, is that arising from the government, or from persons invested with its authority. Against all other depredators there is hope of defending oneself.[111]

In Western Europe, vigour and *Progress* had stemmed from the existence of independent social institutions as a counterweight to the

[108] John Stuart Mill, *Principles of Political Economy*, ed. Ashley, London, Longmans, 1923, p. 12.
[109] *Ibid.*, pp. 12–13.
[110] *Ibid.*, pp. 18; 113. Marx followed Mill closely in arguing that historically, the development of strong forms of private property was necessary for progress, and that the state could not provide an alternative economic dynamic. On the other hand, Marx and Mill shared an ambivalent attitude towards the disappearance of communal forms of landownership. Mill was to write that: 'the system under which nearly the whole soil of Great Britain has come to be appropriated by about thirty thousand families [...] is neither the only nor the oldest form of landed property, and [...] there is no natural necessity for its being preferred to all other forms', and furthermore, that 'we have done and are still doing, irreparable mischief, by blindly introducing the English idea of absolute property in land into a country where it did not exist and never had existed [...]' (J.S. Mill, 'Mr Maine on Village Communities', *Fortnightly Review*, Vol. IX, New Series, (May 1871), pp. 549 and 550).
[111] Mill, *Principles of Political Economy*, *op.cit.*, pp. 113–114.

state, buttressed by customary right and public opinion.[112] Mill differentiated sharply between the 'nominally absolute' governments of Europe and the absolutisms of Asia. In the former, established usage and social institutions protected the individual from the depredations of the government, and private property was in a relatively strong position.[113]

J.S. Mill shared the opinion of his father and the other British political economists that Asiatic systems had no dynamic principle within them, and that this must be provided by the introduction of exogenous factors; ultimately it was only the invasion by foreign capital which could bring to an end the homeostatic tendencies of such systems. The importation of capital would establish the principle of accumulation, and hence substitute economic progress for the circularity of the old system.

The importation of foreign capital, [...] by instilling new ideas and breaking the chains of habit, if not by improving the actual condition of the population, tends to create in them new wants, increased ambition, and greater thought for the future.[114]

Or as Marx was to put it, the penetration of British capital into India was necessary to break up the 'self-sufficient *inertia* in the villages', each of which had existed 'with a given scale of low conveniences, almost without intercourse with other villages, without the desires and efforts indispensable to social advance'.[115] The other conditions of progress were that the Asiatic form of government should be changed for one that did not impose arbitrary taxation on property, and that economically dysfunctional belief systems should be dispersed through education.[116]

The political economist of this period who was to develop the economic analysis of Asiatic society most systematically was not, however, either of the Mills, but their contemporary Richard Jones. It was Jones who was to exercise the greatest single influence on Marx's idea of Oriental despotism.

Jones shared the basic assumptions of the other political economists

[112] *Ibid.*, pp. 114–115. Cf. Marx, 'The British Rule in India', *N.Y.D.T.*, 25 June 1853, *Karl Marx on Colonialism and Modernization*, p. 85. Here both Marx and Mill compare (favourably) the performance of common tasks by voluntary social organisation in Flanders and Italy, with the performance of such tasks by Asiatic governments.

[113] Mill, *Principles of Political Economy, op.cit.*, p. 115.

[114] *Ibid.*, p. 190.

[115] Marx, 'The Future Results of British Rule in India', *N.Y.D.T.*, 8 Aug. 1853, *Karl Marx on Colonialism and Modernization*, p. 135.

[116] Mill, *Principles of Political Economy, op.cit.*, p. 189.

on what constituted 'Asiatic Despotism'.[117] He claimed that the root cause of this socio-political form lay in the fact that the sovereign was the sole proprietor of the land, and enjoyed exclusive title to it.[118] It was the 'universal dependence on the throne for the means of supporting life' which was the explanation of the unbroken despotism of the East.[119]

Such dependence was detrimental to any economic progress as the rents extracted from the direct producers discouraged the expenditure of skill and energy in agriculture.[120] The ryot rents of the Orient (mixed to some extent with labour and metayer rents) served to perpetuate the despotic system in which they had their origin, in that they prevented any independent accumulation.[121]

The distribution of income in Asiatic despotism was determined by the centralised ownership of the basic means of production (land).[122] From this starting point, Jones developed his analysis of 'labour funds' in East and West, or the functions of different method of distributing wealth. His models represented a significant attempt to develop a comparative science of economics.

Jones divided labour funds (i.e. the amount of wealth devoted to maintaining labour) into three main categories: firstly, the self-produced labour funds found in peasant agriculture; secondly, funds paid out of revenues; and thirdly, funds paid out of capital.[123] Jones used Bernier's description of the fate of Indian craftsmen, completely dependent on the revenue centrally distributed by the sovereign and his servants, in order to illustrate the disadvantage of the second category of labour funds over the third. Payment from capital provided a securi-

---

[117] Jones deals specifically with Persia, Turkey, Hindostan and China, and in his later works with Egypt also.

[118] E.g. Richard Jones, *Essay on the Distribution of Wealth*, London, 1831, reprinted N.Y., Kelley and Millman, 1956, pp. 7–8. Jones relied heavily on François Bernier (see above) for primary source material in regard to this, and in regard to the role of the city and the status of crafts in the East.

[119] *Ibid.*, p. 8.

[120] *Ibid.*, pp. 141–142.

[121] *Ibid.*, p. 138.

[122] Cf. Sir Thomas Stamford Raffles, from whom Marx was to quote liberally in 1853 and in succeeding years: 'There is no hereditary rank, nothing to oppose his will [that of the Islamic despot of Java]. Not only honours, posts, and distinctions, depend upon his pleasure, but all the landed property of his dominions remains at his disposal, and may, together with its cultivators, be parcelled out by his order among the officers of his household, the ministers of his pleasures, or the useful servants of the state. Every officer is paid by grants of land, or by a power to receive from the peasantry a certain proportion of the produce of certain villages or districts.' (*The History of Java*, London, Black, Parbury and Allen, 1817, Vol. I, p. 267).

[123] Richard Jones, *Political Economy*, ed. W. Whewell, London, Murray, 1859, pp. 440–454; pp. 219–221.

ty of remuneration, and the possibility of an efficient division of labour, unknown where artisans were directly dependent on the consumers of their goods. The insecurity experienced by the Eastern craftsman was evidenced in the sudden ruin of Asiatic cities when the sovereign, with his monopoly of the revenues of the soil, decided to change his capital.

The influence of Jones' analysis of labour funds on Marx will be discussed elsewhere. One might note here, however, Marx's criticism of the limiting of types of (non-self-produced) labour funds to the type derived from revenues 'belonging to classes distinct from the labourers', and the capitalist type. Marx claimed that Jones had overlooked both the Asiatic community, with its unity of agriculture and industry, and the medieval city corporation. [124]

Jones did, in fact, describe the Indian village community, quoting the same *Report of the Committee on East India Affairs* as Marx did.[125] Jones described the support of village craftsmen from communal revenue as follows: 'The artizans in rural districts are, however, provided for there in a peculiar manner [...] Such handicraftsmen and other non-agriculturalists as were actually necessary in a village were maintained by an assignment of the joint revenues of the villagers, [...] The villagers were stationary and abiding [...] and so were their handicraftsmen [...]'[126]

According to Jones the village system on the one hand tended to support the ryot against the pressure of a despotic government, but on the other hand functioned to keep the level of industry and agriculture stationary, by its exclusion of competition. The division of labour remained hereditary and immutable within its enclosed world, and the villagers were cut off from any more general division of labour within society as a whole, which could only have been brought about by the exchange of commodities. The village was, in fact, the 'substratum of the Hindoo social system, and the cause and pledge of its character and permanency'.[127]

---

[124] Marx, *Theories of Surplus Value, op.cit.*, Part III, p. 417.

[125] *The Fifth Report of the Committee on East India Affairs*, 1812. This section of the parliamentary report seems to have captured the contemporary imagination. Jones (*Political Economy, op.cit.*, pp. 214–215) quotes it via George Robert Gleig's *The History of the British Empire in India*, 4 vols., London 1830–35. Marx reproduces it (in 'The British Rule in India', *N.Y.D.T.*, 25 June 1853, and in *Capital*) from Sir Thomas Stamford Raffles' *The History of Java, op.cit.*, Vol. I, p. 285. He would also have encountered it in one of his major sources on India, George Campbell's *Modern India: A Sketch of the System of Government*, London, Murray, 1852, pp. 84–85.

[126] Jones, *Textbook of Lectures on the Political Economy of Nations*, Hertford, 1852, pp. 73–74, quoted by Marx in *Theories of Surplus Value, op.cit.*, Part III, p. 435.

[127] Jones, *Political Economy, op.cit.*, p. 446.

As for the Asiatic town or city, we have already noted Jones' account of the complete dependence of the townspeople on the expenditure of the sovereign and his servants. Politically, also, industry and commerce suffered in Asiatic despotisms from the absence of independent urban corporations.[128] As a contemporary historian (from whom Marx was to borrow) put it: 'The towns had no common funds or real self-government, so that large non-agricultural municipalities cannot be said to have existed.'[129] J.S. Mill had also commented on the different functions of Oriental and Occidental cities in his explanation of why a bourgeois class had emerged in the West but not in the East.[130]

Here one finds the beginnings of the comparative analysis of the role of the city in feudalism and in Eastern society. This was to become of major significance in the work of Marx and Weber, in explaining the unique historical development which brought into being Western capitalism. Further on this subject, Jones observed that Eastern sovereigns did not have the need, which had existed in Western feudalism, to foster the political influence of the towns (and hence of an emergent bourgeoisie) as a counterbalance to a body of powerful landed proprietors.[131]

With regard to the future of Asiatic despotism, Jones followed Malthus, whom he succeeded at Haileybury, in believing that the necessary 'cure' for it was the development of a landed aristocracy with status-based power.[132] As we have seen, this idea had been current at least since the rise of absolutism in Europe, and was popularised in particular by the opponents of Mazarin and Louis XIV, and by Montesquieu. It occurred naturally to those itinerant noblemen, de Custine and Von Haxthausen, when observing Tsarist bureaucracy

---

[128] Jones, *Essay on the Distribution of Wealth, op.cit.*, pp. 138–139.

[129] George Campbell, *Modern India . . . , op.cit.*, p. 78. Campbell, who was recommended by Marx (*Capital*, Vol. I, p. 358, fn. 1), provided a classic definition of the distinction between Oriental despotism and feudalism. He wrote that the tendency of the Mahommedans has always been 'to the formation of great empires, having nothing feudal in their composition, but everything centralised – the only aristocracy being official, and the officials the creatures of the sovereign'. (*Ibid.*, p. 75). Marx himself chose to excerpt this sentence in his June 1853 conspectus of Campbell (Held at the IISG). Campbell added that the throne was subject to 'the irregularities of revolutions and changes of dynasties common to all Oriental despotisms'. (*Ibid.*, p. 76).

[130] Mill, *Principles of Political Economy, op.cit.*, pp. 17–18.

[131] Jones, *Essay on the Distribution of Wealth, op.cit.*, p. 139.

[132] *Ibid.*, p. 59. As we have seen, the Mills, while advocating the Europeanisation of Asiatic society were selective in respect to which aspects of European society they wished to see transplanted overseas. They were strongly opposed to the creation in India of a class of aristocratic landowners, a class they regarded as already anachronistic in the European context.

in the nineteenth century.[133] Jones, viewing Russia from a greater geographical and social distance than de Custine or von Haxthausen, believed, unlike them, that the aristocracy *had* succeeded in providing a check on Russian absolutism 'sufficient to distinguish it from Asiatic despotism'.[134]

Jones in fact borrowed heavily from Montesquieu in his analysis of the political aspects of Asiatic society. He copied in particular the latter's emphasis on the unhappy consequences of a lack of intermediary bodies between the sovereign and the direct producers: it was the atomisation of the population *vis à vis* the central power which constituted the political framework for a self-perpetuating despotism.[135]

The key to the Asiatic form of society remained, however, for Jones, the economic explanation – i.e. the government monopoly of land. Nonetheless, in explaining the first causes of this exclusive proprietorship, Jones fell back on a non-economic explanation, that of the 'right of conquest'. State ownership had arisen from the fact that all these countries had been conquered by foreigners.[136] As already mentioned, this idea had been employed by earlier colonial apologists, such as Alexander Dow (*On the Origin of Despotism in Hindostan*, 1772) who used it as a justification for the confiscation of land.

Jones did not posit any prior factors to account for the singular results of such conquests in Asia, apart from a half-hearted attempt to establish that the conquering hordes of the East were inured to habits of military submission because of the dangers of the exposed plains, whereas the Germanic hordes had contracted habits of freedom in the security of the 'fastnesses and morasses of [their] native woods'.[137] Hence the differing results of conquest in the case of the Germanic and Eastern hordes.

Where the British political economists, and Richard Jones in particular, succeeded was in investing the concept of Oriental despotism with an element of systematic economic analysis which previously it had

[133] De Custine, *Russia*, abridged edn, London, Longmans, 1855, passim; von Haxthausen, *The Russian Empire, its People, Institutions and Resources*, 2 vols, London, Chapman Hall, 1856, reprinted Frank Cass, 1968, Vol. II, Ch. VIII (pp. 200–217).

[134] Jones, *Essay on the Distribution of Wealth, op.cit.*, p. 59.

[135] *Ibid.*, p. 113.

[136] Jones, *Political Economy, op.cit.*, p. 221. Popular arguments were that it was either conquest by steppe nomads or by Islamic nations that instituted despotic systems. Both of these arguments are reflected in Marx's work, though they are not included in his central model of Oriental despotism. The conquest theory goes back to Jean Bodin and Montesquieu (see above).

[137] Jones, *Essay on the Distribution of Wealth, op.cit.*, p. 110. Marx noted down this explanation in his 1851 conspectus of Jones' *Essay*, and it is to be found on p. 76 of the Notebook catalogued as B58 by the IISG.

lacked. This in turn was only made possible by developments in the science of economics associated with the progress of capitalism. As Marx said:

... bourgeois economics arrived at an understanding of feudal, ancient, oriental economics only after the self-criticism of bourgeois society had begun.[138]

The political economists did not however arrive at the idea that the Oriental political system derived from the need for the state to provide the conditions of production.[139] Although Jones, and for that matter Adam Smith and the Mills, described the expenditure by Asiatic governments on public works, they did *not* treat such expenditure as symptomatic of the need for state intervention in providing the conditions of production in the East. The general argument, from the Physiocrats through Adam Smith, had been that the interventionist role of the Asiatic state in agriculture derived from its controlling interest in agricultural productivity, not *vice versa*.

---

[138] Marx, *Grundrisse*, Introduction, p. 106; and used by Marx in *A Contribution to the Critique of Political Economy*, tr. S.W. Ryazanskaya, Moscow, Progress, 1970, p. 211.

[139] Wittfogel's account of Jones, (e.g. Karl A. Wittfogel, 'The Marxist View of Russian Society and Revolution', *World Politics* Vol. 12 (1959–1960), p. 490, fn. 21), misleadingly suggests that Jones saw the need for irrigation as the key to Asiatic despotism. What Jones actually said in the passage referred to by Wittfogel is that, because of the special need for irrigation which existed in Persia, 'some valuable *modifications* [my emphasis] of the Asiatic system of ryot rents' had been introduced there. (*An Essay on the Distribution of Wealth*, *op.cit.*, p. 119). These modifications comprised more secure guarantes of property, in order to encourage the building of 'cannauts'. The Persian despots wished to encourage the productivity of the soil because, as elsewhere in Asia, they were the 'supreme owners' of the produce of the soil, by right of conquest.

CHAPTER II

THE MARXIAN CONCEPT OF THE ASIATIC MODE OF PRODUCTION

> Absichtlich ist es vermieden worden, an dem für uns weitaus wichtigsten Fall idealtypischer Konstruktionen zu demonstrieren: an Marx.
>
> MAX WEBER

MARX'S PERCEPTION OF THE NON-WESTERN WORLD

Marx and Engels took no specific interest in the nature of non-Western society before 1853. Up till then they simply adopted Hegel's characterisation of the Orient as the relic of a past era of human history, destined to succumb to the more dynamic civilisation of the West.[1] The impact of capitalist commodities was already bringing about a revolution in the social structure of India and China, for example, forcing these countries out of their ahistorical vegetation. This is the point that Engels makes in his report to the London Workingmen's Educational Society on the effects that the discovery of America has had on the opening up of a world market:

Since the English have made themselves masters of world trade and brought the state of their manufacturing to such a height that they can furnish almost the entire civilised world with their products, and since the bourgeoisie have attained political power, they have also succeeded in making further progress in *Asia*; the bourgeoisie have achieved ascendancy there also. Through the rise of machinery the barbarian condition of other countries is continually ruined. We know that the Spanish found the *East Indies* at the same level of development as did the English, and that the Indians have nevertheless continued to live for centuries in the same manner, i.e. they have eaten, drunk and vegetated, and the grandson has tilled his soil just as the grandfather did – with the exception that a number of revolutions have taken place which however, amounted to nothing more than a conflict between various races for the government. Since the arrival of the English and the spread of their commodities the Indians have had their livelihood torn from their hands, and the consequence has been that they have departed from their stable situation. The workers there are already migrating and through mingling with other peoples are becoming for the first time acces-

---

[1] Marx and Engels refer specifically to Hegel's account of Oriental society only in *The German Ideology* (written 1845–1846), Moscow, Progress, 1968, pp. 176–183. Hegel's characterisation of Oriental society, however, colours everything that Marx and Engels wrote on the subject in this period.

sible to civilisation. The old Indian aristocracy is completely ruined, and the people are being set against each other as much there as here.

Subsequently, we have seen how *China*, the land which has stubbornly resisted development and all historical change for more than a thousand years, has now been overthrown and dragged into civilisation by the English and their machines.[2]

In Engels' report, one can observe both the theme of the revolutionary impact of Western capitalism on countries which had resisted change for millennia, and the theme of the contrast between the superficial (political) turbulence of traditional Oriental society and its fundamental (social) changelessness – a theme already encountered in relation to Herder and Hegel, and which was to reappear in Marx's articles for the *New York Daily Tribune*.

The theme of the revolutionary effects of the capitalist world market on countries previously 'more or less strangers to historical development'[3] was also developed by Engels in his *Principles of Communism* and became part of the *Communist Manifesto*. Western capitalism, in compelling 'all nations, on pain of extinction, to adopt the bourgeois mode of production',[4] also brought the possibility of socialism to the non-Western world. Moreover, its role in bringing all nations of the world into contact with one another ensured that:

Whatever happens in civilised countries will have repercussions in all other countries. It follows that if the workers in France and England now liberate themselves, this must set off revolutions in all other countries – revolutions which sooner or later must accomplish the liberation of their respective working classes.[5]

The *Communist Manifesto* describes the impact of capitalism on traditional societies both in terms of the destruction of traditional manufactures *and* in terms of the stimulation of material wants, long underdeveloped in Eastern societies. Marx and Engels followed Hegel in the belief that man developed his potential powers in the process of satisfying everchanging and diversifying material needs. Hegel wrote that:

An animal's needs and its ways and means of satisfying them are both alike restricted in scope. Though man is subject to this restriction too, yet at the same

---

[2] See the [Protokollauszüge über die von Marx und Engels in der Londoner Bildungs-Gesellschaft für Arbeiter am 30. November und am 7. Dezember 1847 gehaltenen Vorträge], *MEGA* I/VI, p. 637.

[3] Engels, *Principles of Communism* (written October 1847), tr. Paul M. Sweezy, London, Pluto, n.d., p. 8.

[4] Marx and Engels, *Communist Manifesto*, *MESW*, Vol. I, pp. 36–37.

[5] Engels, *Principles of Communism*, *op.cit.*, p. 9.

time he evinces his transcendence of it and his universality, first by the multiplication of needs and means of satisfying them, and secondly by the differentiation and division of concrete need into single parts and aspects which in turn become different needs, particularised and so more abstract.[6]

Marx and Engels applied this idea to the functions of the world market:

> In place of the old wants, satisfied by the productions of the country, we find new wants, requiring for their satisfaction the products of distant lands and climes. In place of the old local and national seclusion and self-sufficiency, we have intercourse in every direction, universal inter-dependence of nations. And as in material, so also in intellectual production. The intellectual creations of individual nations become common property. National one-sidedness and narrow-mindedness become more and more impossible . . .[7]

Marx and Engels were also interested in the non-Western world from the point of view of its role in prolonging the life of European capitalism (through the provision of raw materials and markets). This argument became particularly important to Marx and Engels in and after 1850, with the disappointment of their early revolutionary hopes.

But although Marx and Engels foreshadowed their later analysis of the dynamics of interaction between East and West during this period, they did not as yet attempt any explanation of the special character of the Oriental world (as they understood it from Hegel). This was in spite of the fact that their reading in these years encompassed many of the authors referred to in Chapter One, who put forward explanations of the character of Oriental society. Marx had taken copious notes from Montesquieu's *De l'esprit des lois* as early as 1843, and in the following years he began his study of the British political economists.[8] He read and made extracts from Richard Jones' *Essay on the Distribution of Wealth* in 1851, though the latter's analysis of Asiatic society only made

---

[6] Hegel, *Philosophy of Right*, tr. T.M. Knox, Oxford, Clarendon Press, 1942, § 190, p. 127.

[7] Marx, Engels, *Communist Manifesto, loc.cit.*, p. 36. Cf. Marx's later description of the impact of British capitalism on the traditional Indian village – a community which had 'existed with a given scale of low conveniences, almost without intercourse with other villages, without the desires and efforts indispensable to social advance. The British having broken up this self-sufficient *inertia* of the villages, railways will provide the new want of communication and intercourse'. ('The Future Results of British Rule in India', *N.Y.D.T.*, 8 Aug. 1853, *Karl Marx on Colonialism and Modernization*, p. 135).

[8] For details of Marx's reading in these years see Maximilien Rubel, 'Les cahiers de lecture de Karl Marx: 1840–1853', *International Review of Social History*, New Series, 2, 1957, pp. 392–420. Marx's notes on Smith are reproduced in *MEGA* I/3, pp. 457–492. Other writers on the subject of Asiatic despotism with whom Marx came into contact at this time were the Physiocrats, Linguet, and W.A. Mackinnon. (The latter of whom argued that the basis of Oriental despotism was the ownership of all land by the sovereign combined with a lack of moral principle brought about by the absence of a middle class.) See W.A. Mackinnon, *History of Civilisation and Public Opinion*, 2 vols., 3rd edn, London, Henry Colbourn, 1849, Vol. II, pp. 185–215.

a real impact on Marx after he had read Jones' most important source, François Bernier, for himself in 1853.[9]

In 1853, in connection with his articles for the *New York Daily Tribune*, Marx began for the first time to consider seriously the socio-economic nature of Oriental society. It is then that the impact of his earlier reading becomes apparent, in conjunction with the further research he now undertook.[10] Through looking at Marx's correspondence with Engels, it is possible to observe fairly closely the formation of the working model of Asiatic society which was to serve Marx for the rest of his life.

Marx's starting point was Bernier, whose writing convinced Marx that the essence of Oriental society lay in the fact that the '*king is the one and only proprietor of all the land in the kingdom* [...]'[11] 'Bernier', Marx wrote to Engels, 'correctly discovers the basic form of all phenomena in the East – he refers to Turkey, Persia, Hindostan – to be the *absence of private property* in land. This is the real key even to the Oriental heaven [...]'[12] Engels raised the question *why* the 'Orientals did not arrive at landed property, even in its feudal form'.[13] Geographical factors in the East, he declared, made irrigation 'the first condition of agriculture' and that this was 'a matter either for the communes, the provinces or the central government'.[14] Private property in land did not develop, in other words, because the private individual, as such, was unable to supply the conditions of agriculture.

In his article 'The British Rule in India', Marx took over Engels' explanation of why Oriental society had assumed its particular features – the need for the government to perform 'an economical

---

[9] See Marx to Engels, 2 June 1853, *Karl Marx on Colonialism and Modernization*, pp. 450–451. The notes which Marx took from Jones in 1851 cover most of the features of Asiatic society incorporated by Marx into his 1853 model. For example, Marx copied out and underlined Jones' statement that the Ryot rents of Asia were produce rents paid by the labourer to the sovereign as proprietor of the soil. Marx also noted down other statements by Jones on the position of the Asiatic sovereign as sole proprietor of the soil and direct landlord of the peasant tenants; on the zemindaree system; on the village system; on the character of Asiatic towns; on the absence of independent intermediary classes, whether of landowners or burgesses, and on the need for irrigation to make the soil fertile over large tracts of Asia. (See pp. 76–79 of Notebook B58, referred to above in the last section of Chapter One, p. 38).

[10] The IISG holds three unpublished notebooks dating from this period, catalogued as B63, B64 and B65, which contain Marx's notes on his research into the nature of Oriental society. The works read by Marx in 1853 included Bernier's *Voyages* ..., Mark Wilks' *Historical Sketches of the South of India*, George Campbell's *Modern India* and Raffles' *History of Java*. For further details of these see the previous chapter.

[11] Marx to Engels, 2 June 1853, *loc.cit.*, p. 450.

[12] *Ibid.*, p. 451.

[13] Engels to Marx, 6 June 1853, *Karl Marx on Colonialism and Modernization*, p. 451.

[14] *Ibid.*, p. 452.

function' in providing public works such as irrigation.[15] Complementary to the 'centralizing power of Government' was the dispersal of the population in small villages, each representing a self-sufficient world in which agricultural and manufacturing pursuits were combined.[16]

Thus by June 1853 Marx had already developed the distinctive Marxian model of Oriental society. This model was similar to that employed by the political economists, in that the central feature of Oriental society was seen as the government monopoly of land (soon to be expressed by Marx in terms of the government monopoly of surplus value), but the explanation given for this monopoly was new. The idea that the state had attained its economic pre-eminence in Asiatic society because of the need for the central power to provide the conditions of production such as irrigation and communication appears to be original to Marx and Engels.[17]

Marx almost immediately began to modify his initial thesis concerning the absence of private property in land in the Orient.[18] As he came across the controversy among British writers on this subject Marx revised his opinion about the complete 'absence of property in land' in the East. He arrived at a more complex argument which distinguished nominal and symbolic ownership from traditional rights of possession and usufruct, and which allowed for communal and even individual title to the land. Since the 1840s Marx has stressed that the first form of ownership was tribal/communal, and by 1857 he had returned to the position that such communal property preceded the rest of the system of Oriental despotism.[19]

Asiatic society had its genesis in a form of communal ownership more resistant to the evolution of private property than either the Greco-Roman or Germanic forms.[20] Hence the development of private-

---

[15] Marx, 'The British Rule in India', *N.Y.D.T.* 25 June 1853, *Karl Marx on Colonialism and Modernization*, p. 90. See also *Capital*, Vol. I, p. 514, fn. 2: 'One of the material bases of the power of the State over the small disconnected producing organisms in India, was the regulation of the water supply.'

[16] Marx, 'The British Rule in India', *loc.cit.*, pp. 92–94.

[17] There are, of course, inconsistencies in Marx, as when he claims that 'it seems to have been the Mohammedans who first established the principle of "no property in land" throughout the whole of Asia.' (I.e., a combination of the religious and conquest explanations of Oriental despotism). See Marx to Engels, 14 June 1853, *Karl Marx on Colonialism and Modernization*, p. 457. See also *Capital*, Vol. III, p. 791, fn. 44, for another instance of Marx's employment of the conquest explanation of Oriental despotism.

[18] See Marx to Engels, 14 June 1853, *loc.cit.*, pp. 456–457.

[19] See Marx and Engels, *The German Ideology*, *op.cit.*, p. 33; Marx, *Grundrisse*, pp.472–473; p. 484. 'Amidst Oriental despotism and the propertylessness which seems legally to exist there, this clan or communal property exists in fact as the foundation ...'. (*Ibid.*, p. 473).

property based classes did not precede or coincide with the creation of state power, as in Western societies. In Asiatic society, the state came into being to perform certain public tasks which could not be fulfilled at the village level. Furthermore, these public tasks included vital economic functions which in the West could be fulfilled by the voluntary association of private enterprise, but not in the Orient, because there 'civilization was too low and the territorial extent too vast to call into life voluntary association.'[21] The low level of civilization was itself conditioned by the communal village structure, which inhibited the development of a more complex social division of labour; and which brought about instead the multiplication of homologous, self-sufficient communities united only through their common relationship to the central power and individually too weak to undertake large public tasks.

The importance of the economic functions which thus devolved on the central government enabled the state to exert a claim prior to that of the commune over the surplus produced by its members. ('The [higher] unity is the [. . .] real presupposition of communal property').[22] Hence the commune, although the original 'owner' of the land, which its members possessed in virtue of their membership of the community, was reduced to the status of intermediary in the appropriation of the surplus value from the direct producers by the central government.

The key feature then of Marx's mature model of Oriental society was that the state, rather than the slave-owner or feudal lord found in Western pre-capitalist societies, was the 'principal owner of the surplus product'.[23] This, together with the general absence of 'strong' private-property rights which could give rise to powerful social classes was the basic distinction which Marx was to draw between the pre-capitalist societies of the East and of the West. The Eastern system conserved, and was conserved by, an archaic social base – villages, which in their communal arrangements bore some relationship to the primitive kinship communities in which men first settled on the land.

---

[20] Marx, *Grundrisse*, pp. 471–498.

[21] Marx, 'The British Rule in India', *loc.cit.*, p. 90.

[22] Marx, *Grundrisse*, p. 473.

[23] E.g., *Capital*, Vol. III, pp. 326; 331; 791; 794. The translation of *Tributverhältnis* as 'vassalage' (*ibid.*, p. 326) is quite inaccurate in the context – Marx is here contrasting the role of the 'tribute-collecting state' with that of the slave-owner or feudal lord. As he wrote elsewhere, 'In Europe, im Unterschied vom East, in *place of the produce tribute* was substituted a *dominion over the soil* – the cultivators being turned out of their land u. reduced to the condition of serfs or labourers.' (Marx's conspectus of Sir John Budd Phear, *The Aryan Village in India and Ceylon* [London, 1880, notes written Aug.-Sept. 1881], Lawrence Krader ed., *The Ethnological Notebooks of Karl Marx*, Assen, Van Gorcum, 1972, p. 284).

The combination of the monopoly by the state of economic initiative and the surplus product, and the lingering on of village communalism (which also inhibited the rise of the private entrepreneur), meant that, in Marx's view there was a complete lack of *dynamism* within the Oriental system. There was the possibility neither of the development of commodity production, as in the Western slave-holding formation, nor of the development of the urban commune, and urban manufacture, as in Western feudalism.

ALTERNATIVE INTERPRETATIONS:
THE QUESTION OF THE CONTINUITY OR DISCONTINUITY OF
MARX'S MODEL OF ASIATIC SOCIETY

It has been argued by Donald M. Lowe that three *different* models of the Asiatic mode of production appear in the work of Marx and Engels: one dating from 1853, one from *Capital*, and one from the *Anti-Dühring* of Engels. According to Lowe:

The 1853 version used the self-enclosed village community and the state water works to explain the persistence of the political phenomenon of Oriental despotism. The *Capital* version used the self-enclosed village community and the state consumption of surplus value to explain the economic phenomenon of under-development in commodity exchange. The *Anti-Dühring* version emphasized the self-enclosed village community, but pointed to the eventual transition from communal landownership to small-peasant landownership [sic].[24]

The implications which Lowe draws from this alleged change of models are as follows:

The shift in argument away from state water works and Oriental despotism, I believe, has to be explained basically by the change in approach from that of political economy to that of economics. Therefore, the political-economic approach indicated the interaction between Oriental despotism and Asiatic economy, and the economic approach explained the Asiatic mode of production in purely economic terms.[25]

Lowe's argument for a shift in models, and the reasons he adduces for this shift, stem basically from a misapprehension concerning the model Marx arrived at in 1853. This misapprehension centres around the term 'Oriental despotism', which Lowe appears to interpret in the Wittfogel

[24] Donald M. Lowe, *The Function of 'China' in Marx, Lenin, and Mao*, University of California Press, 1966, p. 14. Lowe's interpretation of *Anti-Dühring* will be dealt with in a later section of this chapter which is devoted specifically to Engels.
[25] *Ibid.*

manner, as signifying a system of political totalitarianism. But already in 1853, thanks to his acquaintance with political economy, 'Oriental despotism' signified for Marx not so much a *political* phenomenon, as a non-progressive *economic* form marked by state intervention in the economy. In fact Marx went to some pains in 1853 to explain how *little* the central government impinged on the archaic self-governing institutions of the Oriental village community. Thus Marx quoted this description of the village:

> The inhabitants gave themselves no trouble about the breaking up and divisions of kingdoms; while the village remains entire, they care not to what power it is transferred or to what sovereign it devolves; its internal economy remains unchanged. The potail is still the head inhabitant and still acts as the petty judge or magistrate, and collector or rentor of the village.[26]

Moreover, as we have seen in the previous chapter, the political economists did not, as Lowe implies, regard the governmental control of water works as the key to the Oriental system. They described the essence of the Asiatic system as being the state monopoly of the land and land revenue, probably stemming from the conquest of the native people by nomadic invaders.[27] Because the Asiatic state had a direct interest in the revenue of the soil, it frequently provided public works such as irrigation schemes to enhance productivity, but this was not seen as the *cause* of its exclusive proprietorship.

Marx never seriously took up the conquest explanation of how the state came to achieve its dominating position in the Eastern economy. He argued on the contrary that the Asiatic system of exploitation owed less to foreign conquest than did Western forms of exploitation such as slavery and serfdom.[28] The explanation he did adopt from 1853 on was Engels' idea that the Asiatic state owed its economic position to the fact that it played a necessary entrepreneurial role in providing the

---

[26] Marx, quoting from the *Fifth Report of the Committee on East India Affairs (1812)*, in 'The British Rule in India', *loc.cit.*, p. 93. Cf. 'In the East, under the village system, the *people practically governed themselves* . . .' (Marx's conspectus of Sir John Budd Phear, *The Aryan Village in India and Ceylon*, *loc.cit.*, p. 284). The italicised words are those underlined by Marx. Jean Chesneaux sees the capacity of the central power to reduce its intervention at the village level to a minimum as indicative of the high development of the art of government in 'Asiatic' society: 'le caractère élaboré, rationalisé, conscient, des mécanismes de la société "asiatique", dans laquelle le pouvoir central tirait parti au maximum de la capacité "automotrice" des communautés de village et grâce à sa science, réduisait au maximum son intervention'. (Jean Chesneaux, "Où en est la discussion sur le 'mode de production asiatique'?", *La Pensée*, No. 122 (Aug. 1965), pp. 54–55 fn.

[27] E.g., '. . . all the great empires of Asia have been overrun by foreigners; and on their rights as conquerors the claim of the present sovereign to the soil rests.' (Richard Jones, *Essay on the Distribution of Wealth*, 1831, reprinted N.Y., Kelley and Millman, 1956, p. 110).

[28] Marx, *Grundrisse*, p. 493.

conditions of production, a role forced on it by geographical conditions.

It is true, as Lowe points out, that Marx does not continue the discussion in *Capital* concerning *why* the Asiatic state came to have an effective monopoly over the land. In the *Grundrisse*, however, where pre-capitalist formations are specifically under analysis, as they are not in the published sections of *Capital*, he does discuss this issue, and irrigation functions are listed prominently among the factors giving rise to Oriental despotism.[29] Likewise, in an article of 1858 Marx wrote that works of public utility were 'more indispensable in Asiatic countries than anywhere else [. . .]'[30]

Hence there is a continuity in Marx's explanation of the Eastern system which Lowe overlooks. Marx did not *cease* to believe that the state monopoly of the surplus in the East was closely linked with the need for the Eastern state to play an organising role in actualising the productivity of the soil.[31] It was simply that in *Capital* itself he was looking more closely at the *consequences* of such a state monopoly of revenue, although in a way completely foreshadowed in 1853 (the lack of development of Western-style cities etc.).[32] The role of the village system in hampering the development of nation-wide division of labour and commodity exchange was also foreshadowed in 1853.

Eric Hobsbawm, in his introduction to the first English translation of the *Pre-Capitalist Formations*, pursues an argument which is apparently the source of Lowe's three models of the Asiatic mode of production. Hobsbawm writes as follows:

Ignorance of the *Formen* has resulted in the discussion of the oriental system in the past being based chiefly on Marx and Engels' earlier letters and on Marx's articles on India (both 1853), where it is characterised – in line with the views of the earliest foreign observers – by 'the absence of property in land'. This was thought due to special conditions, requiring exceptional centralisation, e.g. the need for public works and irrigation schemes in areas which could not otherwise be effectively cultivated. However, on further consideration, Marx evidently held that the fundamental characteristic of this system was 'the self-sustaining unity

[29] *Ibid.*, pp. 473–475.

[30] Marx, [Taxes in India], leading article, *N.Y.D.T.*, 23 July 1858, *Karl Marx on Colonialism and Modernization*, p. 335.

[31] Or providing the 'communal conditions of real appropriation through labour' as Marx expressed it in the *Grundrisse*, pp. 473–474.

[32] The continuity of Marx's analysis is particularly evident in his handling of the question of the effects of the centralised distribution of revenue on the Oriental city. His first letter on the subject of Oriental society stressed Bernier's description of this, while his later work utilised Richard Jones' systematisation of Bernier's material. (See Marx to Engels, 2 June 1853, *loc.cit.*, the *Grundrisse*, pp. 474, 479; *Theories of Surplus Value*, Part III, London, Lawrence and Wishart, 1972, pp. 401, 416, 435).

of manufacture and agriculture', which thus contains all the conditions for re-
production and surplus production within itself [. . .].[33]

Pace Hobsbawm, the 'self-sustaining unity of manufacture and agriculture' in no way explains what Marx regarded as the key to any
socio-economic formation – i.e., the way in which the 'unpaid surplus-
labour is pumped out of direct producers'.[34] Marx continued to believe
that in Asiatic society the major proportion of the surplus value
accrued to the state, in contrast with the situation in Western socio-
economic formations, and that this was primarily because the Asiatic
state had a special role in providing the communal conditions of production. Indeed Marx suggested that the particular conditions of production in Asia which rendered the state the chief exploiter of labour were
also the reason why the original Oriental village community was so
much more resistant to the forces of dissolution than were the Western
forms of communal ownership. In the West, circumstances arose in
which individual property did not require communal labour for its
valorisation.[35] In Asiatic society, by contrast, the individual was
doubly dependent on the community, i.e. the community both in the
forms of the village community and of the state, for the provision of
the conditions of production. Thus exploitation by representatives of
the larger community took the place of exploitation by the private
individuals who in the West came to control access to the means of
production.

Hobsbawm's and Lowe's reaction to Marx's use of the term 'Oriental
despotism' and their desire to prove that Marx moved away from such
a concept towards a more 'consistently economic and more cogent'[36]
argument epitomises the many attempts to 'save' Marx from Wittfogel.
These attempts are misguided insofar as Marx used the terms 'Oriental
despotism', 'Asiatic despotism', 'Oriental despot' etc., all his life,
although he did not mean by them what Wittfogel means.

What Marx says in the section on Labour Rent in *Capital*, for
example, is that 'there need exist no stronger political or economic
pressure' on the direct producer where the state is his direct landlord,
and rent and taxes coincide, than where he is confronted by a private
landowner, as in the West.[37] Marx regarded contemporary Western

[33] Introduction to Marx, *Pre-Capitalist Economic Formations*, ed. Eric Hobsbawm, London, Lawrence and Wishart, 1964, p. 33.
[34] Marx, *Capital*, Vol. III, p. 791.
[35] Marx, *Grundrisse*, p. 475. Nicolaus' translation is not directly quoted here, as it is
exceptionally awkward, and furthermore renders 'verwertet' rather loosely as 'realised'.
[36] Donald M. Lowe, *The Function of 'China' in Marx, Lenin, and Mao, op.cit.*, p. 14.
[37] *Capital*, Vol. III, p. 791.

governments as more potentially oppressive than Oriental despotisms
– to get free of an oppressive social situation was much more difficult
in the conditions of social interdependence of modern centralised
government than under 'the much more *"fluid"* Asiatic despotism or
feudal anarchy'.[38]

In any 'Asiatic' system the exploitation of the direct producers was
limited, as in the feudal systems of the West, by the predominance of
natural economy. Marx analysed the situation in the following manner:
'It is, however, clear that in any given economic formation of society
where not the exchange-value but the use-value of the product pre-
dominates, surplus-labour will be limited by a given set of wants which
may be greater or less, and that here no boundless thirst for surplus-
labour arises from the nature of the production itself.'[39]

Accordingly, where rent rather than profit is the chief means of
accumulation (i.e. where the capitalist mode of production has not yet
become predominant) the direct producer not only retains that part of
his production equivalent to his own wages, but is almost always able
to retain a proportion of the surplus value he creates. As Marx wrote:

...as long as the greater part of the surplus labour and surplus product which
does not accrue to the worker himself, goes to the landowner (the State in Asia)
and, on the other hand, the worker reproduces his labour fund himself, i.e., he
not only produces his own wages himself, but pays them to himself, usually,
moreover, (almost always in that state of society) he is also able to appropriate
at least a part of his surplus labour and his surplus product ...

This is contrasted by Marx with the capitalist mode of production,
where:

...the capitalist directly appropriates the whole surplus labour and surplus
product in the first instance, although he has to hand over portions of it to the
landowner...[40]

Because of the centralisation of revenue, the Asiatic state had the
power to command large-scale co-operation, but:

This power of Asiatic and Egyptian Kings, Etruscan theocrats, & c, has in
modern society been transferred to the capitalist, whether he be an isolated, or
as in joint-stock companies, a collective capitalist.[41]

Marx took over from Hegel and other sources the notion that the East

[38] Marginal note by Marx on H.C. Irwin's *The Garden of India*, London, Allen, 1880, p. 263,
see *Ex Libris*, p. 103.
[39] *Capital*, Vol. I, p. 235.
[40] Marx, *Theories of Surplus Value*, Part III, *op.cit.*, pp. 420–421. Note that in Asia rents
and taxes coincide.
[41] Marx, *Capital*, Vol. I, p. 334.

was stagnant. What he sought from political economy was a 'scientific' explanation for this Oriental stagnation, not an explanation for Oriental political oppression or excessive economic exploitation. Marx perceived Oriental government as arbitrary, but as intervening less than Western governments with respect to the underlying structure of society. In his treatment of the Oriental village system, as we shall see, he was to reject all suggestions that the state played an active role in moulding the infrastructure of society.

Basically Marx never added very much to the model of Oriental society he derived from the political economists, apart from his explanation of the origins of the system, which he had already arrived at through Engels in 1853. In *Capital* Marx simply adds some points of detail to the model, like the effects of the Asiatic tax in kind in further inhibiting the development of commodity exchange.[42] Marx *did* go beyond the political economists in his investigation into the kinship origins of the community property forms found in the Orient, but this did not affect his working model of Oriental society. There are also some discontinuities in Marx's attitude towards the potential development of the Oriental village system, which will be discussed elsewhere.

The continuity of Marx's thought about Asiatic society stemmed from the fact that in political economy Marx found an explanation for the backwardness, or non-developmental character, of the Orient which fitted in completely with his own life-long anti-étatist views. The monopoly of economic initiative by entrepreneurial state power resulted in stagnation, as would be argued by any nineteenth-century liberal, including Marx who shared the views of the liberals about the role of state power.

MARX'S ANALYSIS OF ASIATIC SOCIETY IN THE
GENERAL PERSPECTIVE OF HIS SOCIAL THEORY

Marx acknowledged the Asiatic mode of production to be a socio-economic formation of comparable historical importance to the ancient, feudal and 'modern bourgeois' modes of production.[43] At first sight

---

[42] *Capital*, Vol. I, pp. 140–141; Vol. III, p. 796.

[43] Marx, Preface to *A Contribution to the Critique of Political Economy*, tr. S.W. Ryazans-kaya, Moscow, Progress, 1970, p. 21. Other problems raised by this passage, relating to whether Marx saw these formations as logically or chronologically progressive, and how this notion of progression can be fitted into a multilinear theory of history, will be discussed below in Chapter Five.

this acknowledgement appears to be an anomaly within Marx's theory of society. The anomaly arises because in the Asiatic mode of production, as defined by Marx, the development of self-conscious classes and class struggle was of negligible importance, whereas according to his social theory 'The history of all hitherto-existing society is the history of class struggles.'[44]

One approach to the problem has been to read the concept out of the Marxist canon, as was done in the Soviet Union between 1931 and 1964. As one of the spokesmen who presided over the exorcism was to say:

The concept of a special 'Asiatic' mode of production [. . .] is theoretically unfounded, because it contradicts the foundations of the Marxist-Leninist teaching on classes and the state.[45]

The apparent anomaly *can* be eliminated on a facile level by resorting to Marx's notion that Asiatic society was in fact incapable of history or only of perpetuating 'unhistorical history', precisely because of the absence within it of classes and class struggle. However, a further problem then arises concerning the functions of state power. According to Marx's analysis, the state form, as contrasted with primitive kinship organisation, was essentially part of the superstructure of society, brought into existence when class antagonisms had become so severe that they could only be held in check by a repressive power. But Marx did not attempt to relate the rise of state power in Asiatic society to the repressive functions required by class society.

In Marx's model the Asiatic state is not only part of the superstructure of society, but also part of the productive base, the state being required to provide the communal conditions of production, such as irrigation. As the soil was unproductive without the entrepreneurial or organisational role of the state, the state assumed a controlling interest in the soil and its surplus product. Agriculture in Asia could not be sustained 'on the British principle of free competition, of *laissez faire* and *laissez aller*'.[46] This was unlike the situation in slave or feudal societies, where state intervention was *not* an economic necessity in order to make land productive, and stronger forms of private appropriation of the land developed.[47] In these societies the slave-owner or the feudal lord were able to establish the private control of the means of production, and hence to enjoy that surplus product of the

---

[44] Marx and Engels, *Communist Manifesto, MESW*, Vol. I, p. 33.

[45] E. Iolk, in *Diskussiia ob aziatskom sposobe proizvodstva*, Moscow, Gos. sots.-ekon. izd., 1931, p. 70.

[46] Marx, 'The British Rule in India', *loc.cit.*, p. 91.

[47] See the passage already cited in Marx, *Grundrisse*, p. 475.

land which in the East was monopolised by the state.[48] The relationship of the state to the base was mediated by dominant economic classes, which largely discouraged direct state intervention in the economy.

In his analysis of Western society Marx treated social and political power as being in a dependent relationship to the (private) ownership of the dominant means of production. Political structures were shaped in accordance with the interests of property-owning classes, and political ruling groups represented these interests, protecting them where need be by force. In the East, where the *state* 'owned' the dominant means of production, and hence itself formed part of the economic base,[49] this situation was reversed. Economic and social privilege derived from political function, and were dependent on service to the state rather than on the ownership of private property;[50] the system of benefices did not become hereditary and independent of service as in the West.

Hence there is a basic difference between the role of the state in Marx's general model, of society and in his model of Asiatic society. In his general model the state bore only an indirect relationship to the productive base; a relationship which consisted in the function of the state in maintaining the exploitative (private) relations of production that were necessary for economic progress up to the socialist stage. In his model of Asiatic society, for the reasons given, it was state rather than private exploitation which lay at the base of the system.

Marx has been criticised on the factual grounds that the Asiatic state had far less significance in providing the direct conditions of production (e.g. irrigation, communication) than he assumed. For example, Barrington Moore has argued, in relation to India, that the Asiatic state was economically superfluous; that it did not even have to perform minimal state functions (like the Western state) such as keeping order, as this was done by the caste system; and that it played no positive role in local production.[51] Marx himself commented that

---

[48] For the comparison between the appropriation by the slave owner and feudal lord in the West, and the state in the East, see, in particular, *Capital*, Vol. III, pp. 326; 331.

[49] 'It is always the direct relationship of the owners [in this case "owner"] of the conditions of production to the direct producers [...] which reveals the innermost secret, the hidden basis of the entire social structure ...' (*Ibid.*, p. 791).

[50] Cf. G.V. Plekhanov: 'The ruling classes we meet with in the history of these countries held their more or less exalted social position owing to the state organisation called into being by the needs of the social productive process.' (*The Materialist Conception of History*, first published in *Novoe Slovo*, 1897, No 9, Moscow, Foreign Languages Publishing House, 1946, p. 21.)

[51] Barrington Moore, *Social Origins of Dictatorship and Democracy*, London, Penguin Press, 1967, p. 791.

where independent natural production communities existed, as in India, the surplus could only be extorted from them by 'other than economic pressure, whatever the form assumed may be'.[52] The non-economic pressure Marx had in mind here was that deriving from conquest,[53] although elsewhere he also discusses the role of social norms:

> ... surplus labour takes the form of tribute etc., as well as of common labour for the exaltation of the unity, partly of the real despot, partly of the imagined clan-being, the god.[54]

Marx's model of Asiatic society certainly contained an exaggerated view of the role of the state in providing the direct conditions of production, and as we see, he became aware of this exaggeration to a certain extent. However he was unable to find an alternative economic and hence to him ultimately satisfying explanation of how the Asiatic state came to 'own', or control the means of production in such a way that it could wrest the surplus product from the direct producers. Here, as with other aspects of the concept of the Asiatic mode of production, Marx provides only hints, which need to be considerably developed by others (and many have contributed to this process) to provide a satisfactory Marxist historiography of non-Western society. These difficulties present in Marx's analysis do not, however, affect the fundamental distinction he drew between Western society, where control over the social surplus was exercised by social classes comprised of the private owners of the means of production, and Eastern society where such control was ultimately monopolised by the state.

Max Weber was to attempt to resolve Marx's problems by retaining an economic or entrepreneurial explanation of the genesis of the Oriental state, but adding to it a concept of the autonomous development of political institutions. Once a state structure (i.e. bureau-

[52] *Capital*, Vol. III, p. 791.

[53] 'Following the conquest of a country, the immediate aim of a conqueror was to convert its people to his own use.' (*Ibid.*, fn. 44).

[54] Marx, *Grundrisse*, p. 473. Cf. Nikolai Bukharin, who analysed the symbolic functions of the Asiatic state *vis à vis* the direct producers as follows: 'Why, for instance, was so vast a quantity of national labour in ancient Egypt devoted to the construction of the huge pyramids, great Pharaonic statues, and other monuments of feudal [sic] art? For the simple reason that Egyptian society could not have maintained itself without constantly impressing upon the slaves and peasants the sublimity and divine power of their rulers.' '[...] it was therefore a *sine qua non* for this society and took an enormous share of the country's labor budget.' I.e., non-economic pressure was the most important factor in the extortion of surplus value from the direct producers in this particular socio-economic formation. (Nikolai Bukharin, *Historical Materialism*, (first published Moscow, 1921), N.Y., International Publishers, 1925, p. 220).

[55] Max Weber, *Economy and Society*, Vol. III, N.Y., Bedminster Press, 1968, pp. 1260–1262.

cracy) was set up to deal with some large economic task, in the absence of competing social agencies, it would continue to expand its area of control, with or without a more general economic rationale.[55] Marx had already argued that these bureaucratic governments came into existence where there was an absence of alternative social organisations capable of dealing with large-scale corporate tasks.[56] He thus assumed that there were no strong countervailing forces which might check the expansion of state structures beyond their original (economic) purpose. In fact Weber's argument is implicit in Marx, and explains his constant emphasis on the correlation between the village system, which inhibited the development of any large-scale social communication or social organisation, and Oriental despotism. Marx failed to make this argument *explicit* because here, as elsewhere, he was reluctant to place too much weight on the internal momentum of political institutions as an explanatory variable.

Although Marx attributed to the Asiatic state a more direct role in production than he did to the Western state, he by no means regarded this as a virtue. As already seen, Marx shared with the liberal political economists the view that the state could not, by definition, be the engine of human progress. The notion that the state monopoly of the surplus and the weak development of private property might prove an advantage in the modernisation of Asiatic society was quite alien to his theoretical premises. Although Marx stressed the role of the state in the process of primitive accumulation in the West, he never conceded that the state might play a positive role as an industrial entrepreneur. (His comments on Russia in this connection suggested that state enterprise of this kind was doomed to a revolutionary overthrow which would liberate private enterprise – in the language of contemporary political science, once characteristic industrial roles had been artificially introduced, these stimulated the appearance of the structures and functions with which they were originally associated.)

One of the fundamental premises of Marx's mature political theory was that social progress took place as the consequence of the struggle of coherent social groups. Social groups arose embodying new modes of production, and struggled to impose a new configuration on society, appropriate to their needs (and the needs of progress). Asiatic society lacked this historical dynamic.

Thus for Marx the East was stagnant because the state, with its

[56] Marx, 'The British Rule in India', *loc.cit.*, p. 90.

monopoly of surplus value, prevented the growth of competing economic classes. For the liberals it was stagnant because the state monopoly prevented the growth of individual competition and incentive. Both Marx and the liberals saw private property in land as the 'great desideratum of Asiatic society'.[57] Marx believed as strongly as the political economists that a self-regulating capitalist system (or one free from the state intervention typical of the East) was necessary in order:

[...] to create the material basis of the new world – on the one hand the universal intercourse founded upon the mutual dependency of mankind, and the means of that intercourse; on the other hand the development of the productive powers of man and the transformation of material production into a scientific domination of natural agencies.[58]

The difference of course was that Marx saw this material basis as provising the foundation of socialism rather than simply of the universalisation of capitalism.

THE CITY IN EAST AND WEST

According to Marx, the effects of a state monopoly of surplus value were such as to preclude any autochthonous advance towards industrial capitalism. For example, the rise of town communes, one of the prerequisites of Western capitalism in his account, could not take place within this system.

Marx relied heavily on the analysis of the Oriental town to be found in Richard Jones. Jones provided Marx with a ready-made analysis of the evidence of their common source, François Bernier, in terms of political economy.

According to this analysis the Oriental town was no more than an ancillary structure of state. Except where the location was particularly favourable to external trade, it was simply an administrative centre or garrison; a point where:

[57] 'The Future Results of British Rule in India', loc.cit., p. 133. At least one Indian communist has employed Marx's analysis of Asiatic society to quite opposite effect. Palme Dutt wrote: 'In India, as we have seen, landlordism is an artificial creation of foreign rule, seeking to transplant Western institutions, and has no roots in the traditions of the people. In consequence, landlordism is here more completely functionless than in any other country, making no pretence even of fulfilling any necessary role of conservation or development of the land, but, on the contrary, intensifying its misuse and deterioration by short-sighted excessive demands. It is a purely parasitic claim on the peasantry [...]' (Rajani Palme Dutt, *Indiv Today*, 2nd rev. Indian edition, Bombay, People's Publishing House, 1949, p. 248).
[58] 'The Future Results of British Rule in India', loc.cit., p. 138.

...the head of the state and his satraps exchange their revenue (surplus product) for labour, [and] spend it as labour-fund.[59]

As a consequence,

In Asiatic societies, where the monarch appears as the exclusive proprietor of the agricultural surplus product, whole cities arise, which are at bottom nothing more than wandering encampments, from the exchange of his revenue with the 'free hands', as Steuart calls them.[60]

The diagram below, taken from Ignacy Sachs,[61] shows up neatly the comparative role of the city in the Marxist models of Western feudalism and the Asiatic mode of production.

a)

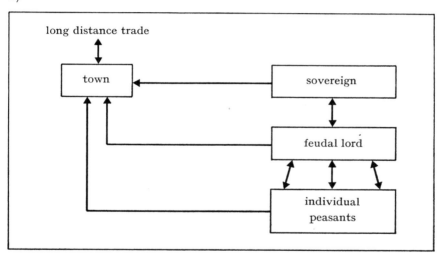

[59] Marx, *Grundrisse*, p. 474. See also *ibid.*, p. 479. In Russia Chaadayev had already written: 'in our towns we are like nomads – more nomadic than the tribes who graze their animals in our steppes, because those tribes are more attached to their steppes than we are to our cities ...' [First Philosophic Letter], 1829, *Sochineniia i pis'ma*, ed. M. Gershenzon, Vol. I, Moscow 1913, p. 78. This theme was to be developed by Trotsky and Parvus, who explained contemporary Russian history in terms of the absence of the Western-style city.

[60] Marx, *Grundrisse*, p. 467. I.e. the revenue of the monarch is the exclusive source of the wages fund for the workers in manufactures (here hand crafts) – those workers 'freed' from agricultural labour.

[61] Ignacy Sachs, 'Une nouvelle phase de la discussion sur les formations', *Recherches internationales à la lumière du marxisme*, No. 57–58 (Jan.-April 1967) (special volume devoted to 'Premières sociétés de classes et mode de production asiatique'), pp. 304–305. Sachs was at the time of writing the article the director of the Institute for the Study of Developing Economies in Warsaw.

b)

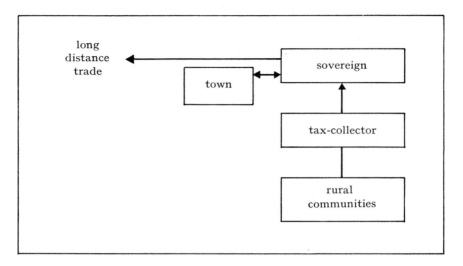

As represented in this diagram, the Eastern city did not enjoy the
same range of economic relations as the Western city. In the West,
the city had a plurality of sources of revenue, and hence was able to
achieve a far greater economic and political independence. Within it
there developed corporative political life and burgher rights. All this
enabled the kind of economic and social innovation which led to
Western capitalism.

Once again, it was to be Max Weber who developed the hints found
in Richard Jones and Marx into a full-blown theory.[62] Weber accepted
the notion that the role of the city was of crucial significance in explaining the particular historical development which brought capitalism
into being. He was more eclectic, however, than Marx, in his explanation of why the Oriental city did not achieve the independent and
innovative role of its counterpart in the West.

Weber's explanation attributed great importance to religious variables. He claimed equal importance, however, for the political factors
brought into play by the conditions of production in the East. As seen,
he argued that the need for irrigation, for example, brought into being
patrimonial bureaucracies. These were initially intended for con-

---

[62] See, in particular, 'The City (Non-Legitimate Domination)', in Max Weber, *Economy
and Society*, Vol. III, *op.cit.*, pp. 1212–1339.

struction tasks only, but they soon absorbed all political life, including that of the city.[63]

Both Marx and Weber believed that Asiatic society was incapable of giving rise to the kind of urban formation which developed within Western feudalism. Hence the East was also incapable of giving rise to that historically most revolutionary class – the bourgeoisie.

THE ANCIENT EAST

Marx's paradigm of the Oriental city was not only of relevance to an explanation of the contemporary backwardness of the East; it was also of relevance to an explanation of the origins of human civilisation. The Oriental city had provided in the distant past the particular environment in which the development of written culture, the codification of law, etc., first took place. Within Marxist theory, the Oriental city is a vivid illustration of the dialectical process of history, whereby structures appropriate to a certain stage of human history become obstacles to further progress.

Marx never *directly* concerned himself with the question of why it should have been Oriental despotism and its associated type of city which provided the framework in which 'civilisation' first developed. He did, however, write that:

It is the necessity of bringing a natural force under the control of society, of economising, of appropriating or subduing it on a large scale by the work of man's hand that first plays a decisive part in the history of industry.[64]

The harnessing of 'natural forces' on a large scale meant the difference between famine and plenty in some areas inhabited by ancient man. Hence there was a strong impulse towards such large-scale organisation. This in itself represented a great step forward in human history, in that the development of co-operation multiplied the effectiveness of human labour power.[65] The institutional corollary of this early large-scale organisation of the work-force was the centralised 'despotic' state which directed it.

The primary relationship between Oriental despotism and the founding of the ancient civilisations appears, then, to reside in the

[63] *Ibid.*, pp. 1260–1262.
[64] *Capital*, Vol. I, p. 514.
[65] *Ibid.*, pp. 333–334.

creation of an organised work-force. The harnessing of a natural force (such as the great rivers associated with the early civilisations) by means of this organised labour brought about a tremendous upsurge in productivity. The fact that the despotic state, through its organising role in production, was able to exercise a monopoly over the surplus meant that this increase in productivity was not absorbed in increased consumption by the direct producers. Rather, it provided the means for the state to support an army of non-agricultural labourers within the Oriental town, and hence the specialised development of arts and crafts.[66]

In the long run, however, the monopoly of the surplus by the state tended to keep the development of agriculture, on which the whole edifice depended, at a standstill. The ossification of a crude division of labour, through its reinforcement by caste, provided another brake on development.[67]

The question of the relationship of Oriental despotism to the development of the ancient civilisations was to be treated more fully by G.V. Plekhanov, for example in his review of Mechnikov's book, *La Civilisation et les grands fleuves historiques*.[68] Mechnikov argued in this book that civilisation first arose within the political framework of Oriental despotism simply because the circumstances which first led man to harness a great natural power also led to despotism.

In the fertile river valleys of the ancient world flood control meant the difference between disaster (floods) and high productivity. Mechnikov suggested that such flood control required a precise allocation of social tasks by a central authority. The absolute power of the latter over society was both a condition and a consequence of its power over nature. The close co-operation and work discipline demanded of all sections of society by the central authority provided the basis for the first flowering of civilisation.

Plekhanov fully endorsed this part of Mechnikov's argument, which stressed the importance of central planning in this early phase of man's economic development. Such central planning first came into existence in response to the challenge provided by the great historical rivers, and

---

[66] *Ibid.*

[67] *Ibid.*, pp. 357–358 (India); pp. 366–367 (Egypt). See also Marx and Engels, *The German Ideology, op.cit.*, p. 52.

[68] Plekhanov's review was published in *Sotsial-Demokrat*, No. 1, 1890, and in *Neue Zeit*, Jg. IX., No. 1 (1891), pp. 437–448. Other aspects of Plekhanov's and Mechnikov's views on ancient civilisation will be discussed in subsequent chapters.

it was only when the technological progress it had fostered gave rise to the need for a more flexible system that it became an encumbrance.

An approach to the question of the ancient civilisations, which supplements that of Mechnikov and Plekhanov, is to be found in the work of the late V. Gordon Childe. Childe chose to stress a different aspect of Marx's analysis of the ancient East; he employed the idea of the concentration of the surplus, rather than the idea of the organised nature of the economy, to explain the first flowering of civilisation.

By the third millennium B.C., Childe argued, the 'urban revolution' had taken place in Sumer, Egypt and the Indus valley. In all these areas, according to Childe, conditions of production had given rise to characteristic institutional correlates. These were, on the one hand, a state apparatus, which typically consisted of a god/king and a functional elite of priest/bureaucrats, and on the other hand a village system. The former accumulated despotic power at the expense of the latter.

The despotic power of the state apparatus brought about the concentration of large economic surpluses, pumped out of the direct producers by agents of the state. These surpluses, in turn, supported the growth of specialised crafts, and the development of technology, most importantly, of metallurgy.[69] The increasing technical sophistication of the basic agrarian economy brought in its train the development of writing (largely used for administrative purposes) and of the exact sciences (e.g. mensuration).

There were definite limits, however, to the economic progress which could take place within the archaic despotic states; they were doomed to decay. Childe filled out Marx's explanation of the fate of these empires with the help of Weber, adopting the latter's emphasis on the corporate goals of institutional structures, particularly with regard to self-maintenance.

As we have seen, Marx's own account of the sources of retardation was presented on two levels: above, the monopolisation of economic initiative and surplus value by a centralised state apparatus; below, the perpetuation of a natural economy in socially isolated, self-sufficient village communities. Childe saw a causal link between these two levels in the corporate striving by state functionaries to consolidate the existing social base. The further economic and intellectual development

---

[69] V. Gordon Childe, *Man Makes Himself*, London, Watts, 1948, pp. 146–178 ('The Urban Revolution').

of society at large would be an almost certain threat to their own position.

On one point, the language used by Childe led him into a position apparently counter to his general acceptance of the Marxist view of social dynamics. He asserted that it was the establishment of a *ruling class* in Oriental society that was responsible for the retardation of progress.[70] According to Marxist historiography, the establishment of class divisions, and hence of a ruling class, was an essential concomitant of *progress* rather than a retarding factor.

The apparent discontinuity in Childe's analysis arises from the fact that what he called a ruling class in the context of the ancient East differed in type from Marx's model of a ruling class. The latter consisted of a class which, owning the dominant means of production, moves into politics mainly for its *protection* value. The priestly corporations and public servants about whom Childe was talking, on the other hand, derived their power and economic perquisites from their 'functional' state roles. If they were in a position to cause social stagnation, it was, on Childe's own argument, not because they formed a ruling class as such, but because they embodied the state power in a society where monopolistic political structures had hypertrophied at the expense of other forms of social structure.

Marx himself did not describe the office-holders of the East as a ruling class.[71] He regarded Oriental society as being antithetical to the real development of the private ownership of the means of production, on which his definition of class rested. Although military and civil officials might be beneficed, their tenure remained precarious and the state was always 'the real landlord'.[72]

If the priestly corporations of the East were able to hamper the progress of rational science and the dissemination of knowledge as

[70] *Ibid.*, p. 229ff.

[71] This was not, as Wittfogel implies, because Marx was afraid that a parallel might be drawn between the ruling bureaucracy of Oriental society and a similar elite likely to be brought into existence under his proposed 'state socialism' (Wittfogel's expression). (See K.A. Wittfogel, *Oriental Despotism*, New Haven, Yale U.P., 1957, pp. 380–388). *Pace* Wittfogel, Marx did not commit a 'sin against science', and obscure the facts of bureaucratic rule because he 'could scarcely help recognizing some disturbing similarities between Oriental despotism and the state of his program'. (*Ibid.*, p. 387). Rather than attempting to conceal any similarity between Oriental society and state socialism, Engels, who is also alleged to have 'sinned', made the comparison quite explicitly in his letters to Bebel, 18 Jan. 1884, and to Kautsky, 16 Feb. 1884. (*Werke*, Vol. 36, pp. 88 and 190). 'State socialism', however, had nothing to do with Marxist *principles*, regardless of Bakunin's accusations.

[72] Marx, 'Indian Affairs', *N.Y.D.T.*, 5 Aug. 1853, *Karl Marx on Colonialism and Modernization*, p. 130.

completely as Childe argued,[73] then on both the traditional and the Marxist analysis it would be because of the particular relationship of the state to society as a whole, rather than because of the establishment of a ruling class. The same applies to the overconcentration of purchasing power, which Childe claimed was another reason for the eventual retardation of growth in the states of the ancient East.[74]

The Oriental city, as the point where surpluses were accumulated on a scale never seen before in human history, provided the forcing ground for the technological inventions of the Bronze Age. The factor which brought about the original pre-eminence of the Oriental city was, however, in the Marxist analysis also responsible for its eventual decline: that is, the assumption by the state of the role of economic entrepreneur, and all the consequences of this.

THE ASIATIC VILLAGE SYSTEM: PASSPORT TO THE FUTURE?

The village system, which formed the social base of the system of Oriental despotism, aroused conflicting attitudes in Marx.[75] On the one hand, he held that the particularistic and inward-looking nature of these small village communities was at least partially responsible for the fact that the unity of Asiatic society was only realised within the despotic state. Moreover, in Marx's account the Asiatic village community was a fossilised form of one of the earliest and most primitive forms of social organisation: within it the principle of individuality had not yet developed; it also perpetuated man's subordination to nature and to tradition which ruled him as a natural force.

On the other hand, the Asiatic village represented to a certain extent what we would now call the *Gemeinschaft* principle of solidarity and co-operation, as opposed to the competitive and divisive principle of society based on private property and the cash nexus. It provided some kind of mutual defence against exploitation, and above all, the

[73] E.g. V. Gordon Childe, *What Happened in History*, London, Max Parrish, 1960, pp. 110–111; *Man Makes Himself*, op.cit., pp. 230–231.
[74] *What Happened in History*, op.cit., p. 113.
[75] Cf. Stepniak (S.M. Kravchinsky) on the Russian village community: 'The common folk live in their liliputian republics like snails in their shells. To them official Russia – the world of *tchinovniks*, soldiers, and policemen – is a horde of foreign conquerors who from time to time send their agents into the country to demand the tribute of money and the tribute of blood – taxes for the Tzar's treasury and soldiers for his army. Yet by a startling anomaly ... these rudimentary republics, which enjoy so large a measure of social and personal freedom, are at once the surest foundations and the strongest bulwarks of despotic power.' (*Russia under the Tzars*, tr. W. Westall, first published 1885, new edn, London, Downey, n.d., p. 9).

possibility of a bridge into socialism, which would obviate some of the worst excesses of capitalism.

During the 1850s it was the negative aspects of the village community which were given the most prominence in Marx's writing; in this period he assumed the progressive nature of the impact of Western capitalism on these structures.[76] In his later writings, however, Marx placed more stress on the positive aspects of the village communities, and apparently became less convinced of the historical necessity of their destruction. By the 1870s the ambivalence in his views had become at least partially resolved in favour of *Narodnichestvo*.[77]

Some signs of this change in emphasis are visible by at least 1859. In his article, 'Trade with China', Marx described the advantages held by communal production over the 'most advanced factory system in the world'.[78] He argued that such communal production would continue to hold off the challenge from the mass-produced commodities of British and American capitalism. The economic advantages of the old communal forms of production, deriving from co-operation and from the absence of the *faux frais* of circulation, were to be discussed further by Marx in *Capital*.[79]

Thus, already in 1859, Marx was to a certain extent denying his earlier view, that pre-capitalist communal forms of production would naturally decay under the impact of capitalism, and that this could not be avoided. He wrote that the British had only succeeded in converting the self-sustaining village communities of India into mere commodity-producing farms through their position as supreme landlords in the country; in China they were unlikely ever to wield this power.[80]

[76] Although even at this time Marx wrote that it must be sickening 'to witness these myriads of industrious, patriarchal and inoffensive social organisations disorganized and dissolved into their units, thrown into a sea of woes, and their individual members losing at the same time their ancient form of civilization and their hereditary means of subsistence . . .', 'The British Rule in India', *loc.cit.*, p. 94. In the original *N.Y.D.T.* text there is a comma after 'civilization'. This is but one example of the many minor errors in the Avineri edition, like the spelling of 'village community' without the hyphen it had in the original, further on in this sentence. The advantages of the Avineri edition, however, outweigh its disadvantages, in the absence of a definitive edition of Marx's works in the original languages they were published in.

[77] Cf. George Lichtheim, 'Oriental Despotism', in *The Concept of Ideology*, N.Y., Random House, 1967, p. 75. Marx's early ambivalence was reinforced by the fact that in his mind the Russian village community, or *obshchina* was inextricably linked with Herzen and Bakunin; with the idea of the special historical mission of holy Russia; and with Pan-Slavism. As he wrote of Alexander Herzen: 'in his hands the Russian community only serves as an argument to prove that rotten old Europe should be regenerated by the victory of Pan-Slavism.' (Marx to the Editors of *Otechestvennye Zapiski*, Nov. 1877, *MESC*, p. 311).

[78] Marx, 'Trade with China', leading article, *N.Y.D.T.*, 3 Dec. 1859, *Karl Marx on Colonialism and Modernization*, p. 396.

[79] *Capital*, Vol. I, p. 328; Vol. III, pp. 333–334.

[80] *Ibid.*, p. 398.

In 1881, in the third draft of his famous letter to Vera Zasulich, Marx went so far as to say that the forcible breaking up of the village community in East India by the British had been an act of vandalism, which meant a step backwards rather than a step forwards for the natives.[81] Again, in the first and third drafts of this letter, Marx praised the form of the community developed by the Germans as having been the only refuge of popular freedom through the middle ages. By inference, if the village community could survive as a refuge for popular freedom through different social epochs in the West, it might also survive social change in the East.

Marx's *Narodnik* sympathies also emerge in his notes on Kovalevsky, composed at about the same time as the Zasulich letter. Marx was particularly interested in Kovalevsky's account of the French rule in Algeria, and the treatment of communal property by the colonial power. According to this account, the French had been quite ruthless in their destruction of communal forms of private property, partly because private property was the 'indispensable condition of any progress in the political and social sphere',[82] and partly for less disinterested reasons.

In his own comments, Marx described as 'outright robbery' the appropriation by the colonial government of the wastelands which had been in the communal use of the Arab clans; he contrasted the tender regard of the French for the sacredness and inviolability of private property with their rampant pillaging of communal property.[83] Marx added that:

Through the individuation of landed property a political goal is also achieved – the elimination of the foundation of this [clan] society.[84]

Nonetheless, in spite of these sympathies, Marx's writing on Asiatic communal forms is permeated by an impatience with the enslavement to nature and tradition perpetuated by these forms. Engels records Marx's views on primitive communalism as follows:

...the tribe, the gens and their institutions were sacred and inviolable, a superior power, instituted by nature, to which the individual remained absolutely subject in feeling, thought and deed. Impressive as the people of this epoch may appear

---

[81] *Werke*, Vol. 19, p. 402.
[82] Marx's conspectus of M.M. Kovalevsky's *Obshchinnoe zemlevladenie, prichiny, khod i posledstviia ego razlozheniia* (Moscow, 1879, notes made 1880–1881), *Problemy Vostokovedeniia*, No. 1, 1959, p. 9. Marx adds, 'in the eyes of the French bourgeois'.
[83] *Ibid.*, p. 17.
[84] *Ibid.*

to us, they differ in no way from one another, they are still bound, as Marx says, to the umbilical cord of the primordial community.[85]

In the same period (i.e. the height of Marx's adherence to *Narodnichestvo*) Marx stressed in his notes on Maine, the naive and *unreflecting* relationship of primitive men to their social environment, and their submersion in the satisfying and comforting bondage of the primitive community.[86] Marx linked the emergence of mankind out of prehistory with the breaking loose from this bondage, and the creation of its antithesis – a one-sided development of individualism.[87]

Thus co-operation within these communal forms as they survived in the self-enclosed village structures of the East was not synonymous with *socialist* co-operation. The latter could only signify a conscious, self-determined relationship of the individual to the community, a historically produced relationship. Primitive co-operation, on the other hand, was a *natural* relationship; it took place in the unfree situation where the individual was not yet *differentiated* from the community, and indeed the latter assumed the form of natural necessity.[88]

In *Capital* itself, despite his comments on the advantages of the natural production communities cited above, Marx was damning on the subject of the economic stasis associated with the communal structures.[89] The natural economy perpetuated in these self-enclosed communities meant that man remained through the ages a 'mere accessory to the land' – a slave of, instead of the master of, nature.[90] The conditions for the development of social labour as well as the conditions for the development of individuation were absent:

The original unity between the worker and the conditions of production ⟨abstracting from slavery, where the labourer himself belongs to the objective conditions of production⟩ has two main forms: the Asiatic communal system

---

[85] Engels, *The Origin of the Family, Private Property and the State*, *MESW*, Vol. II, p. 255. Engels himself tended to adopt a less Hegelian and more Rousseauan approach towards the primitive communities. Cf. Erhard Lucas, 'Marx's Studien zur Frühgeschichte und Ethnologie 1880–82', *Saeculum*, Vol. 15 (1964), pp. 327–343.

[86] 'Erst Losreissung der Individualität von d. ursprünglich *nicht despotischen Fesseln* (wie blockhead Maine es versteht), *sondern befriedige(n)den u. gemüthlichen Banden der Gruppe*, der primitiven Gemeinwesen, – damit d. einseitige Herausarbeitung der *Individualität*'. Marx's conspectus of Sir Henry Sumner Maine's *Lectures on the Early History of Institutions* (London, 1875, notes made 1880–81), *The Ethnological Notebooks of Karl Marx*, ed. Lawrence Krader, *op.cit.*, p. 329.

[87] *Ibid.*

[88] Cf., Eric Hobsbawm, Introduction to Marx, *Pre-Capitalist Economic Formations, op.cit.*, pp. 14–16, for an account of how Marx viewed capitalism as dissolving all social relationships into commodity relationships, but at the same time creating the preconditions of social relationships between fully developed individuals.

[89] *Capital*, Vol. III, p. 796.

[90] *Ibid.*, p. 616.

(primitive communism) and small-scale agriculture based on the family (and linked with domestic industry) in one form or another. Both are embryonic forms and both are equally unfitted to develop labour as *social* labour and the productive power of social labour. Hence the necessity for the separation, for the rupture, for the antithesis of labour and property (by which property in the conditions of production is to be understood). The most extreme form of this rupture, and the one in which the productive forces of social labour are also most powerfully developed, is capital. The original unity can be re-established only on the material foundation which capital creates and by means of the revolutions which, in the process of this creation, the working class and the whole society undergo.[91]

What happened, in the 1870s in particular, was not that Marx changed his mind on the *character* of the village communities, or decided that they could become the basis of socialism as they were; rather, he came to consider the possibility that the communities could be revolutionised not by capitalism but by socialism.

In the 1870s socialism suddenly appeared to be making unexpected headway in a country which still had a largely pre-capitalist economy – namely, Russia – and this opened up a new line of approach to the village community. Marx's hesitations on this question are well known, but he does seem to have entertained seriously the hope that with the intensification of social communication and the modernisation of production methods the village system could be incorporated into a socialist society. In 1882 this still appeared to Marx to be a genuine alternative to the complete disintegration of the *obshchina* under the impact of capitalism.[92]

Marx suggested that social communication between the isolated villages of Russia could be quite easily intensified, for a start, by the substitution of peasant assemblies for the existing units of local government. Such assemblies would be elected by the various village communities comprising the district, and serve as district-level economic and administrative organs.[93] The increase in social interaction thus brought about would create a supra-village social consciousness, and

[91] Marx, *Theories of Surplus Value, op.cit.*, Part III, pp. 422–423.

[92] See the Preface written by Marx and Engels for the 1882 Russian edition of the *Communist Manifesto, MESW*, Vol. I, pp. 23–24. The Russian Marxists were shortly to expend much effort in proving that the *obshchina* was no longer economically viable, and had disintegrated beyond reclamation.

[93] First draft of Marx's letter to Zasulich of 8 March 1881, *Werke*, Vol. 19, p. 390. Bakunin had discussed the problems involved in surmounting the isolation of the village communities, and in intensifying social communication between them, in terms strikingly similar to those used by Marx, in a letter addressed to Nechaev, 2 June 1870. Bakunin suggested that a federal structure, organised from village commune upwards was necessary to raise the level of popular awareness. See Michael Bakunin, letter to Sergei Nechaev, 2 June 1870, published for the first time in *Encounter*, July 1972, pp. 89–90.

bring an end to that particularism, or 'rural idiocy', which Marx attributed to the traditional peasantry. It may be extrapolated that Marx assumed a further federal structure based on these assemblies, similar to the proposals he discussed in *The Civil War in France*.[94]

The modernisation of methods of production within the Russian village community would be simplified, according to Marx, by the fact that the Russian peasants were already to a degree prepared for collective work. The configuration of the Russian countryside also lent itself to large-scale, mechanised cultivation.[95]

Among the many qualifications that Marx attached to this optimistic view of the future of the *obshchina* was the stipulation that a successful proletarian revolution must take place in the West before the process of dissolution had become irreversible; such a revolution would 'show the way' to Russia.

Engels tended to be less restrained than Marx in his attitudes towards primitive communalism. He went so far as to attribute a defeat inflicted by Bulgaria on Serbia to the fact that gentile institutions (the vestigial Southern Slav communalism) had survived in the former but not in the latter. In Serbia, independence from Turkey had meant the substitution of a bureaucracy and legislature (on the Austrian model) for the old gentile constitution; Bulgaria, thanks to the continued overlordship of the Turks, had so far escaped this fate.[96] Moreover, the Serbian case was unfortunate because 'the gentile institutions would have provided a striking link for the passage to communism.'[97]

With the passing of the years, it appeared less and less likely, even to Engels, that the remants of primitive communalism would survive into the new age. In 1893 he summed up the possibilities which the socialist discovery of vestigial communism had opened up for a time as follows:

...no more in Russia than anywhere else would it have been possible to develop a higher social form out of primitive agrarian communism unless – that higher form was *already in existence* in another country, so as to serve as a model.[98]

[94] E.g. Marx, *The Civil War in France*, Peking, Foreign Languages Press, 1966, p. 69.

[95] First draft of Marx's letter to Zasulich, *loc.cit.*, p. 405. Interestingly, Marx added that Russian society, which had fed for so long off the village community, at least owed it the necessary advance for this transformation.

[96] Here, as elsewhere, the rule of Oriental despotism preserved archaic forms of social organisation; the appropriation of the surplus by the state was not accompanied by the kind of legislative intervention in social relations found in European states.

[97] Engels to Bernstein, 9 Oct. 1886, *Cahiers de l'I.S.E.A.*, Vol. III, No. 7 (July 1969), pp. 1442–1443.

[98] Engels to N.F. Danielson, 17 Oct. 1893, *MESC*, p. 464. In letters written to Danielson on 29–30 Oct. 1891; 15 March 1892, and 18 June 1892, Engels had already conceded that the chance to bypass the full development of capitalism in Russia had been lost.

THE CONTRIBUTION OF ENGELS TO THE MARXIAN
ANALYSIS OF THE NON-WESTERN WORLD

As seen earlier, Marx's mature model of Oriental society was originally evolved in partnership with Engels in 1853, and Engels continued to employ this model intermittently until the end of his life. Nonetheless, Engels' treatment of the subject created certain problems which later contributed to the eclipse of the concept of a specifically 'Asiatic' mode of production – Oriental despotism.

As Wittfogel has pointed out,[99] Engels' two major pieces of writing on the state, *Anti-Dühring* and the *Origin of the Family, Private Property and the State*, served to confuse the relationship between the concept of Oriental despotism and the (Western-oriented) Marxian theory of the state. These works of Engels assumed a special importance in the Marxist tradition because Marx himself never wrote his projected work on the state.[100]

In *Anti-Dühring* Engels did initially outline a theory of the development of state power which could accommodate the Marxian model of Oriental society.[101] According to this theory, state power was cognate with the delegation by a community of the performance of public tasks to certain of its members.[102] State power arose where productivity was high enough to support such a specialised stratum, and it was destined to exist as long as productivity was not high enough to enable all members of the community to participate in performing public functions.[103]

[99] K.A. Wittfogel, *Oriental Despotism, op.cit.*, pp. 383–386.

[100] In January 1845 Marx concluded a contract with the German publisher, Leske, promising to produce within a few months a work entitled *A Critique of Politics and Political Economy*. This work did not materialise, and neither did the section on the state projected for his major work, of which *Capital* was the first section. (See the Introduction to the *Grundrisse*, pp. 108–109.)

[101] Engels, *Anti-Dühring*, tr. E. Burns, London, Lawrence and Wishart, n.d. printed with minor revisions from the 1934 edition, pp. 167; 200–206; 309–310.

[102] This explanation of the development of state power was to be seized upon by Plekhanov for the very reason that it *was* consistent with the Marxist concept of Oriental despotism. Plekhanov linked the development of the state power in the East with the fulfilment of the public function of irrigation; and the development of the state power in Russia with the fulfilment by the prince and his *druzhina* of the public function of defence. See G.V. Plekhanov, *History*, pp. 53, 77.

[103] An idea vividly alluded to in the following note by Marx: 'Maine ignores das viel Tiefere: dass d. scheinbare supreme selbständige Existenz des *Staats* selbst nur *scheinbar* u. dass er in allen seinen Formen eine *excrescence of society* is; wie seine *Erscheinung* selbst erst auf einer gewissen Stufe der gesellschaftlichen Entwicklung vorkommt, so verschwindet sie wieder, sobld d. Gesellscft eine bisher noch nicht erreichte Stufe erreicht hat.' (Marx's conspectus of Maine, *loc.cit.*, p. 329).

The delegation of public functions occurred first of all in the small agricultural communities themselves, and then later in larger aggregates of such communities. General functions performed by this administrative stratum included, in particular, military functions in the West, and water-control functions in the East. The public servants performing these generalising functions achieved a position of mastership over the primitive communities of direct producers they were supposedly serving. Correspondingly their positions tended to become hereditary.[104]

At this point Engels went beyond Marx, in that he stated that these public servants became an actual ruling class:

> ...this independence of social functions in relation to society increased with time until it developed into domination over society; [...] what was originally the servant developed gradually, where conditions were favourable into the lord [...] finally the separate individual rulers united into a ruling class.[105]

Engels, however, made no attempt to reconcile such a function-based definition of class with the Marxian definition of class in terms of ownership of the means of production.[106] The analogy between political/administrative elites and economic classes becomes most troublesome where the development of the two forms of ruling class are made concomitant. Engels appears unable to relate them except through the implications of crude juxtaposition. Thus: 'alongside of this development of [administrative and administered] classes another was taking place' – i.e. the development of private-property based slavery.[107]

To begin with, it becomes clear from the subsequent paragraphs that this concomitant development was posited as taking place only in the West, and that in the East (including Russia) private-property based classes did not emerge, but on the contrary the ancient communes continued to exist for 'thousands of years'.[108] Engels seems to have been trying to say that in the West the original class divisions between rulers and ruled based on political/military functions *gave way* to divisions based on the ownership or non-ownership of private prop-

---

[104] Engels, *Anti-Dühring, op.cit.*, pp. 201–202.
[105] *Ibid.*, p. 201.
[106] Engels found another function-based class in contemporary Russia. He described the 'large army of bureaucrats which overflows Russia' as a 'real class'. See his 'Soziales aus Russland', *Der Volksstaat*, 1875, tr. as 'Russia and the Social Revolution', *The Russian Menace to Europe*, p. 208.
[107] Engels, *Anti-Dühring, op.cit.*, p. 202.
[108] *Ibid.*, p. 203.

erty.[109] In the East, *per contra*, the original class division based on political/economic functions perpetuated itself, and the original communal forms of property did not give rise to private-property based classes.

According to Engels, the original type of class division corresponded to the 'heroic' period of Western society, and elsewhere to 'the most barbarous form of state, Oriental despotism', which had held sway from 'India to Russia'.[110] In this primitive form of the state 'political force has made itself independent in relation to society', whereas in the more advanced forms of state, based on the institution of private property, political force became the instrument of the dominant economic class.

Unfortunately, a few paragraphs later one finds that Engels has forgotten that he had described the primitive division between rulers and ruled as a class division; he goes on to say that in the historical conditions of the *ancient world* (in particular, Greece) 'the advance to a society based on class antagonisms could only be accomplished in the form of slavery.'[111] Thus the idea of class division in societies based on communal property is scrapped. The reference to the ancient world also appears to be an attempt to modify, by specifying the particular historical environment in which it holds good, his original argument that the introduction of slavery was the natural solvent of primitive communalism – an argument untenable in the light of his understanding of the transition from tribal communalism to feudalism in German history.[112]

The composite analysis of the state which emerges from *Anti-Dühring* is confused because Engels does not resolve the tension between the analysis of the state as the natural consequence of the delegation of communal tasks to a specialist stratum, and the analysis of the state as 'an organisation of the exploiting class at each period for the maintenance of its external conditions of production'.[113] The most that he does is to separate temporally and geographically the areas of reference of the two analyses.

---

[109] And that in this process functional elites sacrificed their distinctive 'class' interests in favour of the economic class they came to represent.

[110] Engels, *Anti-Dühring, op.cit.*, p. 203.

[111] *Ibid.*, p. 204.

[112] See for example, his essay on the Mark, *Werke*, Vol. 19, pp. 315–330.

[113] Engels *Anti-Dühring, op.cit.*, p. 308. Or to put it another way, he does not resolve the idea of the state as 'the product of the irreconcilability of class antagonisms' (Lenin, *State and Revolution, Selected Works*, Vol. 2/1, p. 205), and the idea of class antagonisms as the product of the creation of a state structure.

This confusion is not present in Engels' *Origin of the Family, Private Property and the State*, for the good reason that in this work Engels does not mention the concept of Oriental despotism, or the analysis of the origin of state power with which it was linked.

Engels wrote this book shortly after Marx's death, on the basis of the notes Marx had made on Morgan's *Ancient Society*. Morgan had outlined a schema of the development of human society, largely based on his research into the social structure of the Iroquois Indians. His schema was a stadial one, with an emphasis on the universal progression from gentile social organisation to political society which took place in the course of civilisation.[114]

This universal progression was associated by Morgan with improvements in methods of production, which led in turn, to increased personal property, and to the desire to institutionalise private property and inheritance through the 'monogamian family'. The social stresses and strains introduced by the institutionalisation of private property could not be dealt with satisfactorily within gentile social structures.[115] Hence there came about a necessary transition to political society based on the territorial unit rather than on the kinship unit, and based on private property rather than on communal forms of property.

Engels interpreted this transition stage as representing the alienation of public powers from the community as a whole, and the creation of a state power separate from the community.[116] In the *Origin of the Family* ... Engels tied the alienation of public powers strictly to the rise of private property and slavery, and the need for a coercive power to maintain such exploitative relations of production. Although mentioning briefly the transformation of elective military offices in the gens into hereditary offices, etc., he insisted that 'the first great social

[114] Lewis H. Morgan, *Ancient Society*, Bellknap Press of Harvard U.P., 1964 (reprinted from the 1878 edition), pp. 290–291.

[115] Engels quoted directly from Marx's notes the comment that: 'property differences in a gens changed the community of interest into antagonism between members of a gens'. (Engels, *The Origin of the Family, Private Property and the State, loc.cit.*, p. 314).

[116] *Ibid.*, p. 252. Morgan's own account of the initiation of political society was much more sympathetic. He saw Greek and Roman democracy as inheriting the spirit and principles of gentile democracy, the form of government natural to man, which became perverted only through excessive greed for private property. In general, Morgan held an evolutionary view of human history, according to which continuous human progress was hampered only by the evils arising from excessive preoccupation with private property. Engels tended to idealise the primitive community to a greater extent than Morgan, and to be more critical of the ensuing stage of human development in which class society was held together by the state. According to Engels' dialectic, the final synthesis towards which history was leading was a synthesis of primitive communalism with the technical progress made during the period of private property and the state.

division of labour, and hence the first great division of society was into the two classes of masters and slaves'[117] – i.e. not the division between public functionaries and free direct producers.

Thus, in the *Origin of the Family* ..., Engels simplified his previous analysis of the origins of state power, and at the same time, following Morgan, he attempted to outline a universal pattern of social development. Quite apart from the general demerits of unilinear schemas, to be discussed in a later chapter,[118] the use of the gentile constitution of the Iroquois tribes as a paradigm for the early stages of all human societies made necessary an extremely selective treatment of European and Asian prehistory. In this work Engels did not mention the early river-basin agricultural civilisations, presumably because they did not fit neatly into the pattern according to which communal property equals gentile constitution and private property equals the state.[119]

Before reading Morgan, Marx and Engels had concluded that the key to the original forms of communal constitution, those present when tribal communities first became settled, was to be found in Asia or India.[120] Vestiges of later forms were still to be found in Eastern Europe, etc., but it was presumed that these had all developed from the original 'Asiatic' forms. After reading Morgan, Engels, at least, was convinced that the key to the original forms of communal constitution was to be found in America.[121]

---

[117] Engels, *The Origins of the Family* ..., *loc.cit.*, p. 310.

[118] The term unilinear is used here and throughout later chapters not in its technical sense, indicating an unbroken curve on a graph, but rather to convey the idea of a single, universally occurring sequence. Hence the use of the term unilinear is not meant to deny the existence of radical breaks in the progression.

[119] Paradoxically, although both Morgan, and Marx's notes on Morgan, on which Engels' work was based, suggested a unilinear pattern of human development, Plekhanov was to use this work to argue that Marx had become converted to a multilinear theory. Plekhanov took the fact that a version of social development was being outlined here in which there was no stage of Oriental despotism (as in the preface to the *Contribution to the Critique of Political Economy*) to mean that these were alternative models rather than that one unilinear pattern was being replaced by another. Gentile society might evolve into either ancient society, as depicted in *The Origin of the State* ... or into Oriental society as suggested by Marx and Engels previously. See G.V. Plekhanov, *Fundamental Problems of Marxism*, tr. J. Katzer, Moscow, Foreign Languages Publishing House, n.d., pp. 63–64.

[120] E.g. Marx to Engels, 14 March 1868; *Pre-Capitalist Economic Formations*, ed. Eric Hobsbawm, *op.cit.*, p. 139.

[121] In a footnote to the 1888 English edition of the *Communist Manifesto*, Engels wrote: 'In 1847, the pre-history of society, the social organization existing previous to recorded history, was all but unknown. Since then, Haxthausen discovered common ownership of land in Russia, Maurer proved it to be the social foundation from which all Teutonic races started in history, and by and by village communities were found to be, or have been the primitive form of society everywhere from India to Ireland. The inner organization of this primitive Communistic society was laid bare, in its typical form, by Morgan's crowning discovery of the true nature of the *gens* and its relation to the *tribe*.' (*MESW*, Vol. I, p. 33).

A reflection of this change of paradigm appears in a variation in the text between the third German edition of *Capital*, Vol. I, and the English edition which was based on it, and prepared under the general supervision of Engels (after reading Morgan). The English text reads as follows:

> Peasant agriculture on a small scale, and the carrying on of independent handicrafts [...] also form the economic foundation of the classical communities at their best, after the primitive form of ownership of land in common had disappeared, and before slavery had seized on production in earnest.[122]

The German edition reads:

> [...] after the primitive *Oriental** form of ownership [...] had disappeared [...][123]

Nonetheless, although Engels abandoned the Indian village community as the paradigm of early social forms, and although his preoccupation with patterns of development based on the development of the American gentile system led him, in his most important work on the state, to neglect alternative modes of development based on the Asiatic paradigm, he continued to find useful the concept of Oriental despotism.

In 1882 Engels wrote:

> From Ireland to Russia, and from Asia Minor to Egypt – in a peasant country the peasant exists only to be exploited. It has been so since the Assyrian and Persian empire. The satrap, alias pasha, is the chief Oriental form of the exploiter, just as the merchant and the jurist represent the modern Western form.[124]

The description of Oriental society in this letter encompasses both the state appropriation of the surplus and another important feature, the lack of effective class structure. Marx and Engels shared the view that the peasantry, as such, could never form an effective class; correspondingly, the population in predominately peasant countries consisted of an undifferentiated mass of atomised social units, particularly susceptible to despotic control from the centre.[125] Although in the West the state did not have the same economic monopoly, countries with a predominantly peasant population had a tendency towards a

---

[122] *Capital*, Vol. I, p. 334, fn. 3.

[123] *Das Kapital*, Vol. I, Berlin, Dietz, 1953, p. 350, fn. 24. See Daniel Thorner, 'Marx on India', *Contributions to Indian Sociology*, Dec. 1966, p. 60. Another example of the 'suppression' of the idea of a specific Asiatic mode of production in the English edition appears on p. 79 of *Capital*, Vol. I. Here the German 'In den altasiatischen, antiken usw. Produktionsweisen ...' (*Das Kapital, op.cit.*, Vol. I, pp. 45–46) is rendered as 'In the ancient Asiatic and other ancient modes of production ...' – thus blurring the distinction between the Asiatic and the ancient modes of production.

[124] Engels to Bernstein, 9 Aug. 1882, *Karl Marx on Colonialism and Modernization*, p. 472.

[125] Whether these units are individual, or communal as in the original Marxist model.

political form of despotism – a relatively independent role for the state apparatus *vis à vis* the population.[126]

In 1890, Engels went on the describe 'Turkish, like any other Oriental domination' as being incompatible with a capitalist economy because property was insecure, and the surplus was liable to be appropriated by representatives of the state.[127] As already stated, the concept remained an essential part of his vocabulary up till the end of his life.[128]

Engels' continued reliance on the concept of Oriental despotism as an analytical tool was not however to be of such importance as his essential failure to integrate the concept into the Marxian theory of the state. This failure foreshadowed the neglect of the concept by the Marxist movement in general. Marx's own analysis of the non-Western world came to be superseded by Marxist theories of imperialism, in particular after the publication of Lenin's pamphlet in 1917. Lenin's theory tended to suggest that colonial areas such as Asia had enjoyed the normal (i.e. Western) pattern of historical development until being subjected to the effects of Western imperialism.[129] 'Backwardness' thus became extrinsic rather than intrinsic to Asiatic society; and a conceptual weapon against Western colonial policies rather than an argument for their historical necessity.

'ASIATIC FEUDALISM'

In general, then, the Marxism of the third world ignored Marx's own analysis of non-Western society. Marx's belief that Western capitalism was fulfilling an essential role in 'the annihilation of old Asiatic society, and the laying of the material foundations of Western society in

[126] See in particular, Marx, *The Eighteenth Brumaire of Louis Napoleon*, *MESW*, Vol. I, *passim*.

[127] Engels, 'The Foreign Policy of Russian Czarism', *Sotsial-Demokrat*, No. 2, 1890, *The Russian Menace to Europe*, p. 40. For reasons outlined earlier in this chapter, Marx and Engels were unable to construe 'Oriental despotism' as providing a possible framework for the industrialisation of the East.

[128] See for example Engels' 'Soziales aus Russland', which he had had republished, with a new afterword confirming his original view, in the collection *Internationales aus dem Volksstaat (1871–1875)*, Berlin, 1894.

[129] Lenin did in fact quote approvingly in his pamphlet a passage from Hilferding which followed Marx in describing imperialism as the force destined to bring the non-European nations back into history: 'The old social relations become completely revolutionized, the agelong agrarian isolation of "nations without history" is destroyed and they are drawn into the capitalist whirlpool.' (Lenin, *Imperialism, the Highest Stage of Capitalism, Selected Works*, Vol. 1/2, pp. 560–561.) This aspect of the theory was not incorporated into the Marxism-Leninism of the third world.

Asia'[130] was unacceptable in view of the rising mood of nationalism in the East. But instead of taking Marx's model of Oriental society and giving it a positive rather than a negative evaluation as an alternative, non-Western way forward into industrialism and socialism, non-European Marxists imposed a European pattern on their own history. If class struggle was the dynamic factor which was to bring about the desired transition to socialism in Europe, then equivalent classes and forms of class struggle had to be discovered in Asia. Social revolution could then, at least, be conceptualised as the end-product of an indigenous development parallel to that of the West rather than as a by-product of Western imperialism.

The desire to eliminate completely the notion of Asiatic exceptionalism and its connotations of Western paternalism resulted in the following type of methodological approach being offically prescribed in the Soviet Union from 1931:

For us, there exists no division of peoples and countries into an Orient and an Occident, which are opposed to one another and which it would be appropriate to study in a different manner. In our Union, the Orient has the same rights as the Occident, and we study it with the same Marxist methodology as the Occident. There has been, and there is, class struggle in the East, just as much as in the West. The history of the Orient knows the same formations as those of the West. Such are the fundamental principles which govern our study of the Orient.[131]

These principles, based on the notion that any concession to Asiatic particularism would be a weapon in the hands of the Western colonial powers and their native allies, remained unchallenged as the official line in the Soviet Union until about 1964.

One result of such an approach was that the agrarian social system which Marx had termed Oriental despotism was relabelled by Soviet and Eastern Marxists as feudalism,[132] or at least as 'Asiatic feudalism' – a slightly modified version of the historical Western European

[130] Marx, 'The Future Results of British Rule in India', loc.cit., pp. 132–133.

[131] S. Ol'denburg (Secretary of the Soviet Academy of Sciences), statement made in 1931, quoted in J. Pečirka, 'Discussions soviétiques' (first published in German, Eirene [Prague] 1964, No. III), Recherches internationales à la lumière du marxisme, No. 57–58 (Jan.–April 1967), p. 65. For an almost identical formulation thirty years later see D.G. Reder and R.A. Ul'ianovsky's entry on the AMP in the Sovetskaia istoricheskaia entsiklopediia, Vol. I, Moscow, 1961.

[132] Georg Lukács, shortly before his death in 1971 was to describe the effects of this as follows: 'Il en résulte que nous nous sommes mis dans la situation d'examiner le cas de la Chine à partir d'un système économique qui n'y a jamais existé.' Lukács went on to say that contemporary China could only be understood when an analysis was made of the transition from the AMP to capitalism, such as Marx had done of the transition from feudalism to capitalism in Europe. ('Entretien avec Georg Lukács', L'Homme et la Société, No. 20 April–June 1971), p. 9.

formation, but one which had basically the same dynamic qualities. For example, M.S. Godes was to write that, in India and China, the process of primitive accumulation began:

...on the basis of the disintegration of feudal relations and the birth of new forms of production; it began independently of the direct influence of European capital [...]. The misfortune of Asia, and of the two greatest of its peoples – the Indians and Chinese – consists in the fact that the period of the completion of the process of primitive accumulation in Europe found China and India in the first stage of this process.[133]

Soviet authors were to admit that the state played an important economic role in 'Asiatic feudalism', but they argued that the existence of state ownership of the means of production was insufficient reason to categorise the Asiatic formation as a mode of production distinct from feudalism. One form of the Soviet argument has been that modes of production are distinguished by characteristic forms of exploitation – the subjection of the individual by violence in slavery, exploitation through monopoly of the possession (sic) of the soil in feudalism, and exploitation through wage-labour in capitalism.[134] According to this argument the question of property relations, or *who* monopolises the soil – i.e., the state or private landowners – is not central.[135] Another form of the argument, which however retains the essence of the above, has been that:

...given the cultivators work on their own land with the aid of their own implements, and that they alienate their surplus labour in the interest of a third person or third persons, they are therefore subject to feudal exploitation.[136]

But as stressed earlier, Marx believed that it was the relationship between those who owned the conditions of production and the direct producers which provided the key to any given social epoch.[137] The 'public ownership' and 'public' appropriation of the surplus value in the Asiatic formation clearly distinguished this formation from 'feu-

[133] M.S. Godes, *Spornye voprosy metodologii istorii. Diskussiia ob obshchestvennykh formatsiiakh*, Kharkov, 1930, pp. 216–217. Cf. Marx, 'However changing the political aspect of India's past must appear, its social condition has remained unaltered since its remotest antiquity, until the first decennium of the nineteenth century.' ('The British Rule in India', *loc.cit.*, p. 91).

[134] See, for example, V.N. Nikiforov, 'Zakliuchitel'noe slovo po dokladu' in *Obshchee i osobennoe v istoricheskom razvitii stran Vostoka*, Izd. 'Nauka', 1966, tr. in *Recherches internationales à la lumière du marxisme*, No. 57–58 (Jan.–April, 1967), p. 243.

[135] Cf. S.M. Dubrovsky, *K voprosu o sushchnosti 'aziatskogo' sposoba proizvodstva, feodalizma, krepostnichestva i torgovogo kapitala*, Moscow, Izd. Nauchnoi Assotsiatsii Vostokovedeniia, 1929, *passim*.

[136] From the account given by L.A. Sedov, 'La société angkorienne et le problème du mode de production asiatique', *La Pensée*, No. 138 (March–April 1968), p. 72.

[137] *Capital*, Vol. III, p. 791.

dalism', which for Marx was characterised by the private ownership and private appropriation of surplus value.

Marx himself frequently protested against what he regarded as erroneous comparisons between Oriental society and Western feudalism (for example, 'La Touche d. facts verfälscht dch phraseology borrowed from feudal Europe'[138]). Such comparisons were based partly on the fact, as he observed, that institutions of commendation and benefice could be identified in e.g. India.[139] Many of the early writers on Western feudalism had drawn an analogy between the early phases of the system of fiefs in Western Europe (before they became heritable) and the Turkish timar system – which could in turn be assimilated to the Persian/Indian jaghir system.[140]

Marx's own specific rejection of the analogy between feudal forms of benefice and the timar or jaghir forms[141] has not inhibited later Marxists, with access to the relevant material, from providing definitions such as the following:

Jagirdars – representatives of the Moslem feudal gentry in the Great Mogul Empire who received in temporary use big estates (jagirs) for which they did military service and supplied contingents of troops. When the Empire disintegrated the jagirdars became hereditary feudal owners.[142]

One of the most important reasons why Marx shunned the analogy between Oriental society and Western feudalism was that his approach to social analysis was couched in terms of the potential development of systems. According to his model of Eastern society, the institutions of benefice existing there did not have the same potential for development which had been intrinsic to their Western counterparts, and hence they were of a completely different character.

One of the specific differences between Western feudalism and Oriental society which was enumerated by Marx was the absence in the latter of anything approaching the Western system of *feudal law*.

[138] Marx's conspectus of Sir John Budd Phear, *The Aryan Village in India and Ceylon*, loc.cit., p. 283. For other examples see *ibid.*, pp. 256, 262.
[139] Marx's conspectus of Kovalevsky, *op.cit.*, *Sovetskoe Vostokovedenie*, 1958, No. 5, p. 12.
[140] See J.G.A. Pocock, *The Ancient Constitution and the Feudal Law*, Cambridge U.P., 1957, pp. 30, 82, 97, 132, 134. Pocock observes that the analogy drawn in the sixteenth and seventeenth centuries between the Turkish system of timars and early European feudalism was based on the 'apparently universal delusion that "feudal law" was an hierarchical system imposed from above as a matter of state policy.' (*Ibid.*, p. 97.) In fact the Turkish system *was* a matter of state policy, but European feudalism arose from the *collapse* of the state, a fundamental difference between European and non-European systems of benefice.
[141] Marx's conspectus of Kovalevsky, *Problemy Vostokovedeniia*, 1959, No. 1, p. 7.
[142] Marx and Engels, *On Colonialism*, Moscow, Foreign Languages Press, n.d. (published during the 1960s), pp. 356–357, fn. 38.

Marx followed Palgrave in describing feudal law as being based on the assumption of the right of the individual, whether free or enserfed, to legal protection from his feudal lord.[143] Moreover in the empire of the Great Mogul, for example, civil law excluded patrimonial justice (the exercise of juridical functions by the feudal lord),[144] whereas in Western feudalism 'the functions of general and judge, were attributes of landed property'.[145]

The work which stimulated many of Marx's strictures on applying the concept of feudalism to Asiatic society was that of M.M. Kovalevsky on communal land-tenure, a copy of which the author sent to Marx on publication in 1879. Elsewhere in his book, Kovalevsky stated that under Mohammedan rule in India, allodial land tenures had tended to change into feudal ones, and free landowners had become dependent. Marx rejected the inferences which had led Kovalevsky to this conclusion. He argued that the mere fact that under the Mogul benefice system the land tax was paid to an appointee of the treasury rather than directly to the treasury, by no means implied the feudalisation of India. In general, the Indian land tax no more converted landed property into feudal property than did the land tax in contemporary France.[146] The fact that the tax was used by the government as a payment to its appointees did not make the latter into feudal lords. Marx also observed that in the East there was no poetisation of the soil (*Bodenpoesie*) comparable to that of Western feudalism, and the principle of *nulle terre sans seigneur* did not obtain, land being alienable to other than nobles.[147]

More evidence concerning Marx's views on the notion of 'Asiatic feudalism' can be gleaned from the material he copied from Kovalevsky and heavily emphasised, in particular, Kovalevsky's account of why Turkish rule in Algeria did not lead to feudalisation. Feudalisation was:

... impeded by the *strong centralisation* of the civilian-military administration of Algeria; the latter excluded the *possibility of the hereditary seizure of local posi-*

[143] Sir Francis Palgrave, *The Rise and Progress of the English Commonwealth*, The Anglo-Saxon Period, Part 1 (first published 1832), new edn, Cambridge U.P., 1921, p. 11; Marx's conspectus of Kovalevsky, *Sovetskoe Vostokovedenie*, 1958, No. 5, p. 12.
[144] *Ibid.*
[145] Marx, *Capital*, Vol. I, p. 332. As will be seen, E. Varga, one of the most important Soviet proponents of the concept of the Asiatic mode of production, also stressed this distinction; Western feudalism was characterised by the private appropriation (e.g. by the feudal lord) of those administrative, juridical and symbolic functions which in the Asiatic formation were monopolised by the state. (E.g. Y. [E.] Varga, *Politico-Economic Problems of Capitalism, op.cit.*, pp. 345–346).
[146] Marx's conspectus of Kovalevsky, *Sovetskoe Vostokovedenie*, 1958, No. 4, p. 18.
[147] Marx's conspectus of Kovalevsky, *Sovetskoe Vostokovedenie*, 1958, No. 5, p. 12.

tions, or the conversion of the holders of them into huge landowners almost independent of the 'dayi'.[148] *The local dayis and qa'ids who customarily had the lease of the collection of taxes in the districts transferred to them, all retained these functions for only three years. The law strictly prescribed this change*, and in practice it took place *even oftener*.[149]

I.e., there was nothing resembling the 'motley pattern of conflicting, medieval plenary powers' which Marx saw as characterising French feudalism;[150] the state guarded jealously its monopoly over surplus value.

Marx's analysis of the non-Western world was far too closely tied to earlier concepts of Oriental despotism for the notion of an Asiatic feudalism to be acceptable to him, except in the special case of Japan:

Japan, with its purely feudal organisation of landed property and its developed *petite culture*, gives a much truer picture of the European middle ages than all our history books, dictated as these are, for the most part, by bourgeois prejudices.[151]

Otherwise, Marx categorically denied the relevance of his categories of pre-capitalist Western society to non-European areas.

THE ASIATIC MODE OF PRODUCTION AND SINO-SOVIET RELATIONS

Apart from the more general rejection of the idea of Asiatic exceptionalism for the reasons outlined above, the fortunes of the concept of the Asiatic mode of production have also been closely tied to the state of Sino-Soviet relations. The disappearance of the concept from Soviet writing in 1931 reflected what both the Chinese communist leadership and their Soviet allies saw as the needs of the Chinese revolution. The reappearance of the concept in 1964 was, in part, governed by the Soviet desire to discount the claims of the Chinese model of socialism, by demonstrating the particularity of Chinese history.

Between 1925 and 1931 there were widespread discussions in the Soviet Union on the topic of the Asiatic mode of production, reaching a peak in terms of published material in 1930.[152] The discussions

---

[148] 'Dayi' was an honorific title given to janissaries of certain ranks. In Algeria it was used specifically for the janissary who held the regency, but also apparently for lower-ranking janissaries.

[149] Marx's conspectus of Kovalevsky, *Problemy Vostokovedeniia*, 1959, No. 1, pp. 8–9.

[150] Marx, *The Eighteenth Brumaire of Louis Bonaparte, MESW*, Vol. I, p. 301.

[151] *Capital*, Vol. I, p. 718, fn. 1.

[152] For a recent Soviet account of the 1925–1931 'diskussiia' which is reasonably fair, in spite of the fact that the author has been one of the leading opponents of the concept during

touched both on the general historiographical problem of periodisation, and on the specific problem of the nature of the Chinese revolution, first in the optimistic period of 1925–1927 and later in the wake of the 1927 debacle.

1. *The Beginnings of the Debate: 1925–1926*

The debate was opened in a similar way to that in 1964, with an essay by the economist Eugene Varga.[153] In 1925 Varga published an article entitled 'Economic Problems of the Revolution in China'[154] in which he challenged the prevailing orthodoxy that pre-capitalist Chinese society was feudal in nature. He argued that unlike in Europe, state power 'arose in China out of the necessity to regulate the water supply, to provide protection, from floods, and to ensure the irrigation of the land'. I.e., state power arose in China not out of class struggle but rather out of the need to provide certain large-scale public works, and it was of a 'completely pacifist nature'. A 'ruling class was formed of a special type unknown in the sphere of European culture – namely a class of *literati*.'[155] Complementary to this special type of function-based ruling class was the 'tyranny of the clan' at the village level, through which the peasants owned the land, and which prevented the emergence of a native capitalism.

It is not clear what exactly led to this sudden shift on the part of Varga, who had previously adhered to the orthodox position that the structure of pre-capitalist China could adequately be described in terms of the universal feudal stage of development. However Varga did make explicit his indebtedness to Max Weber for the framework of analysis he was adopting; together with its stress on the differences rather than

the second stage of the debate, see V.N. Nikiforov, 'Diskussiia sovetskikh istorikov ob obshchestvenno-ekonomicheskom stroe Kitaia (1925–1931)', *Narody Azii i Afriki*, 1965, No. 5, pp. 75–91. This article forms the basis of Chapter Five of the author's *Sovetskie istoriki o problemakh Kitaia*, Moscow, izd. 'Nauka', 1970.

[153] Eugene or Jenö Varga (1879–1964) had become a professor of political economy at the University of Budapest in November 1918, and was to become People's Commissar of Finance and Chairman of the Supreme Economic Council of the Hungarian Soviet Republic in 1919. With the fall of the Republic he migrated to the Soviet Union where he worked for Comintern and became Director of the Institute of World Economics and World Politics (1927–1947). He returned to Hungary 1949–1956 and was one of the architects of the first Five Year Plan. In 1956 he was restored to his position at the Institute of Economics in Moscow (he had been purged 1947–1949 following censure from Stalin) and worked there until his death. His last book, *Ocherki po problemam politekonomii kapitalizma*, was published in June 1964 and contained a final chapter in which he roundly condemned the eclipse of the concept of AMP after the early discussions.

[154] E. Varga, 'Ekonomicheskie problemy revoliutsii v Kitae', *Planovoe khoziaistvo*, 1925, No. 12, pp. 165–183.

[155] *Ibid.*, p. 174.

the similarities between European and Chinese development and the use of these differences to explain why a native capitalism did not emerge in China.

In the following year (1926) Varga received support from A.Ia. Kantorovich, then engaged in research in China, for his position on the absence of feudalism in Chinese pre-capitalist society. In China there existed instead a combination of peasant or clan ownership and rule by a service estate of *literati*. Kantorovich also brought forward the argument that in the absence of a feudal structure, peasant revolts did not serve to promote system-change, but, rather, maintained the equilibrium of the system: 'revolts should be regarded in the first instance as an element of the social-fiscal-political system of China itself, as the necessary means for maintaining equilibrium in this system ...'[156]

Meanwhile the young German Communist, K.A. Wittfogel, had been undergoing a similar evolution away from the concept of a universally occurring feudal stage, also under the influence of Max Weber. In his earlier work Wittfogel, like Varga, had upheld the orthodox conception of universal stages of development.[157] By 1926, however, he had already adopted the proposition that the classical feudalism of the Chou period had been superseded by the middle of the third century BC by a bureaucratic state system. The intensification of agricultural practices (rice cultivation etc.) had enhanced the importance and power of a class of officials concerned with irrigation and flood-control works. These state officials grew sufficiently strong to prevent a new flowering of a class of feudal lords, while the everpresent threat of peasant revolts served to hold the mandarinate itself in check.

The peasant revolts which studded Chinese history were in fact class struggles directed against excessive exploitation in the form of taxes levied by the ruling official class. The creation of the bureaucratic state was accompanied by the revival of the clan organisation of the peasantry at the village level. The consequences of the destruction of

---

[156] A. Ia. Kantorovich, 'Sistema obshchestvennykh otnoshenii v Kitae dokapitalisticheskoi epokhi (V poriadke gipotezy)', *Novyi Vostok*, 1926, No. 15, p. 91. Kantorovich's article was introduced by an editorial demurral about the presentation of the bureaucracy as an autonomous group rather than tied to fundamental classes in Chinese society. See *ibid.*, p. 61. Nonetheless articles using the AMP concept were later to appear in *Novyi Vostok*. See, for example, I. Reisner, 'Novyi etap v rabochem dvizhenii Indii', No. 25 (1929) and V. Ditiakin, 'Agrarnye otnosheniia i sel'skoe khoziaistvo vo Frantsuzskom Indo-Kitae', No. 29 (1930).

[157] E.g., K.A. Wittfogel, *Ot pervobytnogo kommunizma do proletarskoi revoliutsii*, 1. Pervobytnyi kommunizm i feodalizm, tr. from the German, Kharkov, 1923.

feudalism in China, were that at the same time the machinery was broken which in Europe eventually created free wage-labour.[158]

2. The Introduction of the Term Asiatic Mode of Production

It will be noted that during the period 1925–1926 the term 'Asiatic mode of production' had not yet made an appearance, and that Weber rather than Marx himself was employed to support the concept of the particularistic development of Chinese history. In fact Weber's views on, for example, the importance of the need for public (water) works in determining Chinese development were largely derived from Marx and Engels, but this was not made explicit. Earlier Marxists such as G.V. Plekhanov who had derived the concept from Marx and Engels also did not use the term 'Asiatic mode of production'. Plekhanov, although quoting Marx's 1859 Preface concerning 'the asiatic, the ancient, the feudal and the modern capitalist modes of production', himself preferred to use the terms 'Oriental social system' or 'social order' and in particular the term Asiatic despotism (including the 'economic foundations of Asiatic despotism').

The term seems to have been used for the first time by Lenin, in his Report on the Unity Congress, when he was attempting to reconstruct the logic of Plekhanov's argument about an Asiatic restoration, and to destroy the argument from within. Lenin wrote, inter alia, that: 'To the extent that there existed (or if there existed) nationalisation of land in Muscovite Russia, then its economic foundation would have been the Asiatic mode of production.'[159] Lenin used the term twice more in the continuation of this passage, but it does not seem to have appeared elsewhere in his work except in the 1859 Preface formulation.

The term seems to have achieved currency only with the publication by David Riazanov of an explanatory preface to Marx's article 'Revolution in China and in Europe' published in *Pravda* on fourteenth of June 1925 (and soon after in *Inprecorr* and elsewhere).[160] In deference to its novelty Riazanov places the term in inverted commas each of the three times he uses it, although he clearly accepts its validity as a Marxian category. It was employed for the first time in an analysis of

---

[158] K.A. Wittfogel, *Probuzhdaiushchiisia Kitai* (tr. from the original German edition published in Vienna 1926 by D. Strashunskii), Leningrad, izd. 'Priboi', 1926, Chapters 3 and 4. For the further development of Wittfogel's position see in particular U. Vogel, *Zur Theorie der chinesischen Revolution*, Frankfurt a. M., Athenäum, 1973, pp. 64–70.

[159] V.I. Lenin, *Doklad ob ob"edinitel'nom s"ezde RSDRP, Sochineniia*, Vol. IX (1930) p. 187.

[160] D. Riazanov, 'Karl Marx et la Chine', *La Correspondance Internationale* (Vienna), Yr. 5, No. 68 (8 July 1925), pp. 563–564.

contemporary China in an article by John Pepper,[161] entitled 'Europo-American Imperialism and the Revolution in China', published in *Pravda* on the first of May, 1927. Meanwhile others, guided by Riazanov, were also going back to Marx's writings for evidence of this newly discovered independent mode of production. S.A. Dalin had come out in its defence at the University of the Workers in China in 1926 and K.A. Wittfogel published an article in the *Vestnik Kommunisticheskoi akademii* in late 1927, in which he drew on Riazanov.[162] In fact, as L.V. Danilova has claimed, from 1926–1927 onwards 'the question of the Asiatic mode of production was never off the agenda'.[163]

In November 1927 the assertion that the AMP had dominated China from the third century BC appeared in the Draft Agrarian Programme discussed at a plenum of the Central Committee of the CPC.[164] The Comintern representative V.V. Lominadze appears to have been responsible for its inclusion, and he repeated his belief in the existence of the AMP in China at the Fifteenth Congress of the CPSU in December 1928. He argued that the Chinese social system was of a type quite unlike that of European feudalism, and had rested upon the performance of vital irrigation and drainage functions by the bureaucratic state apparatus. With the collapse of the centralised state power these functions were no longer carried out; extortionate taxes were still being

[161] John Pepper (Jozsef Pogány) like Varga and the other famous 'Aziatchik' Ludvig Mad'iar (Lajos Magyar) was a Hungarian survivor of the 1919 Revolution. It is not clear why Hungarians should have played such a leading role in promoting the AMP concept in 1925–1931. Pepper was purged, and died in 1939.

[162] K.A. Wittfogel, 'Problemy ekonomicheskoi istorii Kitaia (v poriadke obsuzhdeniia)', *Vestnik Kommunisticheskoi akademii*, Kn. XX, 1927.

[163] L.V. Danilova, Introduction to Ch. XII ('Sovetskoe vostokovedenie'), *Ocherki po istorii istoricheskoi nauki v SSSR*, Vol, IV, ed. M.V. Nechkina *et al.*, Moscow, Izd. 'Nauka', 1966, p. 740. In this Introduction Danilova provides a sensitive account of the way in which early Soviet historiography of the East consciously attempted to overcome the derogatory implications of Asiatic exceptionalism by stressing universal laws of development – and in so doing constricted the facts of Oriental history within a schema basically derived from the experience of Western Europe. I.e., as noted previously, Soviet historiography attempted to overcome a Europocentric bias in Oriental studies through an approach that while purportedly universalistic, in fact concealed an equally European bias.

[164] The Sixth Congress of the CPC in June–July 1928 was to reject the relevance of the AMP concept to China in the following resolution: The attempt to characterise the contemporary socio-economic structure of China as a whole, and of the Chinese village in particular as a transitional structure between the 'Asiatic mode of production' and capitalism must be acknowledged as mistaken. The most essential features of the 'Asiatic mode of production' are: firstly, the absence of private property in land; secondly, the state-directed creation of large-scale public works (above all, a rational system of water-supply) – that is, the construction of works representing the material basis of the power of the central government over the small producers organised in village communities; and finally, thirdly, the durable existence of a village system, resting on the basis of a domestic union between agriculture and industry. All these features, and particularly the first condition mentioned above contradict the reality of China. (*Kommunisticheskii Internatsional*, 1928, No. 43, p. 43).

demanded from the peasants, although the productive functions of state power were no longer being performed; and agriculture was in ruins.

The historical consequences of the existence of the AMP in China were seen by Lominadze as follows. The absence of feudalism meant the absence also of the conditions which could give rise to a native bourgeoisie as a viable political class. In so far as a Chinese bourgeoisie existed it was the child of Western imperialism and incapable of sustaining the reform of Chinese society. The Kuomintang, for example, had degenerated into a self-seeking band of generals. The peasantry and the proletariat on the other hand were ripe for revolution, suffering conditions far worse than those in Europe.[165]

The tactical corollary of Lominadze's argument was of course at variance with official policy, and he was challenged by Stalin, Mif and Bukharin for his 'repudiation' of the Chinese bourgeoisie. The following dialogue occurred during Mif's speech at the Congress.

MIF: 'Comrade Lominadze has attempted to contrast with feudalism the "Asiatic" mode of production.'

LOMINADZE: 'Marx himself contrasted it!'

MIF: 'Marx did not contrast feudalism with the Asiatic mode of production.'

LOMINADZE: 'That means you don't know Marx!'

MIF: 'If you, Comrade Lominadze, read the letters of Engels and Marx on this question you will be convinced that by the "Asiatic" mode of production Marx understood one of the varieties of feudalism; to be specific, that there are here no differences in essence from the usual form of feudalism but that there are secondary differences of a more external kind, in the sphere of the juridical and historical system. This is the way that this question has been understood by us up to now and this is the way that Comrade Lenin understood it.'[166]

Mif went on to quote a passage from Lenin in which China was described as feudal and as his *coup de grâce* suggested that Lominadze had been (vainly) attempting to find contradictions between Marx and Lenin.

Despite the backing Mif received for his position, the AMP concept continued to appeal to influential Comintern activists. Indeed in 1928 the term, even if hedged about with quotation-marks, received an important official imprimatur by being included in the Programme adopted by

[165] *Piatnadtsatyi s"ezd VKP/b: Protokoly*, Vol. 1, Moscow, Gos. izd. pol. lit., 1961, pp. 733–736.
[166] *Ibid.*, p. 805.

the Comintern at its Sixth Congress. The circumstances were as follows.

In May 1928 a draft programme was published, referring to 'colonial and semi-colonial countries [...] with a predominance of medieval/ feudal relations both in the economy and in the political superstructure.'[167] (I.e., no mention of the AMP.) Protestations were made by L.I. Mad'iar, who wished the programme to acknowledge the existence of a distinct 'Eastern society'.[168] In the same month (June), Varga argued in the Comintern organ *La Correspondance Internationale* that 'the employment of the expression "feudalism" to characterise the situation in China was more harmful than useful to the understanding of the Chinese agrarian question.'[169] Furthermore, the erroneous description of China as feudal encouraged a dangerous political opportunism. By analogy with Europe an autochthonous development towards capitalism was expected, rather than there being a clear perception that the transition to capitalism in China could only signify China's submission to foreign capital.[170] A compromise was reached, and in the final version of the programme the relevant sentence read: 'countries .... with a predominance of medieval/feudal relations or of the "Asiatic mode of production" [...].'[171]

L.I. Mad'iar had spent 1926–1927 engaged in diplomatic work in China, where, among his other activities, he had played a leading part in the successful defence of the Soviet consulate in Shanghai against a White Russian attack. While in China Mad'iar collected the materials for his famous book *The Economics of Agriculture in China*, which was published in Moscow in 1928 and became a focal point of the AMP discussions. From 1929 until he was purged in 1934 Mad'iar worked in the Eastern Secretariat of Comintern, where he promoted as far as possible the AMP concept.[172] After 1931 he was forced to drop explicit reference to it, but simply pasted the new label of 'Asiatic feudalism'

---

[167] 'Proekt programmy Kommunisticheskogo Internatsionala', *Pravda*, 27th May 1928.

[168] L.I. Mad'iar, 'K proektu programmy'. 'Diskussionyi listok', *Pravda*, 24 June 1928. Mad'iar argued that the traditions of state provision of the conditions of production and nationalisation of land in this society, lent themselves to propaganda in favour of nationalisation, in the form of dictatorship of the proletariat and peasantry.

[169] E. Varga, 'Les problèmes fondamentaux de la revolution chinoise', Part 1, *La Correspondance Internationale*, Yr. 8, No. 56 (16 June 1928), p. 669.

[170] *Ibid.*, p. 670.

[171] *Stenograficheskii otchet VI kongressa Kommunisticheskogo Internatsionala*, vyp. 6, Moscow/Leningrad 1929.

[172] For biographical details see Nikiforov, who also cites an unpublished manuscript by himself and A.M. Grigor'ev on Mad'iar. The entry written by Nikiforov for the 3rd edition of *Bol'shaia Sovetskaia Entsiklopediia* gives the date of death as 1940 – in his earlier piece Nikiforov gave the date as unknown.

on the old content. When his book was republished in 1931 the section on the AMP was also removed.

The book, in its original format consisted firstly in a theoretical exposition of the AMP concept with many references to Marx and Engels, and secondly in a collection of materials on land-ownership and relations of production in contemporary Chinese agriculture. Unfortunately the empirical evidence, which seemed to show that feudal relations of landownership were strongly entrenched, did not support Mad'iar's theoretical framework. According to the latter the AMP had existed in China up to the beginning of the twentieth century (when feudal and capitalist concepts of private property were imported from Europe), and the survivals of the AMP were of great importance in determining the strategy of the Chinese revolution.

The lack of correlation between Mad'iar's theoretical framework and his empirical materials was acknowledged even in the review by Eugene Varga, who was second only to Mad'iar in his support for the concept as such, and was certainly the most durable of the *Aziatchiki*. Varga wrote: 'This contradiction between the strong theoretical emphasis on the significance of the "Asiatic mode of production" and the almost complete absence of corresponding concrete material represents the weak side of the book.'[173]

However Mad'iar's defence of the Marxist credentials of the concept, taken in isolation from his empirical materials, aroused considerable interest. It was an accurate presentation lacking only the evidence from the *Grundrisse* and some of the notebook materials (such as Marx's abstract of M.M. Kovalevsky) which were not yet available. It is true that Mad'iar went beyond Marx in describing state officials under the AMP as constituting an actual ruling class although their power derived from their function or office rather than from private property.

However in developing this approach Mad'iar was only echoing Engels' account in *Anti-Dühring*[174] as is clear from the following passage:

[173] E. Varga, 'Novaia nauchnaia literatura o Kitae', *Pravda*, 6 Jan. 1929. S.A. Dalin was less critical: 'Comrade Mad'iar's book is a great scientific work. All of the extremely valuable material collected by him is passed through the prism not only of the Marxist point of view in general, but through the prism of the specific evaluation made by Marx, Engels, Plekhanov and Lenin of the majority of Asiatic countries, and which (economic structure) they characterised as a special Asiatic mode of production. Having adopted this position the author succeeds particularly brilliantly in the first part of his book [...].' (S.A. Dalin [Review of L. Mad'iar, *Ekonomika sel'skogo khoziaistva v Kitae*], *Izvestiia*, 4 Oct. 1928).
[174] Engels, *Anti-Dühring*, tr. E. Burns, London, Lawrence & Wishart, n.d., p. 201.

...the fundamental class division of Eastern society occurs between the peasant masses, united in village communes, and the former servants of the communes who have separated themselves out of the communes and constituted themselves as a ruling class (the priests in Egypt, the literati of ancient China, etc.)[175]

Economic exploitation by such ruling classes takes the form of taxation – in the absence of private property in land, rent and taxes coincide.[176]

One way in which Mad'iar's account of Asiatic society differed from the writings of 1925–1927 relying on Weber, was in its rejection of the concept of a kinship-based as distinct from neighbourhood village system. Pepper had retained this clan-based approach but those *Aziatchiki* following him in deriving the concept from Marx on the whole rejected it.

Another very interesting aspect of Mad'iar's work is his treatment of G.V. Plekhanov. Mad'iar paid a warm tribute to Plekhanov for the latter's grasp of Marx's theory of social formations, in particular that of the AMP. This acknowledgement of Plekhanov's important role in the theoretical elucidation of Marx is to be found generally among the *Aziatchiki*, and distinguished their work from the rising school of Stalinist historiography. As a recent Soviet scholar has written:

During the period of the personality cult of I.V. Stalin the rich literary legacy of G.V. Plekhanov, even the works of his Marxist period, were buried in oblivion and his role in the development of the science of history was disparaged and ignored. After the Twentieth Congress of the CPSU this tendency was reversed by the concerted efforts of philosophers, economists and historians, although it has still not been completely overcome.[177]

The repudiation of the applicability of the AMP concept to Russia[178] was hardly surprising considering that the whole legitimacy of Bolshevik rule rested on just such a repudiation. If the chief legacy of the Russian past was the hypertrophy of the state, which reflected and prolonged Russia's backwardness, then the correct antidote was a period of bourgeois democracy. As the historian A.G. Prigozhin, an opponent of the AMP concept, wrote:

---

[175] L. Mad'iar, Preface to *Ekonomika sel'skogo khoziaistva*, Moscow, izd. IKKI, p. iii.
[176] *Ibid.*
[177] Iu.Z. Polevoi, 'G.V. Plekhanov o vostochnom despotizme', *Narody Azii i Afriki*, 1967, No. 2, p. 73. By the same author see also 'Nachalo marksistskoi istoriografii v Rossii', *Istoriia istoricheskoi nauki v SSSR*, Vol. II, Moscow, 1960.
[178] See also for example A.I. Lomakin, Discussion of the Report by S.M. Dubrovsky, *Istorik-Marksist*, Vol. 16 (1930) p. 121. Lomakin wrote that despite this error, Plekhanov's general concept of the AMP 'does not revise but develops Marx, and for us to learn from him is by no means shameful'.

...At the Fourth (Unity) Congress in Stockholm, Lenin raised precisely the objection that Plekhanov was attempting to construct the Menshevik conception of the Russian revolution out of his analysis of the 'Asiatic character of Russian despotism' and of the Russian commune. If Marx and Engels really took the viewpoint of acknowledging an 'Asiatic' mode of production in Russia, then it was not Lenin who was right as we have thought and believed up till now, but Plekhanov: it was Menshevism that was right, and not Bolshevism![179]

The sensitivity felt towards this subject was demonstrated at a discussion held in 1929 by the Society of Marxist historians, when S. Shmonin caused an uproar (noted in the published account) by his claim that Marxists were correct in attributing the AMP to Russia. Shmonin went on to provide his own definition of the concept, which he believed was applicable to any precapitalist formation – even those with a developed form of exchange, which 'incorporated an inner stability which precluded a transition to industrial capitalism'.[180] Shmonin listed five different pre-capitalist formations which could suffer from the condition of stasis he described as the AMP, but he did not regard it as an autonomous formation in the manner of the true *Aziatchik*.

Returning to Mad'iar's appraisal of Plekhanov, we find that he drew particular attention to the fact that: 'Plekhanov introduced a higher and extremely valuable degree of precision into Marx's teaching, in the sense of a correct construction of the order of progression of the stages of the economic formation of society.'[181] Mad'iar was referring to *Fundamental Problems of Marxism* where Plekhanov argued that although Marx originally regarded the Oriental and the Ancient as successive epochs, he changed his views after reading Morgan's *Ancient Society*.[182] Plekhanov's argument rested on the fact that both Morgan, and Marx's notes on Morgan, on which Engels' *Origin of the Family, Private Property and the State* was based, depicted a transition from clan society to the slave-based state with no intervening 'Oriental' stage. Plekhanov took this to indicate that Marx had been converted to the view that clan society could develop into *either* Oriental society (as in the 1859 Preface) *or* into Ancient society (as in the *Origin of the Family*).

---

[179] A.G. Prigozhin, 'Problema obshschestvennykh formatsii', *Pod znamenem marksizma*, 1930, No. 7–8, p. 165.
[180] Discussion of A. Efimov's report entitled 'Kontseptsiia ekonomicheskikh formatsii u Marksa i Engel'sa i ikh vzgliady na struktura vostochnykh obshchestv', *Istorik-Marksist*, Vol. 16 (1930), p. 154.
[181] Mad'iar, Preface, p. LVI.
[182] G.V. Plekhanov, *Fundamental Problems of Marxism*, tr. J. Katzer, Moscow, Foreign Language Publishing House, n.d., p. 63.

Plekhanov's reasoning was in fact faulty in that the impact of Morgan on Marx and Engels was to strengthen not to weaken their belief in a unilinear pattern of history. Morgan's work provided independent corroboration of such a universal schema, although it varied from that put forward by Marx and Engels in 1859. The respect felt by Marx and Engels towards Morgan's work led them to substitute his version of the early development of history for their own working hypothesis.[183]

All this does not detract from Plekhanov's correct conclusion, which Mad'iar built on, that whenever Marx and Engels actually turned their attention to Oriental society they were speaking in terms of an alternative form of social production determined by particular geographical and historical circumstances rather than of a universal stage. There was an ambivalence in Marx and Engels between a unilinear and a multilinear perception of historical progress, and it was this ambivalence which Plekhanov with his systematising approach was unable to comprehend.

Plekhanov's rejection of the unilinear model of history, like that of Mad'iar and other *Aziatchiki*[184] was essentially based on knowledge of the work *published* by Marx and Engels on Asiatic society and their letters on the same subject. Hence they arrived at an essentially bilinear (East/West) view of historical development. Access to the *Grundrisse* has now revealed that Marx, when paying close attention to the forms of pre-capitalist development rather than writing polemical excurses, believed in the possibility of at least three major alternative forms of development out of the primitive community (the Asiatic, classical and Germanic) and other mixed forms of development such as the Slavonic.[185]

Meanwhile S.A. Dalin, who had reviewed Mad'iar's book in *Izvestiia*, and was to survive to review E. Varga's book which reopened the debate in 1964 in *Novoe Vremia,* had published an important essay on the Taiping Rebellion in which he employed Mad'iar's theoretical framework. Dalin described the Taiping revolution as an aspect of the

---

[183] Cf. M. Godes, *Diskussiia ob aziatskom sposobe proizvodstva*, Obshchestvo marksistov vostokovedov, Moscow/Leningrad, 1931, p. 24. Godes omits to remark that if a unilinear pattern is to be retained, the 1859 hypothesis was more plausible than Morgan's schema, in that the latter was at odds with what we now know about Mycenaean civilisation in Greece – which preceded the classical epoch and had some similarities with the AMP. This point has been made by the contemporary Soviet scholar M.A. Vitkin.

[184] M.D. Kokin, G.K. Papaian and A.I. Lomakin all followed Mad'iar in rejecting the unilinear conception.

[185] Marx, *Grundrisse*, tr. M. Nicolaus, Penguin, 1973, p. 471 ff.

equilibrating mechanism of the AMP, already mentioned above in connection with A. Ia.Kantorovich. The rebellion represented a striving to return to the 'original primitive forms of "Asiatic" society, rather than creating a new mode of production'.[186] Varga followed Dalin in this respect in an article which reflected the post-1927 emphasis on Marx rather than Weber as the authority for regarding the AMP as an autonomous (non-Western) social formation.[187] Another *Aziatchik* who was to argue that peasant rebellions were one of the mechanisms ensuring the durability of the Asiatic system was A.I. Lomakin, who claimed that: '[popular revolutions] were the fundamental cause of the equilibrium of Eastern societies, condemning them to an immobile, stagnant condition, broken only by the incursion of imperialism'.[188] The popular revolutions acted as a safety-valve when the tendencies of officials to transform themselves into a feudal ruling class became too strong, and they brought about the 'formation of a new "popular" government, with the whole inevitable bureaucratic hierarchy'.[189]

Taken as a whole, the 1927–28 period saw the expression of various views about Oriental and in particular Chinese society, which had previously been regarded as incompatible with the Marxist conception of historical progress. These views were now brought forward under the umbrella of the AMP concept, which was legitimised by numerous newly discovered references in the works of Marx and Engels.

3. The Peak of the Debate 1929–1931

The year 1929 opened with the long-overdue publication of Lenin's most explicit treatment of the problem of the sequence of social formations – the lecture on *The State* delivered at Sverdlov University on the eleventh of July 1919.[190] In this lecture Lenin argued that:

The development of all human societies for thousands of years, in all countries without exception, reveals a general conformity to law, a regularity and consistency in this development; so that at first we had a society without classes – the original patriarchal, primitive society, in which there were no aristocrats; then we had a society based on slavery – a slaveowning society[...]
This form was followed in history by another – feudalism. In the great majority of countries slavery in the course of its development evolved into serfdom[...]
Further, with the development of trade, the appearance of the world market

---

[186] S.A. Dalin, *Taipiny* (Sbornik statei), Moscow, 1928, pp. 15–16.
[187] E.S. Varga 'Osnovnye problemy Kitaiskoi revoliutsii', *Bol'shevik*, 1928, No. 8, pp. 17–40.
[188] Discussion of the Report by S.M. Dubrovsky, *Istorik-Marksist*, Vol. 16 (1930), p. 123.
[189] *Ibid.*, p. 122.
[190] Published in *Pravda*, 18 January, 1929.

and the development of money circulation, a new class arose within feudal society – the capitalist class.[191]

This posthumous utterance by Lenin provided a timely confirmation of the kind of rigid historical schema approved by Stalin, and which was to be given its definitive statement in the latter's 'Dialectical and Historical Materialism'. (1938) It had the great advantage over Marx's 1859 preface of excluding the problem-creating AMP. Supporters of the AMP concept did not have the advantage of access to Lenin's *Conspectus of the Correspondence of K. Marx and F. Engels 1844–1883* (first published Moscow, 1959), which more recent Soviet *Aziatchiki* have been swift to employ in demonstrating the Leninist credentials of the concept. In these notes Lenin wrote, *inter alia*: 'The "key" to Oriental systems is the absence of private property in land. All land = the property of the head of state.' And, 'The Asiatic villages, self-enclosed and self-sufficient (natural economy) form the basis of Asiatic systems + public works of the central government.'[192]

Nonetheless, following the publication of the lecture on *The State* a series of lively discussions took place on the problem of the historical formations of society, and the *Aziatchiki* were not the only participants to challenge the five-stage scheme now handed down from above.

Many of the discussions centred around the report prepared by S.M. Dubrovsky for the Scientific Association of Oriental Studies entitled 'On the Question of the Nature of the "Asiatic" Mode of Production, Feudalism, Serfdom and Trading Capital'. This report was presented early in 1929 and published as a separate monograph later that year.[193] In it Dubrovksy denied the existence of the Asiatic mode of production, but on the other hand he provocatively introduced new modes of production into the orthodox schema, including the division of feudalism into that mode of production based on small peasant production and that based on serfdom. In the subsequent discussions of the problem of social formations both supporters and opponents of the AMP concept were united in attacking Dubrovsky.

In May 1929 a discussion was held on Dubrovsky's report at an open session of the Sociological Section of the Society of Marxist Historians. In the same year a report was presented by M. Godes to Leningrad historians on the subject, and there was another Leningrad discussion,

191 Lenin, *The State*, Peking, Foreign Languages Press, 1970, pp. 8–9.
192 Taken from M. Trush, [V.I. Lenin, Konspekt *Perepiski K. Marksa i F. Engel'sa 1844–1883 gg*], *Kommunist*, 1960, No. 2, p. 50.
193 S.M. Dubrovsky, *K voprosu o sushchnosti 'aziatskogo' sposobe proizvodstva, feodalizma, krepostnichestva i torgovogo kapitala*, Moscow, Izd. nauchnoi assotsiatsii vostokovedeniia, 1929.

again with a report from Godes in 1931.[194] In January 1930 Mad'iar presented a report and Dubrovsky a dissenting report on the AMP to the Eastern Section of the All Union Conference of Marxist Agriculturalists.[195] Also in 1930 a discussion was held at Kharkov, and one at Baku and Tiflis, where T.D. Berin, an *Aziatchik*, presented reports based on his (never eventually published) work, entitled 'Feudalism and the Asiatic Mode of Production'.[196] Berin's report consisted in a large number of citations proving the existence of the AMP concept in Marx's work. The discussion on his report at Tiflis was extremely interesting in that his opponents (for example, A.A. Bolotnikov and M.P. Zhakov) argued not so much that the concept did not exist in Marx's works but that the concept did not correspond to historical facts and hence Marx was wrong on this. Marxist methodology in approaching the facts of history was held to be more important than Marxist citology.[197] Alagardian drew an analogy between the AMP and the concepts of primitive communism and of matriarchy – in his view it was possible to be a Marxist and yet to deny the existence of these categories.[198]

At the discussion held by the Society of Marxist Historians another interesting issue was raised by I.M. Reisner, who on the basis of his own historical work believed that Mogul India was definitely 'Asiatic' rather than feudal in character. At the conclusion of his exposition Reisner made the following remarks:

It is necessary for us to turn back directly to Marx. The charge against us 'Aziatophiles' of Eastern chauvinism is quite groundless. Our task, despite the Indian nationalists who blanket Indian history with the fog of mysticism, consists in discovering in this history the laws of class struggle.[199]

Reisner's formulation may have been quite deliberately paradoxical, for the concept of the AMP was unpopular with Eastern communists from the beginning of the debate, not because of its implications of

[194] The latter was published under the title *Diskussiia ob aziatskom sposobe proizvodstva po dokladu M. Godesa*, Moscow, Leningrad, 1931. An accompanying report was presented by M.D. Kokin.

[195] Mad'iar's report was entitled 'Obshchestvennye formatsii i agrarnyi vopros', and included Theses on the AMP.

[196] The Tiflis discussion was published in the form: *Ob aziatskom sposobe proizvodstva. Stenograficheskii otchet diskussii po dokladu t. Berina*, Tiflis, Zakkniga, 1930. Berin's report at the Baku discussion was entitled: 'Vostochnyi feodalizm ili aziatskii sposob proizvodstva' (4 April 1930). In it he applied the concept to the history of Persia and pre-Revolutionary Azerbaijan. The conference materials were not published.

[197] *Ibid.*, p. 98.

[198] *Ibid.*, pp. 85–86.

[199] 'Preniia po dokladu S. Dubrovskogo', *Istorik-Marksist*, Vol. 16 (1930), p. 115.

Eastern chauvinism, but because of the fear discussed above in the section on 'Asiatic Feudalism' that it was a weapon in the hands of Western chauvinism and paternalism.

Apart from the discussions held in 1929–1931, at which the *Aziatchiki* put forward their claims for the concept, a number of monographs were to appear in 1930 – the high tide mark of the respectability of the concept. These included a new book by L.I. Mad'iar, *Essays on the Economy of China*, which was edited by E. Varga and contained a foreword and closing article by him; A.I. Shtusser's *Marx and Engels on India* (edited by and with a foreword by Mad'iar); *Ching t'ien; The Agricultural Structure of Ancient China*, by M.D. Kokin and G. Papaian, edited by and with a foreword by L. Mad'iar. The English Marxist Paul Fox, who was then working in the Institute of Marxism-Leninism in Moscow published a very detailed study entitled 'The Views of Marx and Engels on the Asiatic mode of production and their sources'.[200] In this study Fox argued that, as his researches showed, there was no doubt that the AMP was a Marxist concept. There was also no doubt that a qualitative difference existed between Eastern and Western society. What Fox refused to commit himself to was whether the theory of the AMP, as understood by Marx and Engels, elucidated this difference in a definitive way, although he suggested that external evidence supported their point of view.[201]

The book by Kokin and Papaian, which represented their degree work as students of the Leningrad Institute of Oriental Studies, was of particular interest as an effort to show, by using old Chinese sources, that Chinese society of the Chou period was based on the AMP. The book opened with the preface of seventy-five pages by Mad'iar on the theory of the AMP – someone described the work of Kokin and Papaian as an 'afterword to L. Mad'iar's foreword'.[202] Kokin and Papaian themselves had a theoretical section on the AMP, in which they, foreshadowing the more recent *Aziatchiki*, opposed Marx's concept of the absolute stagnation of the East. Kokin and Papaian argued that when Marx and Engels were writing there had been insufficient research done to reveal the internal dynamic of Asiatic systems; a

---

[200] P. Foks, 'Vzgliady Marksa i Engel'sa na aziatskii sposob proizvodstva i ikh istochniki', *Letopisi marksizma*, 1930, III (XIII), pp. 3–29.
[201] *Ibid.*, p. 29.
[202] Reported in V.N. Nikiforov, *op.cit.*, p. 231, fn.

dynamic which although different from that of Western European society nonetheless existed.[203]

The rest of the book was devoted in part to an account of the historiographical sources for the Chou period, and finally to a direct account of the social system. The latter they described as based on the 'ching t'ien' or neighbourhood commune, which was exploited by a bureaucratic apparatus. Rent and tax coincided, the state owning the land. The official governing this or that region did not regard himself as the proprietor of the region. The external sign of the Asiatic structure of the society was the high degree of centralisation, which distinguished it from classical feudalism. Kokin and Papaian, like the other *Aziat-chiki*, found the explanation of the AMP to lie in the need for irrigation.

The closing essay by Eugene Varga in Mad'iar's book touched on the more contemporary problem of the relevance of the AMP concept to the strategy of the Chinese revolution. Varga argued that while the AMP no longer existed in China, neither did feudalism, and land-rent was in fact of a usury-capital variety. Feudal land-rent based on feudal rights did not exist in China and there was no class of feudal land-owners distinct from the bourgeoisie such as existed in Europe before the bourgeois revolution.

There were dangerous similarities between this kind of position, denying the relevance of the feudal category to China (and hence denying the relevance of an anti-feudal revolution), and Trotsky's position that the Chinese revolution must be of an anti-capitalist nature. These similarities sealed the fate of the concept in 1931, when the *Aziatchiki* were loudly denounced as Trotskyites (although Trotsky had never used the AMP concept).

4. *The Arguments Used Against the AMP Concept*

The types of criticism made of the AMP concept fall into three main categories, the methodological, the empirical and the pragmatic. All three categories were to be employed by E. Iolk in a vitriolic attack on the concept published in 1931,[204] in which he used every piece of ammunition which was to hand, and summarised many of the arguments put forward at the earlier discussions. The following account largely follows Iolk, but leaves out some of the more idiosyncratic

[203] M.D. Kokin, G. Papaian, '*Tszin'-Tian*'. *Agrarnyi stroi drevnego Kitaia*, Leningrad, Izd. Leningr. vostochnogo instituta im. A.S. Enukidze, 1930, p. 85. Kokin and Papaian's book was translated and published in China in 1933.

[204] E. Iolk, 'K voprosu ob "aziatskom" sposobe proizvodstva', *Pod znamenem marksizma*, 1931, No. 3, pp. 133–156.

attempts to prove that Marx and Engels did not put forward the AMP concept in their work.

(a) *Methodological Arguments*. Methodological arguments concerning the AMP concept have been common both in the earlier and more recent Soviet debates, and stem from the structural differences between this category and others defined by Marx as modes of production.

In the first place, the AMP was, by its very formulation geographically circumscribed, unlike the other modes of production which in the 1920s were regarded as being universal in character.[205] The appearance of the AMP was determined by regionally specific geographic factors (climate, extensive flood plains etc.) rather than by the universal logic of the development of forces of production.

This attribution of a determining role to geographical factors seemed to many of the opponents of the AMP concept to be a denial of the principles of historical materialism. As one of its critics remarked, 'Can one be surprised [...] that a theory built upon water is soggy from the outset?'[206]

The belittling of the significance of geographical factors was characteristic of Stalinist historical materialism as a whole, according to which the role of geographical environment was limited to an 'accelerating or retarding effect'. This aspect of Stalinist historiography was officially renounced in 1963 and a major reassessment of the role of geographical factors in history has been taking place in the Soviet Union.[207]

A different kind of methodological objection concerned the problem of a mode of production in which the defining elements were of a secondary or superstructural character; that is, the functions of the state in providing public works, the state ownership of the land, and the state monopoly of rent in the form of tax. According to a central stream of Marxist thinking the state is always a secondary phenomenon, brought into being as a consequence of class struggle, and subordinate to a dominant economic class. In the AMP thesis, however, the state is part of the economic base in so far as it supplies essential conditions of production and hence achieves a monopoly of surplus

---

[205] In the recent debates, especially within the PCF this position has been more or less reversed, with the AMP being interpreted as a more universally occurring formation than the regionally restricted slavery and feudalism.

[206] M.G. Godes, in *Diskussiia ob aziatskom sposobe proizvodstva*, op.cit., p. 10. Cf. Iolk, p. 149.

[207] See Marian Sawer, 'The Place of Geographical Factors in Historical Materialism', *Political Science*, Vol. 26, No. 2, p. 66.

labour. This thesis was inacceptable and indeed even incomprehensible to the opponents of the AMP concept. S.M. Dubrovsky was to write: 'According to Comrade Lomakin, the mode of exploitation in Asiatic societies amounts to the collection of tribute: but the state collecting the tribute must represent the rule of a definite class.'[208]

A similar refutation was made by one of the reviewers of Wittfogel's book, *China Awakes*:

The officials constituted a class not because they were officials but because they represented the property interests of the ruling class. The administration of the irrigation system was not the basis of the state, but rather the means or instrument of its consolidation.[209]

Dubrovsky also argued, as did Iolk, that while Marx undeniably claimed that in the East the state owned the land, this did not constitute an independent mode of production as both the subject and the relationship were superstructural phenomena.[210] The analysis of the property relationship as superstructural was hardly tenable, as Varga has pointed out – for Marx property relations were the legal expression of relations of production, and the key to any given social formation was the relationship of the direct producers to the owners of the means of production, in this case, the state.

Related to the special role of the state in Asiatic society was the problem of whether the state was a 'supra-class' state, a theory associated with 'bourgeois historiography'; or whether the state could embody a function or office-based ruling class. Mad'iar, as has been pointed out, followed Engels in describing the bureaucracy as a ruling class, but many others of the *Aziatchiki* drew back from this position – involving as it did the apparent rejection of the concept of class as based on the private and hereditary ownership of the means of production. These doubts over whether the concept of a functional class was compatible with Marxism were expressed in the usage of words such as stratum, group, exploiting layers and so on.

Whether or not the bureaucracy associated with the AMP was defined as a class, the supporters of the concept agreed in viewing its role as an exploitative as well as a functional one. This involved the further problem of why this relationship of exploitation did not gener-

[208] S.M. Dubrovksy, 'Preniia po dokladu S. Dubrovskogo', *loc.cit.*, p. 123.
[209] M. Shchukar, [Review of K. Wittfogel, *Probuzhdaiushchiisia Kitai*], *Novyi Vostok*, No. 16–17 (1927), p. 380.
[210] The underlying assumption of the argument being that wherever cultivators worked with their own implements land to which they had certain hereditary rights, and were compelled to alienate surplus labour to a third party or parties, there existed a feudal mode of production.

ate a dynamic class struggle as occurred in the Marxist description of all other historical formations. According to the general principles of Marxist social analysis, relations of exploitation always breed social struggle, and are the locomotive of social change and progress. On the other hand, the concept of the AMP, even as modified by Kokin and Papaian and more contemporary Marxists, has always included the notion of relative stagnation and the failure to develop the prerequisites of industrial capitalism from within. Iolk described the failure of the *Aziatchiki* to perceive the internal dynamic of Eastern societies as due not so much to the backwardness of these societies as to the 'backwardness of the "Eastern" sector of our historical front'.[211] Marx himself appears to have believed that although his general theory of history rested on the premise of necessary progress, lack of individuation and differentiation in the social division of labour could lead to a self-perpetuating system as long as conditions of isolation from expanding capitalism were preserved. These systems existed outside the mainstream of world progress, which provided the justification of Marx's general social theory, but as the critics pointed out, the very acknowledgement of the AMP also tended to destroy the concept of the inevitability of social progressions.

(b) *Empirical Arguments*. Even if the structure of the AMP concept was compatible with the Marxist theory of socio-economic formations, many opponents of the AMP concept believed it to be incompatible with empirical evidence. Marx did not have sufficient data at his disposal to determine whether in fact Eastern societies experienced the same or different modes of production from those in the West. More recent research showed that although the features comprising the AMP concept might have existed to some degree in Eastern societies they were not sufficiently dominant *vis à vis* patriarchal, and/or slavery, feudal and trading capital elements to warrant being defined as comprising an autonomous mode of production.

(c) *Pragmatic Arguments*. Pragmatic arguments raised against the AMP concept dealt in the main with its presumed political consequences, regardless of its methodological correctness or its empirical truth. For a start there was the guilt by association in that G.V. Plekhanov had been the only Marxist to develop and apply the concept system-

---

[211] E. Iolk, 'K voprosu ob "aziatskom" sposobe proizvodstva', *loc.cit.*, p. 155.

atically before the 1925–1931 debate. The Bolshevik school of historiography headed in the 1920s by M.N. Pokrovsky had claimed that Plekhanov's erroneous conceptualisation of the Russian state as relatively autonomous of social classes had led to his 'defencist' position in the First World War. Iolk was to seize eagerly on this ready-made argument as to the detrimental political consequences of the AMP concept.[212]

Secondly there was the argument alluded to in the main body of this essay, that the concept of Asiatic particularism and its connections with the ideology of Western colonialism would alienate potential and actual Asian revolutionary movements. On the other hand, there was the possibility that the AMP concept would 'play right into the hands of various nationalist elements' who argued that Marxism was not applicable to Asia, in that class struggle was something alien to the area, only imported by Western imperialism.[213] In order to combat both these suggestions it was necessary to uncover a history of class struggle similar to that in Western Europe which could be deployed as the heroic antecedent of existing struggles.

A third pragmatic argument raised against the AMP concept was that it lent itself more to the Trotskyist than the Stalinist interpretation of the Chinese revolution. In fact the *Aziatchiki* differed from Trotsky in their understanding of Chinese history although their practical conclusions converged somewhat. Trotsky argued that capitalism was already firmly established in China and hence the revolution must be socialist rather than bourgeois-democratic in character. The supporters of the AMP concept, as noted before, tended to argue that because the native bourgeoisie had only been brought into existence through the influence of Western imperialism they should not be relied upon as a revolutionary force.

Unfortunately, from 1931 the *Aziatchiki* of this period were in no position to answer the arguments of their opponents. However, their efforts helped to fuel the recent debate in the Soviet Union and Eastern and Western Europe. So in a broad sense, the concept of the AMP has continued to act as the leverage point for efforts to resist the conversion of historical materialism from a critical apparatus into rigid ideology. The early AMP debate is perhaps particularly notable for the fact that the leading protagonists had been active participants in at least one

---

[212] Iolk wrote that: 'One could say that the whole theory of "Eastern" society is a mark of the negative aspects of Plekhanov's heritage'. (*Ibid.*, p. 147.)

[213] M. Godes, *Diskussiia ob aziatskom sposobe proizvodstva, op.cit.*, p. 34.

revolution (the Hungarian) and were deeply involved in another (the Chinese): for them, the preservation of Marxism as a critical rather than dogmatic theory was of the greatest importance in both analytic and practical work.

THE IMPACT OF THE SINO-SOVIET RIFT

Since 1964, and the deepening of the Sino-Soviet rift, Soviet historiography has become much more receptive to the idea that Chinese history represents an alternative to and not just an Asiatic version of Western European history. This tendency is crystallised in a recent article by L.S. Vasil'ev which employs the 'Asiatic' concept in analysing Chinese society and does so at a new level of sophistication which betrays in part the influence of the *Grundrisse* (as we have seen, unavailable to the earlier protagonists of the concept).

Vasil'ev begins with an attack on Chinese historiography for its failure to come to grips with the nature of Chinese history. The reason for this failure, Vasil'ev argues, is that Chinese historians have attempted to cram the three thousand years of Chinese civilisation into the framework of the five-stage theory of development 'created on the basis of European material'.[214] One of the most glaring results of working from such a schema and not from 'the facts', according to Vasil'ev, has been a wildly fluctuating periodisation, particularly in relation to the origins of feudalism.[215] The continuation of this argument is that:

... the solution of the problems of the social structure and the tendencies of evolution of ancient Chinese society can only be discovered through determinedly eschewing schemas which have failed to justify themselves. The socio-economic analysis of pre-capitalist societies witnesses to the multilinear evolution, and different paths of development of these societies. But this analysis by itself is insufficient to deal with the whole complexity of the problem. The study of the history of China and of the role within this history of social, political and ethical factors, gives considerable foundation to the point of view, with which the great Sinologist V. Eberhard is in substantial agreement, that the law of dynamics of Chinese society depends to a large degree on socio-political rather than socio-economic factors [momenty].[216]

The way to solve the problems of Chinese history, Vasil'ev suggests, is

[214] L.S. Vasil'ev, 'Sotsial'naia struktura i dinamika drevnekitaiskogo obshchestva', L.V. Danilova *(et al.)* ed., *Problemy istorii dokapitalisticheskikh obshchestv*, Kniga 1, Moscow, Izd. 'Nauka', 1968, p. 456.
[215] *Ibid.*
[216] *Ibid.*, p. 457.

through the concept of the Asiatic mode of production and through the analysis of the role of non-economic factors. In describing the nature of ancient Chinese society, Vasil'ev differs from the earlier Soviet supporters of the concept in that he places less emphasis on the entrepreneurial role of the state in bringing the system into being and more emphasis on the enabling factor of communal property.[217] However, like his predecessors, Vasil'ev makes explicit some of the unstated implications of Marx's model, such as that the bureaucratic elite assumes the functions of a ruling class under this system,[218] and that the state is part of the economic base, rather than being merely part of the superstructure of society.[219] Vasil'ev, unlike Mad'iar or Varga, is careful to describe the bureaucratic elite as assuming the *functions* (including that of economic exploitation) of a ruling class rather than actually *being* a ruling class; he does this because in Marx's model of Asiatic society social stratification stems from social inequality rather than from property differences,[220] and there is an absence of (private-property based) classes or class antagonism in the Western sense. Vasil'ev's terminological nicety extends also to referring to the peasantry in this system as an estate rather than a class. (China's 'most important estate – after officialdom').[221]

Having described the nature of old Chinese society, Vasil'ev turns to the question of its dynamics. The most important factor governing the dynamics, or more properly speaking the lack of dynamics in Chinese society, Vasil'ev sees as the role of Confucian ideology. The influence of Confucian ideology was to inhibit the development of individuation within Chinese society, and substitute for it a backward-looking conservatism.[222]

Here Vasil'ev is touching on one of the most important questions raised by the revival of the concept of the Asiatic mode of production (and one which will be treated at greater length in another chapter). Since the absence of the private ownership of the means of production (land) is central to this concept, and where the importance of the economic functions of the state (in providing irrigation etc.) is denied or belittled as has frequently been the case with more recent exponents

[217] Mad'iar and Varga had discussed the role of the 'tyranny of the clan' in providing the preconditions of a functionally-based rather than a private-property based ruling class.

[218] *Ibid.*, p. 483.

[219] *Ibid.*, p. 495.

[220] Though the former tends to give rise to the latter. See *ibid.*, p. 478.

[221] *Ibid.*, p. 483.

[222] *Ibid.*, p. 511.

of the concept, the role of *non-economic* factors in the expropriation of the surplus and in providing the general dynamic of society looms very large. As Vasil'ev concludes:

> In short, socio-political factors, Confucian ideology in particular, have played an important, and often a decisive role in determining the social structure of China and the dynamics of its further evolution. There is no doubt that conservative Confucian doctrine has impeded the development of China – for example, through the disparagement of the role of trade and traders, the efforts of the state to restrict private initiative and introduce monopolies, the admiration for the institutions of antiquity, the distrust in innovations, etc.[223]

The peculiarities of China's past, including the lack of individuation are now being held responsible in the Soviet Union for the directions taken by the Chinese revolution – i.e., non-socialist directions 'rooted in China's socio-economic and ideological development, and her Confucian traditions and history'.[224]

This situation has to some extent encouraged the re-emergence of the concept of the Asiatic mode of production within the Soviet Union, even to the extent that the third edition of the *Bol'shaia sovetskaia entsiklopediia* includes, for the first time, an entry on the AMP – written, moreover, by a supporter of the concept, N.B. Ter-Akopian.[225] However, there is still far from universal acceptance of it. As used for propaganda purposes in the Sino-Soviet dispute it easily becomes a two-edged weapon, as can be seen from the following:

> ... Marx pointed out with marvellous historical insight that the patriarchal peasant commune which was the social basis for various forms of despotic rule in the past could only become the foundation for 'barrack communism'. This deep insight can now be illustrated by the trend developments have taken in China caused by attempts to substitute a petty bourgeois theory and practice of Maoism for true Marxism.

---

[223] *Ibid.*, p. 515.

[224] E.g., *A Critique of Mao Tse-tung's Theoretical Conceptions*, tr. Y. Sdobnikov, Moscow, Progress, 1972, p. 72.

[225] N.B. Ter-Akopian, 'Aziatskii sposob proizvodstva', *Bol'shaia sovetskaia entsiklopediia*, 3rd edition, Vol. I, 1970. Ter-Akopian provides a factual account of Marx and Engels' development of the AMP as an analytic category, and of the subsequent failures to explore this concept. Ter-Akopian's bibliographical research on the AMP concept within the work of Marx and Engels was published at greater length in a two-part article in *Narody Azii i Afriki*, 1965, Nos. 2 and 3. Ter-Akopian's open affirmation of the Marxian status of the AMP category is in marked contrast to the 1961 entry under 'Aziatskii sposob proizvodstva' in the *Sovetskaia istoricheskaia entsiklopediia*. There it is claimed that: 'The publication of Marx's manuscript, "Precapitalist Economic Formations" (in 1940) has made it fully clear that Marx did not understand by the formula "AMP" a special socio-economic formation supposedly existing in the countries of Asia and peculiar only to them, but only a specific peculiarity in the forms of property constantly appearing in the social structure of these countries.'

Despite all his hate of capitalist exploitation [...] Marx considered capitalism as a historically progressive system serving as a springboard for socialism.[226]

However, as we shall see, propaganda purposes apart, there is great interest among Soviet scholars in the possibilities opened up by the 'Asiatic' concept for a new Marxist historiography; an historiography which does not apply concepts to non-Western history which are appropriate only to West European history; an historiography which also awards a greater significance to the role of non-economic factors in the economic infra-structure. This is one aspect of the present quest taking place in Soviet historical institutes for a new and satisfying framework in which to synthesise the rapidly increasing store of specialised empirical knowledge about the countries outside Europe.

---

[226] A. Milejkovskij [Mileikovsky], 'Marx and economic planning', *Marx and Contemporary Scientific Thought*, The Hague, Mouton, 1968, p. 356. (Mileikovsky is a member of the Soviet Academy of Sciences.)

CHAPTER III

THE ASIATIC MODE OF PRODUCTION IN RELATION TO THE PLACE OF GEOGRAPHICAL FACTORS IN HISTORICAL MATERIALISM

MARX ON THE ROLE OF GEOGRAPHICAL FACTORS IN HISTORICAL DEVELOPMENT

Marx viewed history as the unfolding of successive modes of material production, culminating in industrial capitalism. He did not, however, regard these modes of production as evolving independently of the influence of the natural environment. For him, geographical factors not only provided the necessary conditions of production, but also played an important, and sometimes, crucial, role in determining forms of production and of social organisation.

In this Marx followed Montesquieu and Hegel. As we have seen, Montesquieu had linked geographical factors with forms of political organisation in an analytic and comparative framework,[1] and had stressed the direct influence of environment on man's character and predilections. Hegel, on the other hand, had described the interaction between man and nature in a historical framework, showing the influence of geographical factors on social organisation as taking place through what Marxists were to term the 'mode of production'. For him, too, *different* geographical factors came to be of decisive importance at *different* stages of historical development.[2]

Since the publication of the *Grundrisse* it has become more generally recognised that Marx saw the early stages of human history in terms of a plurality of modes of production developing under the influence of specific local geographic, ethnographic, and historical circumstances. In the *Grundrisse* Marx wrote, for example, that:

---

[1] For the influence on Marx of Montesquieu's emphasis on geographical factors see, for example, *Capital*, Vol. I, pp. 512–515.

[2] See G.W.F. Hegel, *The Philosophy of History*, tr. J. Sibree, London, Bell, 1905, pp. 82–107 ('The Geographical Basis of History').

...the extent to which this original community [the earliest form of landed property, that based on kinship] is modified will depend on various external, climatic, geographic, physical etc., conditions as well as on their particular natural predisposition – their clan character.[3]

Under the influence of such conditions, Marx argued, the original community developed into three major alternative forms, the Asiatic, classical (Greek or Roman) and Germanic, while the Slavonic form appeared as a mixture of the Asiatic and Germanic types.

Marx summarised the major forms of pre-capitalist development, the forms in which free labour did not yet exist, in the following manner:

...these different forms of the commune or tribe members' relation to the tribe's land and soil – to the earth where it has settled – depend partly on the natural inclinations of the tribe, and partly on the economic conditions in which it relates as proprietor to the land and soil in reality, i.e. in which it appropriates its fruits through labour, and the latter will itself depend on climate, physical make-up of the land and soil, the physically determined mode of its exploitation, the relation with hostile tribes or neighbour tribes, and the modifications which migrations, historic experiences, etc. introduce.[4]

MARX'S GRUNDRISSE SCHEMA OF HISTORICAL DEVELOPMENT
(emphasis placed on the geographical factor)

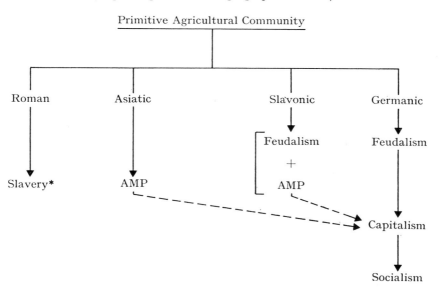

------ Non-progressive, but can develop into capitalism under pressure from pre-existing capitalist sys tem
  * Non-progressive and self-destructing.

[3] Marx, *Grundrisse*, p. 472.
[4] *Ibid.*, p. 486.

The description of human history to be found in the *Grundrisse* might be represented schematically as in the diagram on page 105.

This is in contrast with the description of human history to be found in most accounts of historical materialism,[5] which is presented in the next diagram.

THE UNILINEAR SCHEMA

(emphasis placed on the social factor)

Primitive Agricultural Community

↓

AMP*

↓

Slavery

↓

Feudalism

↓

Capitalism

↓

Socialism

* Has sometimes been omitted as it causes difficulty for a schema of universal application.

The most unequivocal use of a geographical explanation in Marx's writing on pre-capitalist societies is his stress on the need for extensive irrigation in the East. According to Marx, as we have seen in Chapter Two, this factor was largely responsible for the development of a special mode of production, and a corresponding form of political organisation.[6]

[5] See, for example, the following which have all been widely used as text-books: V.I. Lenin, *On the State* (first published 1929); J.V. Stalin, *Dialectical and Historical Materialism* (first published 1938); N. Bukharin, *Historical Materialism*(first published 1921); O. Kuusinen ed., *Fundamentals of Marxism-Leninism* (first published 1959); G. Glezerman and G. Kursanov *Historical Materialism* (Moscow, 1968).

[6] E.g., Marx, *Grundrisse*, p. 474, The Hungarian sinologist Ferenc Tökei has attempted to discover a different geographical explanation of the AMP in Marx, namely the influence of internal (conditioned by the autarchic village system) and external *isolation*. (F. Tökei, *Sur le mode de production asiatique*, Budapest, Akadémiai Kiadó, 1966, *passim*.)

He believed that under this 'Asiatic' mode of production state intervention was necessary to make the land productive. From this economic role, forced upon it by geographical circumstances, the Asiatic state acquired a monopoly position over the surplus product and over economic initiative.

Marx was particularly interested in these institutional correlates from the comparative perspective of Western Europe. In Western Europe communal intervention was not necessary to valorise the soil, stronger forms of private property developed, and a socio-historical dynamic emerged in striking contrast to the apparent stasis of the East. Hence Marx's whole analysis of the differing development of East and West, ultimately rested on the use of a geographical factor as an explanatory variable. The numerous secondary factors mentioned by Marx are never given quite the same prominence. For example, the persistence of self-sufficient village communalism, which gave the Eastern state a special role as the symbolic unity of the whole.

Other geographical factors specifically cited by Marx as playing an important role in determining human history are firstly, propinquity of different natural environments to each other, and secondly, the extensiveness of a given territorial unit. The first factor gives rise to the exchange of goods between tribes inhabiting different natural environments and the development of the division of labour.[7] The second factor, extensiveness of territory, Marx saw as having some connection with the creation of despotic systems.[8] Marx did not, however, follow Montesquieu in arguing that empires of a certain size have definite institutional correlates regardless of other variables.[9] Nor did he take up Hegel's position that:

... States – other things equal [sic] – derive a different qualitative character from magnitudinal difference. Laws and constitution become something different when the extent of the State and the number of its citizens increases. The State has a certain measure of magnitude, and if forced beyond this it collapses hopelessly under that very same constitution that was its blessing and its strength for as long as its extent alone was different.[10] [I.e., the transformation of quantity into quality.]

Marx's theory of history, however, diverged from contemporary theories which stressed the role of geographical factors not so much in the

[7] Marx, *Capital*, Vol. I, pp. 351–352; Vol. III, p. 177.
[8] Marx, Second draft of letter to Vera Zasulich, 8 March 1881, *Werke*, Vol. 19, p. 399.
[9] Montesquieu, *The Spirit of the Laws*, Vol. 1, London, Colonial Press, 1900, p. 122.
[10] Hegel, *Science of Logic*, tr. W.H. Johnston and L.G. Struthers, Vol. I, London, Allen and Unwin, 1929, p. 390.

geographical factors he regarded as of decisive importance[11] as in the temporal limitations he placed upon their importance. According to Marx's conception of historical progress, geographical factors, as contrasted with social factors, diminished in importance *pari passu* with the development of man's productive powers.[12] Progress, for Marx, consisted in the movement from naturally determined human relationships to historically evolved social relationships.[13]

The forms of production originally evolved under the direct impress of natural conditions.[14] But as man developed his technological capacities, the importance of geographical influence moved into the background,[15] and his productive activity assumed forms that contained a historical logic of their own. This process culminated in the development of capitalism which tended to universalise itself, regardless of local particularities.

Marx's concept of the receding importance of geographical factors was to be faithfully reproduced by the Soviet historian Pokrovsky in his widely used textbook, *The Brief History of Russia*. According to Pokrovsky, Russia's natural environment was a prime cause of its economic retardation during the greater part of its history. While agriculture was the basic mode of production, Russia suffered from the disadvantage that the Central European plain could only be cultivated for about five months of the year, for climatic reasons. This disadvantage was overcome with the onset of industrialism, because factories could operate for 12 months of the year, using imported raw materials where necessary. At the same time the creation of a railway network compensated for the lack of natural waterways for the transportation of goods. Hence Russia was able to catch up rapidly with the rest of Europe, and its original geographical disadvantages became increasingly irrelevant.[16]

[11] Or in *how* they exercised their influence on society, whether directly, as Montesquieu tended to claim, or through the mode of production as the Germans, from Kant through Herder and Hegel, had argued.

[12] *Pace* Wittfogel, whose examples of Marx's supposed recognition of the decisive importance of geographical factors in 'advanced' countries are extremely weak (e.g. the shift from the Mediterranean to the Atlantic and then to the Pacific as the centre of world trade). See *Werke*, Vol. 7, pp. 220–21.

[13] Marx, *A Contribution to the Critique of Political Economy*, tr. S.W. Ryazanskaya, Moscow, Progress, 1970, p. 213.

[14] Marx, *Grundrisse*, pp. 472–473.

[15] This is not the case with predominantly agricultural nations which remain to a great extent determined by the natural conditions of production. Marx tended to share Hegel's views on the Slavs as an unhistorical nation restricted in their development of consciousness by their naturally determined mode of production. See also their views on Asiatic nations.

[16] M.N. Pokrovsky, *A Brief History of Russia*, 10th edn, 2 vols., tr. D.S. Mirsky, London, Martin Lawrence, 1933, Vol. I, pp. 31–33.

Or, as a more recent Soviet historian puts it:

...the influence of the geographic environment upon a given society is inversely proportional to the degree to which that society is equipped with technology. In other words, the lower the technological level of society's development, the more strongly it is influenced by the geographical environment, and vice versa. The obviousness of this proposition can hardly be challenged.[17]

The effect of capitalism in eliminating the multiplicity of locally determined modes of production was described by Marx as follows:

Thus capital creates the bourgeois society, and the universal appropriation of nature as well as of the social bond itself by the members of society. Hence the great civilizing influence of capital; its production of a stage of society in comparison to which all earlier ones appear as mere *local developments* of humanity and as *nature-idolatry*. For the first time, nature becomes purely an object for humankind, purely a matter of utility; ceases to be recognized as a power for itself; and the theoretical discovery of its autonomous laws appears merely as a ruse so as to subjugate it under human needs, whether as an object of consumption or as a means of production.[18]

In the same vein Marx wrote:

Nature builds no machines, no locomotives, railways, electric telegraphs, self-acting mules, etc. These are products of human industry; natural material transformed into organs of the human will over nature, or of human participation in nature.[19]

These passages from the *Grundrisse* reflect the general account in Marx's works of history as the progressive 'subjection of Nature's forces to man'.[20] Yet there also exists in Marx's work a different account of the role played by geographical factors in human history, resting on a different type of definition of the natural environment. This subsidiary theme rests on the definition of the 'sensuous world' as not a thing given direct from all eternity, remaining ever the same, but the product of industry and the state of society.[21]

Once one is arguing that the geographical environment is a historical product, changing under the impact of man and reacting back on him, the concept of the receding importance of geographical factors appears less plausible. The intensification of man's technological impact on the

---

[17] M.A. Korostovtsev, 'On the Concept "The Ancient East"', *Vestnik drevnei istorii*, 1970, No. 1, tr. in *Soviet Studies in History*, Vol. IX, No. 2 (Fall, 1970), p. 110.

[18] Marx, *Grundrisse*, pp. 409–410.

[19] *Ibid.*, p. 706. See also *ibid.*, p. 705 for man's 'understanding of nature and his mastery over it' embodied in existing forces of production which only need to be reappropriated by man in order for socialist man to develop on their basis.

[20] Marx and Engels, *The Communist Manifesto, MESW*, Vol. 1, p. 37.

[21] Marx and Engels, *The German Ideology*, Moscow, Progress, 1968, p. 57.

environment no longer appears synonymous with a progressive mastery over an externally conceived nature.

Already under capitalism nature as something independent of human activity no longer existed 'except perhaps on a few Australian coral islands of recent origin'.[22] However the kind of new geographical environment (let alone the social environment) created by the advances of technology under capitalism was not necessarily benign. For example river water ceased to be a suitable medium of existence for the fish:

> as soon as the river is made to serve industry, as soon as it is polluted by dyes and other waste products and navigated by steamboats, or as soon as its water is diverted into canals where simple drainage can deprive the fish of its medium of existence.[23]

Elsewhere Marx wrote in connection with the human mediation of nature that:

> *Climate and the Vegetable World Throughout the Ages, a History of Both*, by Fraas (1847), is very interesting, especially as proving that climate and flora have changed in historic times. [. . .] He maintains that as a result of cultivation and in proportion to its degree, the 'moisture' so much beloved by the peasant is lost, (hence plants migrate from south to north) and eventually the formation of steppes begins. The first effects of cultivation are useful but in the end it turns land into wastes owing to deforestation, etc. [. . .] The conclusion is that cultivation when it progresses spontaneously and is not consciously controlled (as a bourgeois he of course does not arrive at this), leaves deserts behind it – Persia, Mesopotamia, etc., Greece. Hence again an unconscious socialist tendency! [. . .][24]

In the same vein Engels was to write that each 'conquest over nature' brought retribution in some form to the conquerors. (Such as the consequences of the destruction of forests to obtain land to cultivate).[25] Nonetheless the technological optimism shared by Marx and Engels led them to believe – even when writing on this subsidiary theme of the dynamic interaction between man and nature – that geographical environment was destined to become negligible as a variable to be taken into consideration. Under the rational planning of socialism, man would at last manifest the capacity not only to create his own environment, as he had done throughout history, but also consciously to plan his environment in such a way that it would no longer assume hostile forms as an unintended consequence of his activities.

[22] *Ibid.*, p. 59.
[23] *Ibid.*, p. 55.
[24] Marx to Engels, 25 March 1868, *MESC*, p. 202.
[25] Engels, *The Dialectics of Nature*, tr. C.P. Dutt, London, Lawrence & Wishart, 1940, p. 292.

The major rethinking of the place of the geographical environment in historical materialism which has taken place in recent years has had its roots in the loss of faith in the nineteenth-century optimism about man's progress which pervaded Marxism in its original form. Authority for the reassessment has largely been sought in the subsidiary theme described above, that of geographical environment as the historical product of man, but with the consequences of the 'humanisation of nature', even under socialist society, described more pessimistically.

Even within Marx's own treatment of the subsidiary theme there is a certain amount of variation concerning man's relationship with the environment under socialism. In the *Grundrisse* there is a return to the Young Marx theme of the universal appropriation of nature by man under socialism, the complete humanisation of nature. In *Capital* itself, however, a less euphoric picture emerges. The possibility of the full reconciliation of subject and object (man and nature) no longer crowns the dialectical development of world history.[26] Although nature is humanly mediated it still retains an independent objective existence, and still holds man in the grip of necessity in so far as production of the basic means of existence is concerned.

In *Capital*, Vol. I, Marx writes:

The labour-process, resolved as above into its simple elementary factors, is human action with a view to the production of use-values, appropriation of natural substances to human requirements; it is the necessary condition for effecting exchange of matter between man and Nature, it is the everlasting Nature-imposed condition of human existence, and therefore is independent of every social phase of that existence, or rather is common to every such phase.[27]

In this passage Marx projects the continued determination of man by non-human factors. This view is presented even more strikingly in the famous passage in *Capital*, Vol. III, which reads:

Just as the savage must wrestle with Nature to satisfy his wants, to maintain and reproduce life, so must civilized man, and he must do so in all social formations and under all possible modes of production.

---

[26] For a full account of the change in Marx's concept of the ultimate relationship between man and nature, see Alfred Schmidt, *Der Begriff der Natur in der Lehre von Marx*, Frankfurt a.M., Europäische Verlagsanstalt, 1962. Schmidt argues that the young Marx (as for example represented in the EPM) took over from Hegel the view that the dialectical process represented the overcoming, step by step, of everything not identical with the subject (Schmidt, p. 117). Schmidt claims, with some justification, that in Marx's mature materialism this view was replaced by a belief in the ultimate irreconcilability of subject and object.

[27] Marx, *Capital*, Vol. I, pp. 183–184.

Even under socialism this interchange with nature remains a 'realm of necessity'.[28]

Marx also wrote that, apart from the degree of development in the form of social production, the productiveness of labour in general was 'fettered' by physical conditions. Thus in the early stage of human development, productiveness was determined by natural wealth in the means of subsistence, such as fertile soil, while at a higher stage of development it was determined by the accessibility of natural sources of energy.[29] Hence, in *Capital*, Marx appears to have come a little closer to the views on the relationship between man and nature normally ascribed to Engels.

ENGELS' ACCOUNT OF LAWS OF NATURE

Engels had begun like the young Marx with the proposition that socialism represented the 'reconciliation of man with nature and with himself'.[30] However the form which this reconciliation took in Engels' 'mature' works (after he had absorbed the influence of Darwin), is as follows:

> If this were so [if consciousness and thought were accepted as being in contrast to being, to Nature], it must seem extremely remarkable that consciousness and Nature, thinking and being, the laws of thought and the laws of Nature, should be so closely in correspondence. But if the further question is raised: what then are thought and consciousness, and whence they come, it becomes apparent that they are products of the human brain and that man himself is a product of Nature, which has been developed in and along with its environment; whence it is self-evident that the products of the human brain, being in the last analysis also products of Nature, do not contradict the rest of Nature, but are in correspondence with it.[31]

Whereas for Marx the reconciliation of man and nature (where he projects it) represents the assimilation of nature by man, for Engels it appears to represent the *assimilation of man* by nature. Engels interpreted the future in terms of man's increasing recognition of those 'general laws' which govern both man and nature, and in terms of man's increasing ability to apply correctly those laws. In Engels as well as in Marx, the dialectic between man and nature is transcended,

[28] Marx, *Capital*, Vol. III, p. 820.
[29] Marx, *Capital*, Vol. I, p. 512.
[30] Engels, 'Umriss zu einer Kritik der Nationalökonomie', *Werke*, Vol. I, p. 505.
[31] Engels, *Anti-Dühring, op.cit.*, pp. 44–45.

but in Engels this is because when men 'not only feel, but also know, their unity with nature [. . .] the more impossible will become the senseless and anti-natural idea of contradiction between mind and matter, man and nature [. . .]'[32]

It has often been observed that Engels, under the influence of Darwin, came to subsume human history under the operation of general laws of nature. By the time he was writing *Anti-Dühring*, Engels had arrived at views on the relationship between human history and 'laws of nature' that were diametrically opposed to those expressed thirty-odd years before in the *German Ideology*. In *Anti-Dühring*, Engels could make the bald statement that 'Nature is the test of dialectics', thus contradicting all the strictures laid down in the *German Ideology* on the subject of using nature to prove social truths.

In the *German Ideology*, Marx and Engels were criticising the 'true socialists' who, among other failings, ascribed to nature certain features which in fact represented a *'pious wish* about human affairs' (my emphasis).[33] The true socialists imported into nature that harmony which they wished to establish in human society, and then invoked nature as a proof of their social theories.

This is merely one instance given in the *German Ideology* of the ideological treatment of nature. Marx and Engels also described how it was possible for a capitalist to discover in nature the competitive system of capitalism; for a supporter of feudalism to perceive a feudal system, for example in the cosmos; or for a supporter of absolute monarchy (i.e. Hobbes) to see in it the war of all against all.[34] Marx and Engels argued, however, that none of the characteristics ascribed to nature could have any necessary bearing on man's social arrangements or provide additional evidence of the necessity of any given social arrangement. Hence although they found Hobbes' description of the law of nature (the war of all against all) more satisfactory than

---

[32] Engels, *The Dialectics of Nature, op.cit.*, p. 293. Although Engels is inconsistent on this. While in most of his later works he describes man's coming mastery over nature in terms of his increasing knowledge of the laws of nature and of natural necessity, he is also capable of statements such as that socialism represents 'humanity's leap from the realm of necessity into the realm of freedom' (*Anti-Dühring*, tr. E. Burns, London, Lawrence and Wishart, n.d. (reprinted with some minor revisions from 1934 edn.), p. 312).
[33] Marx and Engels, *The German Ideology, op.cit.*, p. 533.
[34] *Ibid.*, pp. 531–533. Cf. Marx's later comment: 'It is remarkable how Darwin recognises among beasts and plants his English society with its division of labour, competition, opening up of new markets, "inventions", and the Malthusian "struggle for existence". It is Hobbes's *bellum omnium contra omnes*, and one is reminded of Hegel's *Phenomenology*, where civil society is described as a "spiritual animal kingdom", while in Darwin the animal kingdom figures as civil society . . .' (Marx to Engels, 18 June 1862, MESC, p. 128).

the assumption of a harmony inherent in nature, they by no means concluded that absolute monarchy rather than socialism was the most satisfactory, or the necessary form of social arrangement for man.

According to *The German Ideology*: 'The same general energies and properties, which man has in common with "all things", are cohesion, impenetrability, volume, gravity, etc., which can be found set out in detail on the first page of any textbook of physics.'[35] None of these properties could be construed as a reason for any particular form of human behaviour.

Nonetheless, in his later works Engels came to see man as part of the eternal movement of matter, governed by those general laws that apply to both the history of nature and the history of society.[36]

But although man would, in the future, continue to be determined by these general laws, local particularities of nature would no longer exercise an important influence on man, or on the forms of his social organisation. For example, the antithesis between town and country perpetuated by the capitalist form of production would be abolished, thus putting an end to the 'present poisoning of the air, water and land'.[37]

Moreover, under socialism the location of industry would no longer be determined by the location of raw materials. Engels wrote that capitalist industry had already 'made itself relatively independent of the local limitations arising from the location of sources of raw materials'.[38] The new productive forces brought into being by socialism would complete this independence.[39]

Thus Marx and Engels, in spite of differences in the views they expressed on the relationship between man and nature, concurred in believing that geographical factors would be of negligible importance in determining future forms of social organisation. Capitalism was in the process of making over the world in its own image and once capitalism was established it was inevitable that the inherent tendencies of the system should unfold, including the basis of its ultimate negation.

The general bias of their views on the historical role of geographical factors was to be quite accurately summed up by Pokrovsky, although

[35] *Ibid.*, p. 532.
[36] See Engels, *The Dialectics of Nature, op.cit.*, pp. 24–6; Engels, *Anti-Dühring, op.cit.*, pp. 157–159.
[37] Engels, *Anti-Dühring, op.cit.*, p. 325.
[38] *Ibid.*
[39] Though neither Marx nor Engels seems to have envisaged the possibility that extractive industry might cease to be the major source of raw materials.

he under-emphasised the relation between geographical factors and socio-economic diversity in the pre-capitalist era, in favour of the retarding/accelerating thesis (discussed in the next section):

Man, then, depends on nature, and the rate of progress of a given nation depends to a considerable degree on its natural environment. But this power of nature over man is not unlimited. Man can master nature, and it is not nature that is the *foundation of his economic activity.* Nature is only the material for this activity. *The foundation of the economic activity of man is man's labour;* the more highly developed his labour, the more persistent and skilful he is, the less does his dependence on nature become. It is easy to foresee that in the future, when science and technique have attained to a perfection which we are as yet unable to visualize, nature will become soft wax in his hands which he will be able to cast into whatever form he chooses.[40]

The passage from Pokrovsky brings out the confusion arising from Marx's failure to provide an adequate definition of the 'natural environment' in which man's productive activity took place. It is clearly stated by Marx that nature is a historical product, changing under the impact of man and reacting back on him. Yet when Marx talks of the receding significance of natural factors, or of the environment, it appears that he is not talking about such factors as themselves products of human activity. This has been a problem of great significance in contemporary Soviet Marxism, as we shall see later in this Chapter; other Marxists such as Plekhanov, to whom we now turn, were concerned about the underestimation of the role of geographical factors, but did not appreciate the central confusion from which it sprang.

THE 'GEOGRAPHICAL DEVIATION': PLEKHANOV

The works of G.V. Plekhanov first introduced into Marxism what I shall call the 'geographical deviation' – i.e., the belief that geographical factors do not necessarily diminish in importance with the development of man's productive powers. (Though for Stalin, emphasising the geographical factor at all was to represent a geographical deviation.) Plekhanov played a pre-eminent role in systematising Marx's philosophy of history, contributing at the turn of the nineteenth century to French, Russian and German socialist journals. He gave authorita-

[40] M.N. Pokrovsky, *A Brief History of Russia, op.cit.,* pp. 33–34. Cf. N.I. Bukharin: 'It has taken man centuries of bitter struggle to place his iron bit in nature's mouth.' (*Historical Materialism*, N.Y., International Publishers, 1925, p. 86).

tive expression to the 'theory of historical materialism' in the following writings: *The Development of the Monist View of History* (1895); *Essays in the History of Materialism* (1896); 'The Materialist Conception of History' (*Novoe Slovo*, 1897); and *Fundamental Problems of Marxism* (1908). In these systematising works Plekhanov strengthened the tendency of the later Engels to subsume human history under more general laws of nature. Thus Plekhanov saw historical materialism as deriving from and finding its philosophical justification in what he was the first to dub 'dialectical materialism'. (See his article 'For the sixtieth anniversary of Hegel's death', 1891.) As Plekhanov put it: '*The history of mankind* is a particular case of *development in general.*'[41] This assumption that historical materialism was one aspect of a more universal scientific outlook was to become the quintessence of Soviet ideology and in 1914, in spite of political differences which had become irreconcilable, Lenin wrote that 'On the question of Marx's philosophy and historical materialism, the best exposition is given by G.V. Plekhanov.'[42]

The most persistent criticism that has been made within the Soviet Union of Plekhanov's systematisation of historical materialism has therefore related not to his linkage of natural and socio/historical laws but to his treatment of geographical factors. Thus in one of the many articles published in honour of the centenary of Plekhanov's birth, M.I. Sidorov wrote that Plekhanov correctly represented the influence of geographical factors in historical development in so far as he:

a) showed these factors as influencing historical development through their retarding or accelerating impact on the growth of productive forces; and

b) showed that the influence of geographical factors was a variable one, decreasing as man developed his productive forces and his concomitant mastery over nature. However, Plekhanov occasionally erred in the direction of an overestimation of the role of geographical factors, viewing them as the ultimate cause of the development of productive forces themselves.[43]

Sidorov's criticism is made from the Stalinist position that geographical environment provides on the one hand the *condition* of any social development, and on the other hand may *retard or accelerate* that

[41] G.V. Plekhanov, [Notes to Engels' book *Ludwig Feuerbach* ...] *Selected Philosophical Works*, Vol. I, Moscow, 1961, p. 519.

[42] V.I. Lenin, 'Karl Marx', *Collected Works*, Vol. 21, p. 86.

[43] M.I. Sidorov, 'Razrabotka G.V. Plekhanovym istoricheskogo materializma', *Voprosy filosofii*, 1956, No. 6, pp. 11–22.

social development, but is never a *determining influence*.[44] This raises a very real problem concerning the role of geographical factors within historical materialism, and to what extent geographical factors may determine, or at least favour the development of certain forms of social organisation. This problem cannot be dismissed as easily as it has been by Z.A. Jordan, who claims that:

While Marx recognized that geographical conditions set limits to social response without determining it, Hegel denied the psychological or even physiological influence of surrounding nature on man but fully accepted its determining influence upon the productive forces. Plekhanov does not seem to have noticed the important difference between the viewpoints of Hegel and Marx.[45] [So that sometimes he appears to endorse only the restrictive role, and at other times he appears to endorse the determining role.]

In fact it is not surprising that Plekhanov does not appear to have noticed this difference because, as we have already seen it is not as clear-cut in Marx as Jordan indicates here.

Jordan is right however, as is Sidorov and other Soviet critics in pointing out that Plekhanov does make statements on the role of geographical factors which vary between the accelerating/retarding formula and a much more determinist line, and that he never resolves the contradiction between these two approaches, which in fact rest on very different premises. The premise which underlies the first approach is that according to the immanent logic of the development of material production a determinate series of social formations will universally occur, and that therefore geographical factors can only retard or accelerate the development of these formations.

The premise which underlies the second approach, however, is that at any given stage of the development of material production a number of alternative forms of social organisation (or modes of production) are possible and that these will depend on a number of geographical, historical and other variables. As pointed out above, this conflict is already present in Marx but it does become particularly apparent in Plekhanov, because of the systematising nature of his work.

The fact that Plekhanov was oblivious to this problem of conflicting premises which lies at the heart of Marx's explanation of history is illustrated by Plekhanov's use of the two different approaches to the role of geographical factors within the same paragraph, with no apparent awareness of their very different implications. Thus he writes that:

[44] Stalin, 'Dialectical and Historical Materialism' (Sept. 1938), *History of the Communist Party of the Soviet Union, Short Course*, London, Cobbett, 1943, pp. 106–107.
[45] Z.A. Jordan, *op.cit.*, pp. 342–343.

Modern dialectical materialism shows that the geographical environment provides men with a greater or lesser possibility of developing their productive forces, and thereby pushes them, more or less energetically, along the path of historical progress.

And one sentence later:

Dialectical materialism reveals that [...] the influence of geographical environment shows itself first of all, and in the strongest degree, in the character of *social relations*.[46]

It would also be fair to say that in general Plekhanov strengthened the elements of geographical determinism which Marx had inherited from Montesquieu and Hegel,[47] and was himself deeply influenced by the work of the contemporary geographical determinists, Mechnikov[48] and Ratzel.[49]

The geographical deviation becomes clearly visible in Plekhanov's analysis of the concept of 'forces of production'. Whereas Marx tends to treat the stage of development of the forces of production as the *terminus ab quo* in the analysis of social relations and social structures, Plekhanov's *terminus ab quo* consists in the natural or geographical determinants of those forces. Plekhanov believed that the primary condition for the development of any given production force must be sought in the properties of the environment.[50] He argued that:

... the properties of the geographical environment determine the development of the productive forces, which in its turn determines the development of the economic forces, and therefore of all other social relations.[51]

The divergence from Marx is brought out quite clearly in the following passage from Marx, and in Plekhanov's interpretation of it. Marx wrote:

[46] G.V. Plekhanov, 'Once again Mr. Mikhailovsky, once more the "Triad"', Appendix 1 to *The Development of the Monist View of History, Selected Philosophical Works*, Vol. 1, *op.cit.*, p. 784.

[47] It is significant that in his tribute to Hegel, Plekhanov singles out Hegel's emphasis on the determining role of geographical factors for special praise. See 'For the Sixtieth Anniversary of Hegel's Death', *Selected Philosophical Works, op.cit.*, pp. 455–483.

[48] See Léon Metchnikoff [Lev Il'ich Mechnikov], *La Civilisation et les grands fleuves historiques*, Paris, 1889. See also a Russian edition, tr. by M.D. Gorodetsky, St. Petersburg, 1898. Interestingly enough, the state publishing house brought out an edition in Moscow in 1924, of which the reviewer in *Pod znamenem marksizma* remarked that it was unnecessary to recommend it any further, after the well-known articles of Plekhanov. As will be seen in the next section, theories of geographic determinism had not yet been denounced as incompatible with historical materialism in the 1920s, and in any case a certain flexibility was displayed in such theoretical matters.

[49] See Friedrich Ratzel, *Anthropo-Geographie; oder Grundzüge der Aufwendung der Erdkunde auf die Geschichte*, Stuttgart, 1882.

[50] G.V. Plekhanov, *Fundamental Problems of Marxism*, tr. J. Katzer, Moscow, Foreign Languages Publishing House, n.d., p. 55.

[51] *Ibid.*, p. 49.

In the social production of their existence, men inevitably enter into definite relations which are independent of their will, namely relations of production, appropriate to a given stage in the development of their material forces of production. The totality of these relations of production constitutes the economic structure of society, the real foundation, on which arises a legal and political superstructure...[52]

Plekhanov's gloss on this passage is as follows:

Marx's reply thus reduces the whole question of the development of the economy to that of the causes determining the development of the productive forces at the disposal of society. In this, its final form, it is solved *first and foremost by the* (sic) *reference to the nature of the geographic environment.*[53]

The geographical construction of Marx's materialism facilitated the *rapprochement* between Marxism and Darwinism illustrated in one of Plekhanov's most notorious statements: 'Marxism is Darwinism in its application to social science.'[54] I.e., where Darwinism shows how the development of animals and vegetable species occurs under the influence of the natural environment, Marxism shows how the development of different types of social organisation takes place under the influence of the natural environment. Elsewhere Plekhanov expressed this analogy in terms of the zoological investigation into the development of natural organs under the influence of the natural environment, as compared with the Marxist investigation into the development of artificial organs (i.e. tools, forces of production) under the influence of the natural environment.[55]

While the Darwinian analogy has a certain superficial appeal, in so far as it is plausible to view man's historical evolution in terms of the differentiation of his artificial organs (the development of the division of labour, specialisation, etc.), its dangers are readily apparent.

One of the reasons why Plekhanov suffered pitfalls of this kind was the fact that most of Marx's early writing, and the relevant sections of the *Grundrisse*, were still unpublished and unavailable. He does not seem to have been aware of Marx's account of the historical dialectic between man and nature; and of the historical creation of the geo-

[52] Marx, *Preface to A Contribution to the Critique of Political Economy, op.cit.*, p. 20.

[53] G.V. Plekhanov, *Fundamental Problems of Marxism, op.cit.*, p. 47.

[54] G.V. Plekhanov, *In Defence of Materialism, The Development of the Monist View of History*, tr. A. Rothstein, London, Lawrence and Wishart, 1947, p. 244, fn. Plekhanov appears to be building here on Marx's statement that: 'Darwin has interested us in the history of Nature's Technology, *i.e.*, in the formation of the organs of plants and animals, which organs serve as instruments of production for sustaining life. Does not the history of the productive organs of man, of organs that are the material basis of all social organisation, deserve equal attention?' (*Capital*, Vol. 1, p. 372 fn.).

[55] G.V. Plekhanov, *Essays in the History of Materialism*, tr. Ralph Fox, reprinted N.Y., Fertig, 1967, p. 213.

graphic environment by man. Plekhanov tended to treat the geographical environment as a given factor, rather than as a historical product, although man's relationship with it would vary from epoch to epoch, depending on the development of man's productive forces. For example, he wrote:

The peoples who inhabited England in the time of Caesar experienced the influence of the same geographical environment as the English of Cromwell's day.[56]

(But Cromwell's contemporaries possessed much greater productive forces than the peoples of the time of Caesar.) This is the kind of argument which Marx rejected utterly in Feuerbach,[57] and it is quite clear that the swamp and forest environment of iron-age Britain had given way to a historically created environment of cleared and cultivated land in the seventeenth century.

A contemporary of Plekhanov's, the philosopher Antonio Labriola, who also played an important part in elaborating the theory of historical materialism,[58] wrote an account of the relationship between man and nature that was in some ways closer to Marx. This was probably because Labriola adhered more closely to the Hegelian philosophical tradition than Plekhanov did.

Labriola took a similar position to Plekhanov's in so far as he postulated man's continued dependence on geographical factors, and did not envisage a lessening of this dependence, or Marx's reconciliation of man and nature. Labriola wrote that the kind of change in the relationship between man and the environment brought about by man's technological development was the change from the primitive dependence on stones and osiers and willows for the raw materials of production, to the advanced dependence on coal and the materials necessary to produce electricity.[59]

However, Labriola was also capable of the following viewpoint: 'History is the work of man in so far as man can create and improve his

---

[56] *Ibid.*, pp. 216–217.

[57] 'He does not see how the sensuous world around him is not a thing given direct from all eternity, remaining ever the same, but the product of industry and the state of society; and, indeed, in the sense that it is a historical product, the result of the activity of a whole succession of generations [. . .]', '[. . .] in the Campagna of Rome he finds only pasture lands and swamps, where in the time of Augustus he would have found nothing but the vineyards and villas of Roman capitalists.' (Marx and Engels, *The German Ideology, op.cit.*, pp. 57, 58).

[58] See, for example, his *Essays on the Materialist Conception of History*, the French translation of which was reviewed favourably by Plekhanov in *Novoe Slovo*, 1897. The book was published in a Russian edition in St. Petersburg, 1898.

[59] A. Labriola, *Essays on the Materialist Conception of History*, tr. Charles Kerr, first pub. Chicago, Kerr, 1903, reprinted N.Y., Monthly Review Press, 1966, p. 119.

instruments of labor, and with these instruments can create an artificial environment whose complicated effects react later upon himself.'[60]

Having established Plekhanov's 'geographical deviation', with regard to the stress he laid on geographical factors as the determinants of *any* given mode of production, one can look at some of the wider consequences of this deviation. According to Plekhanov's theory, given a certain level of productive forces, different geographical environments will have different institutional correlates.

Plekhanov's major example concerns the type of social organisation which develops out of *clan* society when the growth of productive forces in the latter causes its break-down. On the basis of the same level of productive forces there appeared one kind of social system in the West (the slave-based classical state) and another in the East. According to Plekhanov, the Oriental and the ancient modes of production represent two *co-existing types of* economic development, owing their distinctive features to *'the influence of the geographical environment, which in one case* prescribed *one kind* of aggregate production relations [...] and in the other case, *another kind* ...'[61]

This is one of the most significant features of the geographical deviation in historical materialism – the fact that it reinforces a multilinear rather than a unilinear interpretation of history. As we have seen, Marx's own analysis of the early stages of history (where geographical and other local circumstances play a more important role in shaping social institutions than under capitalism) supports a multilinear schema, but one which only applies to the period before technology masters geography.

Although Plekhanov was true to Marx, in suggesting a multilinear, or at least a bilinear schema of pre-capitalist development, he suggested a far more deterministic relationship than did Marx, between geographical factors and social structures. For example, Plekhanov criticised Mechnikov for deferring to the geographical 'possibilism' of Elisée Reclus,[62] as expressed in the view that in ancient Egypt the

---

[60] *Ibid.*, p. 120. Labriola, and Plekhanov in his wake (in his review article of Labriola), generally use the term 'artificial environment' to refer to the social organisation man creates. Here, however, a wider meaning seems to be intended.

[61] Plekhanov, *Fundamental Problems of Marxism, op.cit.*, p. 64.

[62] Like Reclus, Mechnikov was an anarchist, and he was involved in several of Bakunin's secret societies. Anarchist doctrine lent itself to voluntarist rather than determinist views. In the sphere of geography this led towards 'possibilism' – i.e., the idea that: 'nature does not drive man along one particular road, but offers a number of opportunities from which man is free to select' (taking into account his level of technology). The general tone of Mechnikov's writing was, however, determinist.

given geographical factors of the Nile Valley still left open the choice between despotism and a form of association based on the equality of all.[63]

According to Plekhanov, given the geographical factors of the flooding of the Nile, and the narrow margin between successful utilisation of the waters of the Nile and the ruin represented by floods, and on the other hand, given the level of man's technology in ancient Egypt, the creation of a despotic state apparatus was completely determined.[64] Elsewhere Plekhanov quotes approvingly a passage from G. Maspero which concludes with the words 'the Nile thus determined the political as well as the physical constitution of Egypt.'[65]

Having mentioned the links between geographical determinism and the multilinear theory of history, it is necessary to add that Hegel and L. Mechnikov, both influential upholders of theories of the crucial importance of geography, succeeded in uniting these theories with unlinear theories of history. Hegel did so in the following way: each progressive stage of world history corresponded to the working out of one particular natural principle.[66] The first stage of world history, the development of forms of substantial freedom, took place in, and could only take place in, the 'valley plains' of the Orient.[67] The geographical factors here were particularly favourable to the development of agriculture, and hence to the development of the institutions of private property and of the state.[68] However, according to Hegel, the next stage of the unfolding of world history could only take place in a completely different geographical environment. The multiformity and diversity of natural features in the Aegean area, linked by sea, was

[63] G.V. Plekhanov, 'O knige L.I. Mechnikova' *Sochineniia*, Vol. VII, p. 24.

[64] Wittfogel's first articles on the place of natural factors in historical materialism followed Plekhanov closely here. (E.g. 'Geopolitika, geograficheskii materializm i marksizm', *Pod znamenem marksizma*, 1929, No. 2–3 (Feb.-March), p. 8). Wittfogel appears to have modified his position in recent years (by 1971), and has come down in favour of a negative causal relationship between natural conditions and social response. E.g. he suggests that while geographical factors preclude certain options, and may favour one particular form of social response, the possibility remains open of more than one institutional correlative for any given geographical environment.

[65] Maspero had written that the centralised co-ordination of irrigation was essential to overcome the strife between communities arising from one community seizing the supply of water or discharging it at pleasure, regardless of whether this deprived another community of water, or alternatively, flooded it. See G. Maspero, *The Dawn of Civilization*, 14th edn, London, Society for Promoting Christian Knowledge, 1901, p. 70. Quoted by Plekhanov in his *History*, p. 77, fn. 2, from the French edition entitled *Histoire ancienne des peuples de l'Orient classique*, Paris, 1895, Vol. I, p. 70.

[66] G.W.F. Hegel, *Philosophy of Right*, tr. T.M. Knox, Oxford, Clarendon Press, 1942, pp. 217–18. (§ 346–47).

[67] G.W.F. Hegel, *The Philosophy of History*, op.cit., p. 93.

[68] *Ibid.*

essential for the rise of *individualism*, as opposed to the *glorification of the unity* which has arisen naturally in the Orient, where one great natural feature (i.e. the river) dominated an otherwise monotonous plain.[69]

Mechnikov's[70] reconciliation of geographical determinism with the unilinear theory of history differs slightly from Hegel's. Firstly, Mechnikov puts more stress on the incentive to centralised social organisation provided by the river-valley environment, where large-scale planning and work discipline meant the difference between high productivity and disaster (i.e. floods). This strict social organisation in turn gave rise to both civilisation and the despotic state. However, the progress of technology and the growth of wealth, which took place in this epoch, created the need for international relations of exchange, a need which could not be satisfied in the geographical environment of the river valley. The Mediterranean was the environment most suited to the unfolding of the second major epoch in Mechnikov's schema of world history, the epoch based on diversity and exchange – i.e. commodity production. According to Mechnikov, the new geographical environment in which history unfolded its second phase also had its specific socio-political correlates.

Another way in which the transition from the geographical environment of the river valley to the geographical environment of the Mediterranean has been depicted as one of the logical progressions of world history is to be found in the work of the late Professor V. Gordon Childe.[71] According to Childe, the despotic state was the correlate of the needs of production in the river valley. The vast surpluses accumulated by this state form provided the means by which Mediterranean civilisation was able to reach take-off point without a despotic system of its own. Eastern surpluses supported the development of craft specialisation in the West, and precisely the fact that in the West the state did not have to play such a leading role in the economy, meant

[69] *Ibid.*, pp. 234–235. I have not mentioned Hegel's third and fourth stages (the Roman and German worlds) or Mechnikov's third epoch (the Oceanic), as I feel that the transition between the *first* two stages, in both cases, most clearly illustrates how the geographical interpretation of history can still be unilinear.

[70] With the revival of interest in the 'geographical deviation' in the Soviet Union there has also been a revival of interest in Mechnikov. See for example M.A. Korostovtsev, 'On the Concept "The Ancient East"' *loc.cit.*, pp. 107–132. V.A. Anuchin, *Teoreticheskie problemy geografii*, Gos. izd. geog. lit., Moscow, 1960; M.G. Fedorov, *Russkaia progressivnaia mysl' XIX v. ot geograficheskogo determinizma k istoricheskomu materializmu*, Novosibirsk, 1972.

[71] See, e.g., V.G. Childe, *What happened in History*, London, Max Parrish, 1960; *Man Makes Himself*, London, Watts, 1948; 'The Bronze Age', *Past and Present*, No. 12 (Nov. 1957), p. 11.

that in the long run Western civilisation was more adaptable and progressive.

All these efforts to reconcile theories of geographic determinism with a universal schema of world history (consisting of progressive epochs) are interesting in themselves, but as arguments are more difficult to sustain than the equation of geographical pluralism with pluralism of modes of production and social forces not linked in any logical progression. The latter equation is certainly applied by Marx to the earlier phases of human history, and Plekhanov was an important figure in redirecting attention to this.

However, Plekhanov is inconsistent on this point in his own writing, and wavers between a geographically-determined pluralism, and the universal development of a determinate series of social formations according to the immanent logic of material production. When leaning towards the latter view, Plekhanov uses the formula, apparently taken from Elisée Reclus, that nature can have only an accelerating or retarding influence on the development of society. Thus Plekhanov wrote:

The physical environment acts on social man through those social relations which arise on the basis of the productive forces, which at first develop more or less quickly according to the characteristics of the physical environment.[72]

As we shall see, the accelerating/retarding formula was adopted by Stalin, and appeared in all Soviet text-books on historical materialism up till 1963. (And is still appearing in some contexts.)

However, the significance of Plekhanov's contribution to historical materialism lay not in the popularisation of the accelerating/retarding formula, but in the alternative view of geographical factors which dominates his work: that the role of geographical environment is always of fundamental importance in determining the character of social relations.[73] This contribution was significant because it helped to bring out Marx's multilinear perception of pre-capitalist society: that given the same level of productive forces, alternative forms of social organisation or modes of production emerged in accordance with differing local geographical and historical circumstances. Plekhanov's contribution also provided a counterpoise to the view, to be found in Marx and Engels, that technological development in the capitalist era

[72] G.V. Plekhanov, *In Defence of Materialism, op.cit.*, p. 244.
[73] G.V. Plekhanov, 'Once again Mr Mikhailovsky, once more the "triad"', Appendix to *In Defence of Materialism, op.cit.*, p. 291.

led to the nullifying of the natural environment as an independent influence on human societies.

THE 'GEOGRAPHICAL DEVIATION': WITTFOGEL

Although Plekhanov stressed the continuing importance of geographical factors in historical development, he did not go as far as certain twentieth-century Marxists, who have argued that the geographical factor becomes of greater rather than of lesser importance with the growth of the material forces of production.

The first important exponent of this view was K. A. Wittfogel, who expressed it in an article published serially in 1929 in the leading theoretical journal of Soviet Marxism.[74] Wittfogel argued that the more man developed his power to 'actualise' nature, the more important was the role of natural factors in production. This was particularly evident in the sphere of the actualisation of various natural sources of energy which came to replace human labour in the process of production. The fact that these sources of energy could only be 'actualised' not created *ex nihilo* by man meant that he was even more at the mercy of the properties of his geographical environment in respect to the development of his forces of production.

In his early articles, Wittfogel criticised those exponents of historical materialism, such as Kautsky and Lukács, who *dematerialised* history by treating the *social* conditions of production as comprising the *basis* of history.[75] According to Wittfogel, this viewpoint was idealistic, in so far as it involved the underestimation of the natural conditions of production.

Wittfogel later illustrated his argument with the example of the French capitalism. According to his account, the French revolution created all the social preconditions for the expansion of capitalist economic forms in France.[76] Yet, in spite of the existence of the social and technological preconditions French industrial capitalism made little progress throughout the nineteenth century. Wittfogel found the

[74] See K.A. Wittfogel, 'Geopolitika, geograficheskii materializm i marksizm', in *Pod znamenem marksizma*, 1929, No. 2–3 (Feb.-March), pp. 16–42; No. 6 (June), pp. 1–29; No. 7–8 (July-Aug.), pp. 1–28.

[75] K.A. Wittfogel, 'Geopolitika, geograficheskii materializm i marksizm', *Pod znamenem marksizma*, No. 6 (June 1929), p. 17.

[76] K.A. Wittfogel, 'Die natürlichen Ursachen der Wirtschaftsgeschichte', *Archiv für Sozialwissenschaft und Sozialpolitik*, Vol. 67 (1932), Part I, p. 467.

explanation for France's failure to develop at this stage in her natural environment; in the lack of good quality iron ore for the production of steel; in the lack of extensive coal deposits; and in the unfavourable location of those coal deposits that France did have.

In his own account of historical materialism, Wittfogel attempted to establish a clear-cut distinction between naturally-determined forces of production and socially-determined forces of production. In the former category he placed factors such as water, steam, wind, warmth, electricity, etc., and in the latter category factors such as technology, organisation of labour (or co-operation), instruments and machines. The combination of both sets of factors resulted in a particular mode of production, which in turn determined the relations of production, etc.

Wittfogel found natural factors to be of decisive historical importance, though they were not constant in form, different natural factors being actualised at different periods. Thus a natural resource such as falling water might be of determining importance in one era (with the water-powered mill), might be of negligible importance in the next era (with the use of steam-powered machinery), and then come into its own again with the invention of the hydro-electric turbine.[77]

Wittfogel applied his theory of ultimate determination of social relations by the natural forces of production to all of the Marxist stages of history. He began with the Australian aborigines. These tribes had never been able to advance along the path of human history because of the natural absence in their environment of animals suitable for domestication or cereals for cultivation. The mode of production was limited by natural factors, and any development to pastoral and agricultural activity, with their corresponding social forms was thus blocked.[78]

As far as the antique mode of production (which he limits to West Rome) was concerned, Wittfogel saw as the determining natural force the fact that the land was suited to *extensive* agriculture. However, this mode of production led only into a blind alley, as it depended on slave labour, and when slaves could no longer be pumped into the system (because the technical limits of empire had been reached) it collapsed.[79]

While the economy of Western Rome declined to a lower stage, that

---

[77] *Ibid.*, Part I, p. 485.

[78] *Ibid.*, pp. 488–492. See also Ellen Churchill Semple, *Influences of Geographic Environment. On the Basis of Ratzel's System of Anthropo-Geography*, N.Y., Henry Holt, 1911, p. 63.

[79] K.A. Wittfogel, 'Die natürlichen Ursachen der Wirtschaftsgeschichte', *loc.cit.*, Part II, pp. 596–600.

of East Rome remained stable. Once again Wittfogel finds an explanation for this in the constellation of natural forces. In the East, the lack of rainfall meant that irrigation was necessary, and hence intensive methods of agriculture. These in turn precluded the wide-scale use of slaves in agriculture and so the system was more stable.

Where large-scale irrigation/flood-control works were necessary there developed the centralised bureaucratic state which participated directly in the economy. In this situation the 'actualisable' natural forces of production gave rise to a mode of production and social relations which did not permit further development into a higher economic stage. There was an irreconcilable contradiction between, for example, the classic irrigation economy and industrialism. In this case (e.g. China), both the technological level and the raw materials necessary for industrialisation were present, but the bourgeoisie did not have the bulwark of the Occidental city in which to develop their form of production.[80]

The widespread need for irrigation in agricultural society did not necessarily give rise to the institutional complex known as Oriental despotism (i.e. a centralised bureaucratic state); where the natural factors demanded small-scale intensive irrigation, on the Japanese model, the institutional correlate would be a variety of military feudalism.[81] As already mentioned, Wittfogel has modified in recent years these extremely deterministic views on the relationship between natural environment and social development.

One final example of Wittfogel's geographical interpretation of history is his account of why the German bourgeoisie never developed into a strong independent class. He quotes *Revolution and Counter-Revolution in Germany* to support his view that the main cause of the backwardness of German industry up to 1900 was Germany's geographical position; i.e. isolation from the Atlantic Ocean, the highway of world trade since 1500.[82] Wittfogel expands his account of the influence of geographical factors on contemporary history with a geographical interpretation of the next dialectical stage of Germany's development. In the nineteenth century, other natural factors became actualised, such as Germany's advantages in iron and coal, and a concentrated development of industry took place; this belated develop-

[80] *Ibid.*, p. 607.
[81] *Ibid.*, Part II, p. 587.
[82] *Ibid.*, Part III, p. 715. See Marx, *Revolution and Counter-Revolution,* ed. Eleanor Marx-Aveling, London, Unwin, 1971, p. 4. (This series of articles has since been shown to have been written by Engels. See Rubel, *Bibliographie.*)

ment created a significant proletarian class simultaneously with the final emergence of a capitalist class (which was hence forced into the arms of the feudal reaction).

Basically, as we see here, Wittfogel placed much more emphasis on the interaction between man and his geographical environment, which developed under the impact of man's transforming and actualising activity, than on the inner laws of development of material production and its corresponding social institutions.

HISTORICAL MATERIALISM VERSUS GEOGRAPHICAL DETERMINISM: STALIN AND BEYOND

The kind of latitude in the Soviet interpretation of historical materialism, illustrated by the publication (despite editorial reservations)[83] of Wittfogel's article 'Geopolitika, geograficheskii materializm i marksizm', was soon to be brought to an end. Stalin, in the first official statement to be made in the Soviet Union on the subject of geographical determinism, established an official line that was to remain in force until 1963. Stalin wrote that:

Geographical environment is unquestionably one of the constant and indispensable conditions of development of society and, of course, influences the development of society, accelerates or retards its development. But its influence is not the *determining influence*, inasmuch as the changes and development of society proceed at an incomparably faster rate than the changes and development of geographical environment. [...] Changes in geographical environment of any importance require millions of years, whereas a few hundred or a couple of thousand years are enough for even very important changes in the system of human society.[84]

This formula was repeated more or less mechanically in Soviet expositions of historical materialism, even after Stalin's death.[85] It

---

[83] Not only did the editor of *Pod znamenem marksizma* express reservations about the original article (published in three parts), but the follow-up article was rejected, and Wittfogel published it elsewhere. (For the follow-up article, see above, K.A. Wittfogel, 'Die natürlichen Ursachen der Wirtschaftsgeschichte', *Archiv für Sozialwissenschaft und Sozialpolitik*, Vol. 67 (1932), Nos. 4, 5, 6).

[84] Stalin, 'Dialectical and Historical Materialism' (September 1938), in *Problems of Leninism*, Moscow, Foreign Languages Publishing House, 1947, p. 482. This article, and statement on the role of the geographical environment was written for the 1938 *History of the Communist Party of the Soviet Union, Short Course*. (London, Cobbett, 1943, pp. 106–07).

[85] See, for example, O.W. Kuusinen ed., *Fundamentals of Marxism-Leninism*, Moscow, Foreign Languages Publishing House, 1961, p. 145; 'The geographical environment, on the one hand, and population, on the other, form the natural material prerequisites for the process of production. However, although these natural material conditions exercise a considerable influence on the course of social development, either accelerating or delaying it, they do not form the basis of that historical process.'

signified the complete abandonment of any dynamic conception of the interaction between man and nature, and the characterising of the geographical environment as a static given, in which 'changes of any importance require millions of years.'[86] The fact that against this static background different social systems developed and superseded each other showed that the geographical environment by no means exercised a determining influence over human society, but could only accelerate or retard its development. The key to human history consisted in the laws of development of material production, which alone explained:

Why the primitive communal system is succeeded precisely by the slave system, the slave system by the feudal system, and the feudal system by the bourgeois system, and not by some other.[87]

Hence Stalin's denigration of the role of geographical factors served to underpin his five-stage schema of world history.

Stalin's rigid demarcation between 'external nature' and human society, and the overwhelming precedence given to the social factor, also gave rise to 'voluntaristic' attitudes in Soviet planning. Given the correct social relations, Soviet man could transform the face of the environment. It was this aspect of his formulation which was first to arouse criticism, which stemmed initially from geographers.

THE REVOLT OF SOVIET GEOGRAPHERS AGAINST STALIN

While Stalin's line on the geographical environment remained orthodoxy until 1963, the revolt among geographers against his interpretation began quite early. In 1940, N.N. Baransky of Moscow University, read a paper at a theoretical conference of the Geographical Faculty of Moscow University on the subject of 'Marx and Engels on the Geographical Environment'. This paper presented evidence contradicting Stalin's position. The fact that Plekhanov's geographical theory exercised a very important influence on Baransky is evident from his work published as early as the 1920s.[88]

---

[86] Stalin, 'Dialectical and Historical Materialism' (September 1938), in *Problems of Leninism, op.cit.*, p. 582; *History of the Communist Party of the Soviet Union, Short Course, op.cit.*, p. 107.

[87] *Ibid.*

[88] See Ian M. Matley, 'The Marxist Approach to the Geographical Environment', *Annals of the Association of American Geographers*, Vol. 56 (1966), p. 99. Baransky was not only an extremely eminent geographer, but had been a friend of Lenin, which may have helped to preserve him in his outspokenness.

In 1960, when the debate was once more being opened up, Baransky brought forward arguments identical to those expressed by that other disciple of G.V. Plekhanov, Wittfogel, in the 1920s, although of course without direct reference to Wittfogel himself. For example, Baransky criticised the tendency to what he called 'geographical nihilism' on the grounds that by isolating society from its material environment it led to idealism.[89] Thus Baransky employed the same argument against Stalin as Wittfogel had employed against Kautsky and Lukács more than thirty years previously.

Baransky also followed Wittfogel in affirming that advances in technology do not mean a lessening of the influence of natural factors on the mode of production. Instead, new natural factors, such as the location of oil, have a determining influence on, for example, the distribution of industry and transportation.[90]

Baransky died in 1963, and it has been the younger geographer, V.A. Anuchin, who has provided much of the inspiration for the de-Stalinisation of theoretical geography, which in turn has led to the revision of Stalin's interpretation of historical materialism. Anuchin's first critique appeared in *Voprosy geografii* in 1957, and was entitled 'On the essence of the geographical environment and manifestations of indeterminism in Soviet geography'.[91] In this article Anuchin launched an attack on Stalin's nihilistic formulation of the geographical environment as the unchanging background to dynamic social development. He described 'geographical indeterminism' as being much more harmful than geographical determinism; geographical indeterminism led to an 'idealist' conception of the relationship between society and its natural environment, and on the other hand, to the conception of the laws of social development as an absolute.[92] Anuchin was to write of the Stalinist era that:

The opinion became current that nature's role in the development of society was insignificant, that human life was wholly determined by social structure and that nature could be remade almost at will.[93]

Anuchin blamed this anti-environmentalist dogma for the harm done

[89] N.N. Baransky, 'Uchët prirodnoi sredy v ekonomicheskoi geografii', in *Ekonomicheskaia Geografiia – Ekonomicheskaia Kartografiia*, Moscow, 1960, p. 40.
[90] *Ibid.*, p. 54, fn. 49.
[91] V.A. Anuchin, 'O sushchnosti geograficheskoi sredy i proiavlenii indeterminizma v sovetskoi geografii', *Voprosy geografii*, 1957, No. 41, pp. 47–64.
[92] *Ibid.*, pp. 48, 55, 57.
[93] V.A. Anuchin, 'A Sad Tale about Geography', in *Literaturnaia Gazeta*, 18 Feb. 1965, tr. in *Soviet Geography*, Vol. VI, 1965, No. 7 (Sept.), p. 28.

to Soviet land-resources through a stereotyped approach to cropping, etc.[94]

In 1960, Anuchin's doctoral thesis, 'Theoretical Problems of Geography', was published in Moscow. This thesis had been failed at Leningrad, presumably because of its radical character.[95] A large part of the book was taken up with a historical analysis of theories of geographical determinism. Anuchin himself rejected the 'pre-Marxist' form of geographical determinism which made geographical factors into the basic cause of social development. His own position was that while the main impetus for development arose from within social forms, the direction of social development might indeed be altered by the influence of specific geographic factors on the mode of production.[96]

As we have seen, Anuchin strongly criticised the Stalinist dichotomy between nature and society, on the one hand, and between laws of nature and social laws, on the other, and attempted to revive the view of nature as a historical product.[97] He wrote:

Landscapes also follow the laws of nature in their development. But man is able to manipulate natural laws to alter their effect. Therefore any study of landscape simply from the point of view of 'pure' natural science means *limiting the possibilities of cognition* [my emphasis]. It amounts to trying to ascertain the effect while ignoring the causes.[98]

As Marx once said: 'Nature [...] taken abstractly, for itself, and rigidly separated from man, is *nothing* for man.'[99]

In fact, in spite of his formula, Stalin did regard natural laws as subject to human activity; this can be seen from the *Stalin Plan for the Transformation of Nature*.[100] However, the formula of unchanging nature did enable Stalin to dismiss the geographical environment as a dynamic element in human affairs, and in general to belittle its importance as an independent factor. Anuchin's work, on the other hand, is based on the assumption that the geographical environment is an

[94] *Ibid.*, p. 31.

[95] With the change in the official line, Anuchin has since become Deputy Chairman of the Council for the Study of Productive Forces, Gosplan.

[96] V.A. Anuchin, *Teoreticheskie problemy geografii, op.cit.*, pp. 149–150.

[97] V.A. Anuchin, 'O sushchnosti geograficheskoi sredy ...', *loc.cit.*, p. 47.

[98] V.A. Anuchin, 'The Problem of Synthesis in Geographic Science', (in *Voprosy filosofii*, 1964, No. 2), tr. in *Soviet Geography*, Vol. V (1964), No. 4, p. 35.

[99] Marx, [Economic and Philosophical Manuscripts], in *Early Writings*, ed. T.B. Bottomore, *op.cit.*, p. 217.

[100] See S.V. Kalesnik, 'Some Results of the New Discussion about a "Unified" Geography', in *Izvestiia Vsesoiuznogo Geograficheskogo Obshchestva*, 1965, No. 3, tr. in *Soviet Geography*, Vol. VI (1965), No. 7, p. 18. The 'Stalin Plan for the Transformation of Nature' was first publicised in *Pravda*, October 1948; see Ian M. Matley, 'The Marxist Approach to the Geographical Environment', *loc.cit.*, p. 102.

extremely important determinant of social development and stresses the nature of the environment as a developing system formed from a combination of social and natural elements.[101]

Because man's impact on the geographical environment is becoming increasingly complex and intensive, Anuchin argues that it is especially important to establish co-ordinated studies of any given geographical environment, i.e. a 'unified geography'. For:

...without knowledge of these complexes as a whole it is impossible to predict all the possible consequences that may result from man-induced changes in the environment. And if that is so, we will inevitably be confronted with unexpected and undesirable results of man's activity. The likelihood of undesirable consequences *will increase with the level of technological progress* [my emphasis]. An especially serious threat to nature has now arisen as a result of man's assuming control over atomic energy.[102]

(I.e. the environment will take its revenge on man.)

Another Moscow University geographer, who, together with Baransky, supported Anuchin's stand and wrote extremely favourable reviews of his book,[103] was Iu.G. Saushkin. Saushkin agreed that a wall had been built between the natural and social sciences in the 'period of the personality cult' in order 'to provide a "theoretical" justification for voluntarism in the solution of problems in the development of society and in projects for the transformation of nature.'[104] Stalin had bypassed the problems of the interaction between nature and society, which arose from the fact that society creates changes in its geographical environment and is in turn affected by this new environment.[105] Saushkin consciously or unconsciously harks back to the 'young Marx' of the Paris Manuscripts in describing the geographical environment as 'humanised nature', as opposed to a *purely* natural category.[106] Saushkin had tended to take the idea of humanised nature to extremes, as in his notion that in the foreseeable future the geographical environment will be, to a large extent, constructed from synthetics such as plastics.[107]

[101] V.A. Anuchin, 'O sushchnosti geograficheskoi sredy i proiavlenii indeterminizma v sovetskoi geografii', *loc.cit.*, p. 50.

[102] V.A. Anuchin, 'The Problem of Synthesis in Geographical Science', *loc.cit.*, p. 35.

[103] Although Saushkin joined in the widespread criticism of the way in which Anuchin included society in the geographical environment.

[104] Iu. G. Saushkin, 'Methodological Problems of Soviet Geography as interpreted by some Foreign Geographers', in *Vestnik Moskovskogo Universiteta*, No. 4 (1964), tr. in *Soviet Geography*, Vol. V, (1964), No. 8, p. 4.

[105] Iu.G. Saushkin, 'The Interaction of Nature and Society', in *Geografiia v shkole*, 1964, No. 4, tr. in *Soviet Geography*, Vol. V (1964), No. 10, pp. 39–40.

[106] Iu.G. Saushkin, 'Methodological Problems of Soviet Geography ...', *loc.cit.*, p. 62. Saushkin attributes the term to N.V. Morozov.

[107] Iu.G. Saushkin, 'Concerning a Certain Controversy', in *Vestnik Moskovskogo Universiteta, Seriia geografii*, 1965, No. 6, tr. in *Soviet Geography*, Vol. VII (1966), No. 2, p. 13.

The whole debate on the theoretical significance of the geographical environment, which broke out with the publication of Anuchin's book, led to an important reversal of the official 'line' in 1963. In October of that year, an ideological spokesman (and Secretary) of the C.P.S.U.'s Central Committee, L.F. Ilichev, delivered a speech before the presidium of the Academy of Sciences in which the Stalinist definition of the relationship between nature and society was completely renounced and an environmental view put forward. This speech was published in the journal of the Academy of Sciences[108] and, in a briefer version, in *Voprosy filosofii*,[109] and represents the new official line (although Ilichev lost his former position with the fall of Khrushchev).

Ilichev, among other things, denounced the rigid division between the natural and the social sciences, and the Stalinist concept of the geographical environment as something external to society.[110] He stressed instead the mutual interaction of nature and society, as illustrated by the continuous changes taking place in the natural environment as a result of man's activities, and the reciprocal influence of these changes on society. Ilichev blamed Stalin's rigid division between human society and geographical environment, and his onesided definition of the relationship between them, for various errors in planning and in the approach to economic development.[111]

The new line, stressing the need for an integrated study of the interaction between nature and society[112] did not pass completely unchallenged. S.V. Kalesnik, for example, was to maintain the old line that: 'In the development of any form of matter the determining role is played by laws that are specific to that form.' From this axiom it must follow that:

neither can the geographical environment be the decisive factor in social development, nor can society be the decisive factor in the development of the environment, since society is incapable of cancelling the laws of nature.[113]

Despite such rear-guard action, the new approach was widely publicised in the 1960s (even through comparatively popular journals such as the

[108] See *Vestnik Akademii Nauk SSR*, 1963, No. 11, pp. 14–15.

[109] *Voprosy filosofii*, 1963, No. 11, pp. 6–7.

[110] 'L.F. Ilichev's Remarks about a Unified Geography', tr. in *Soviet Geography*, Vol. V (1964), No. 4, p. 32.

[111] *Ibid.*, pp. 32–3.

[112] On the need to create a unified theory of the process of interaction, in order to consciously control such interaction see A.G. Doskach, *et al.*, 'The Problem of Interaction of Nature and Society and Present-Day Geography', *Voprosy filosofii*, 1965, No. 4, pp. 104–115.

[113] S.V. Kalesnik, 'Some Results of the New Discussion about a "Unified" Geography', *loc.cit.*, pp. 20–21. Kalesnik, the editor of one of the two leading Soviet geographical journals, was one of those who failed Anuchin's doctoral dissertation.

Literaturnaia Gazeta) in association with an increasing level of concern over environmental problems (e.g. the Lake Baikal issue). In the sphere of history, the new approach manifested itself in both practical and theoretical writing, intended to redress previous neglect of the role of geographical factors in social development.

THE REASSESSMENT OF THE PLACE OF GEOGRAPHICAL FACTORS IN HISTORICAL MATERIALISM

Since the 1960s, there has been an increasing stress on geographical factors in historical writing.[114] The rejection of the Stalinist formula is reflected in statements such as the following:

[...] the geographic factor was, in the process whereby the most archaic cultures arose, not only an accelerating factor, but in considerable measure a factor determining the political structure of the most ancient states. It is hardly possible to deny this fully obvious connection.[115]

Considerable discussion has also been stimulated by the work of L.N. Gumilev, *Otkrytie Khazarii*,[116] in which he links the rise and decline of the central Asian nomadic civilisations with cyclonic patterns (periods of increased rainfall providing an increase in pasturage for the nomadic herders). His subsequent articles have emphasised the need to take into account the changing geographical background to human history.[117]

The overthrow of the Stalinist conception of the geographical environment as an unchanging external factor with minimal influence on the internal development of human society is demonstrated most clearly in one of the latest Soviet textbooks on historical materialism. In this we find that:

Geographical environment is historical for it is changing ever since the appearance of man, both under the impact of natural terrestrial or cosmic causes and also as a result of the transforming activity of men [...]
    It follows from the above that geographical environment today is not some sort of 'pure' nature, nor the result of the operation of natural laws alone. The present geographical environment is also a result of preceding human activity,

---

[114] See the survey by A.V. Dulov, 'Literatura o roli geograficheskoi sredy v istorii obshchestva', *Voprosy istorii*, 1973, No. 8, pp. 142–148.
[115] M.A. Korostovtsev, 'On the Concept "The Ancient East"', *loc.cit.*, p. 112.
[116] L.N. Gumilev, *Otkrytie Khazarii*, Moscow, 1966.
[117] E.g., L.N. Gumilev, 'Mesto istoricheskoi geografii v vostokovednykh issledovaniiakh', *Narody Azii i Afriki*, 1970, No. 1, pp. 85–94.

of the colossal labour effort of the earlier generations. Consequently it is the result of the interaction of natural and social laws.[118]

The text-book not only echoes Marx's description of how the sphere of 'humanised' nature expands to include the whole earth, but claims that:

man's flight into outer space ushered in the transformation of his natural surroundings from terrestrial into interplanetary environment.[119]

The way in which the new emphasis on geographical environment has been interwoven with the revival of interest in the concept of the Asiatic mode of production, and with the attempts to break free of Stalin's five-stage schema of social development, will be discussed at greater length in subsequent chapters. Here we confine ourselves to mentioning one tentative proposal for the classification of pre-industrial societies that emerged in a discussion on the Asiatic formation at the Institute of the Peoples of Asia (May, 1965). The Soviet historian, L.A. Sedov, suggested that pre-industrial societies might be grouped into three main types: those based on agriculture without artificial irrigation; those based on agriculture with artificial irrigation; and those based on herding. These different productive bases gave rise to different socio-economic structures, which developed according to their own characteristic laws. Thus (large-scale) irrigation agriculture gave rise to a society dominated by a bureaucratic elite, while herding gave rise to a society dominated by a military aristocracy.[120] Sedov's taxonomy here owes much to Wittfogel,[121] and the determining role of the geographical environment is clearly in evidence.

[118] G. Glezerman and G. Kursanov, *Historical Materialism*, tr. D. Fidlon, Moscow, Progress, 1968, pp. 52–53. (The English is their translator's.)

[119] *Ibid.*, p. 55.

[120] See L.A. Sedov, 'O sotsial'no-ekonomicheskikh tipakh razvitiia', in G.F. Kim, V.N. Nikiforov *et al.* ed., *Obshchee i osobennoe v istoricheskom razvitii stran Vostoka*, Moscow, Izd. 'Nauka', 1966, pp. 48–55.

[121] Cf. the later Wittfogel's classification of pre-industrial societies into (a) stratified pastoral societies; (b) hydraulic societies; (c) helotage-based, free peasant-based or slave-based non-feudal societies; (d) feudal societies. (K.A. Wittfogel, *Oriental Despotism*, New Haven, Columbia U.P., 1957, p. 419.) Stratified pastoral societies have been notoriously difficult to fit into the five-stage unilinear schema. As we shall see in Chapter Five, as soon as an alternative mode of production (the Asiatic) was discovered, attempts were made to apply it to the nomadic pastoral societies. However, the Asiatic concept was designed for bureaucratic agricultural societies, and is inapplicable to pastoral societies, which perhaps can best be viewed as Sedov has done, as yet another alternative mode of production determined by local circumstances. At least one passage from Marx could be adduced as authority for this point of view: 'Among the nomadic pastoral peoples, the commune is indeed constantly united; the travelling society, the caravan, the horde, and the forms of supremacy and subordination develop out of the conditions of this mode of life.' (Marx, *Grundrisse*, p. 491).

Thus (the newly-revived) emphasis within Soviet historiography on the importance of geographical factors is once more linked, as it has been in the past in Marxist historiography, with a tendency to view pre-industrial society in terms of a plurality of modes of production, rather than in terms of a logical sequence of stages.[122]

A NOTE ON THE POPULATION FACTOR

Yet another factor, not directly relevant to our theme, was mentioned by Marx in the *Grundrisse*, in association with the role of geographical factors in social development – i.e. the factor of population pressure. The impact of demographic factors on development in primitive society is very much linked to more purely geographical factors, in that it is in the context of an environmentally circumscribed area of usable land that population increase becomes significant.

Despite Stalin's attack on the concept of population pressure as a determining factor[123] (linked with his attack on the concept of geographical determinism), it is clear from the *Grundrisse* that Marx believed that population pressure could operate as an independent variable in economic and social development, at least in that early stage of human history where natural rather than historically-produced factors were the major determinants of development. Marx wrote that:

For example, where each of the individuals is supposed to possess a given number of acres of land, the advance of population is already under way. If this is to be corrected, then colonization, and that in turn requires wars of conquest. With that, slaves etc. [. . .]. Thus the preservation of the old community includes the destruction of the conditions on which it rests, turns into its opposite. If it were thought that productivity on the same land could be increased by developing the forces of production, etc. [. . .], then the new order would include combinations of labour, a large part of the day spent in agriculture etc., and thereby again suspend the old economic conditions of the community.[124]

The concept of population increase as an independent variable in economic development (i.e. the concept here prefigured by Marx) has

---

[122] Soviet historiography has finally been discovering in the *Grundrisse* the view that Asiatic society, slavery and serfdom are simply the consequences of different 'distortions' [izvrashchenii] of the primitive community, determined by particular geographical and historical circumstances. (See Iu.A. Kizilov, 'Predposylki perekhoda vostochnogo slavianstva k feodalizmu', *Voprosy istorii*, 1969, No. 3, pp. 94–104).

[123] Stalin, *Dialectical and Historical Materialism*, N.Y., International Publishers, 1972, pp. 26–27.

[124] Marx, *Grundrisse*, pp. 493–494.

been employed in much recent work on the evolution of primitive societies.

Interest in this concept by anthropologists was reawakened with the publication of Ester Boserup's influential book *The Conditions of Agricultural Growth* in 1965. Boserup's basic argument was that because the intensification of agricultural practices (from hunting and gathering through slash-and-burn agriculture eventually to multicropping) involves an ever lower return per unit of labour input, such intensification does not take place except under the pressure of population increase and corresponding land shortage. If one can assume that the working day of hunters and gatherers averaged about four or five hours,[125] and that of long fallow slash-and-burn cultivators not much more (in the busy season perhaps four hours for men and six hours for women),[126] resistance to intensification of agricultural practice follows as a natural corollary

One might argue that even given the resistance to intensification, technical innovations might be introduced to lower the labour input with given methods of cultivation. Boserup argues that with cross-cultural contact this does indeed happen, for example, the replacement of the stone axe by the factory-made axe among the slash-and-burn cultivators of Indonesia,[127] and the spread of new cereal crops to Oceania, Africa, etc., from South America in the sixteenth and seventeenth centuries.[128] However such technological innovation which takes place without the driving force of population pressure will remain, according to Boserup, within relatively narrow parameters – e.g., the improvement of the tool or cereal crop employed, rather than the introduction of new ones which would involve a more intensive mode of agriculture and a heavier labour input. More radical forms of technical innovation, for example the introduction of the hoe or plough to replace the digging stick, were irrelevant to the forest fallow or slash-and-burn cultivation which prevailed as long as there was sufficient land to allow for regeneration of forest for a twenty-five year period after cropping. Under this kind of cultivation any tool other than the digging stick to make holes for seed or roots was superfluous as the soil was loose and weedless. Where fallow periods are shorter because of population pressure and bush fallow prevails, the hoe becomes neces-

[125] See Marshall Sahlins, 'The Original Affluent Society', in his *Stone Age Economics*, Chicago, Aldine-Atherton, 1972, p. 17.
[126] Ester Boserup, *The Conditions of Agricultural Growth*, Chicago, Aldine, 1965, p. 46.
[127] *Ibid.*, p. 27.
[128] *Ibid.*, pp. 67–69.

sary to clear weeds. When cultivation of given plots has become so frequent that the area has been converted to grassland, the plough becomes indispensable, while the disappearance of the roots of trees and bushes facilitates its use. Also the conversion of an area into a grassland (through the frequency of cropping) encourages the appearance of herbivorous animals which can be employed in ploughing.[129]

Thus Boserup's theory rests on the hypothesis that the intensification of agricultural practices alone leads to technical innovation, and that such intensification does not take place except under the pressure of population growth.[130] This hypothesis provides a new dimension of analysis which may serve to strengthen historical materialism in its application to primitive society, and which, as shown above from the *Grundrisse* extract, is not incompatible with Marx's own approach to the earliest phases of socio-economic development. It may serve as a counterweight to the overly-reductionist view that the means of production always function as the most revolutionary variable within society, the variable which forces change on all the other variables despite the increased exploitation and longer working hours which each innovation brings about.

The new approach, that change in the means of production is only one aspect of a complex of variables that may bring about social transformations is exemplified in the recent historical works published by Perry Anderson.[131] Jürgen Habermas has restated the core of historical materialism as concerned with 'system problems': 'if system problems – economic problems, demographic problems, ecological problems and so on – can no longer be solved within the existing system of social integration, then this itself must be revolutionised in order to provide the basic problem solution.'[132]

The way in which Boserup's hypothesis may be fruitfully incorporated into the analysis of pre-capitalist socio-economic development is

[129] E. Boserup, 'The Interdependence of Land Use and Technical Change', *The Conditions of Agricultural Growth, op.cit.*, pp. 23–27.

[130] See E. Boserup, 'The Vicious Circle of Sparse Population and Primitive Techniques', *The Conditions of Agricultural Growth, op.cit.*, pp. 70–76, for discussion of the 'control' situation in which population increase does not take place. However if Boserup's hypothesis is lifted out of the context of primitive societies and applied to the contemporary world it implies the kind of optimism with regards to the elasticity of world resources which has characterised the critics of the Club of Rome. It is presumed that methods of cultivation of food resources can become even more intensive under the pressure of population increase without vital resources being either used up or destroyed by the byproducts of such activity.

[131] P. Anderson, *Passages from Antiquity to Feudalism*, London, NLB, 1974; *Lineages of the Absolutist State*, London, NLB, 1974.

[132] J. Habermas, 'Historical Materialism Reconsidered' (Address delivered at Purdue University, Lafayette, Indiana, 18 March 1975), *Arena*, No. 38 (1975), p. 73.

shown in a recent essay by the American anthropologist Robert McC. Netting. Netting attempts to demonstrate a causal link between population growth and the emergence of the state in the form of sacred authority.[133] More intensive cultivation of the land leads to higher land value, more complicated rules of ownership, and hence to an increasing number of disputes. The only way in which these disputes may be resolved is through the emergence of some form of sacred authority which is freed from the narrower connection with village, lineage, etc., and which becomes the basis of a permanent, territorially-based state structure and associated specialised roles. Once the prestige of the new, more broadly-based cult and cosmology is established, it will serve other functions (besides that of inter-village dispute resolution etc.) created by increased population pressure. Thus, according to Netting, the new state-promoted symbols and ritual will serve to alleviate the social unease promoted by increased pressure on the land and threat of famine, while the sacred protection offered to markets and trade-routes facilitates the circulation of goods to areas of scarcity.[134] Netting's emphasis on the sacred or symbolic functions of the emergent state structure in African societies is similar to that of the Marxist anthropologists applying the concept of the 'Asiatic mode of production' to the same societies, while the population thesis adds an extra dimension to such a Marxist analysis. Other ways in which the population thesis can enrich the Marxist analysis of the emergence of the state in kinship society will be discussed further in a subsequent chapter. Pressure on land may be viewed as giving rise to intensification of agriculture, the development of private-property rights, inequalities, class divisions, and a repressive state apparatus to hold these in check. On the other hand the impetus to state formation may be viewed as coming from an external source – conflict with an alien society over the diminishing supply of arable land, and the absorption of the defeated party as a slave-class into an expanded political unit.[135]

---

[133] Robert McC. Netting, 'Sacred Power and Centralization: Aspects of Political Adaptation in Africa', Brian Spooner, ed., *Population Growth: Anthropological Implications*, MIT Press, 1972, Ch. 9, pp. 219–244.

[134] Robert McC. Netting, *loc.cit.*, p. 236.

[135] See for example, Robert L. Carneiro, 'From Autonomous Villages to the State, A Numerical Investigation', Brian Spooner, ed., *Population Growth: Anthropological Implications, op.cit.*, pp. 64–77.

CHAPTER IV

MARXIST PERSPECTIVES ON RUSSIAN HISTORY: THE PRACTICAL APPLICATION OF THE CONCEPT OF THE ASIATIC MODE OF PRODUCTION

> For Western Europe and its peoples nature was a mother; for the East and the peoples destined to act out their history there it was a step-mother.
>
> Solov'ev[1]

Russian history provides a convenient case-study for the comparison of two historiographical approaches: the one emphasizing the universal and immanent laws of social production, the other (with roots both in Marx and in nineteenth-century Russian historiography), emphasizing geographical and historical pluralism, particularly as existing between Western European and Asiatic societies.

MARX'S CONCEPTION OF THE CHARACTER OF THE RUSSIAN STATE: RUSSIA CONTRASTED WITH EUROPE

In his analysis of Russian history Marx used a qualified version of his model of Asiatic despotism. In Russia as in Asia, the state had assumed a preponderant role in socio-economic life, and social classes on the Western European model were correspondingly underdeveloped. Geographical factors were largely responsible, on Marx's analysis, for this 'non-European' variant of historical development.

This section confines itself to Marx's analysis of the (non-Western) character of the Russian state. It does not attempt to deal with the separate though related topic of the expectations held by Marx and Engels concerning the possibility and character of a Russian revolution. That topic is comprehensively covered in the recent volume edited by Maximilien Rubel, *Marx/Engels: Die russische Kommune.*[2]

It is true, of course, that the interest Marx and Engels showed in Russian affairs stemmed largely from their conviction that the fall of

---

[1] S.M. Solov'ev, *Istoriia Rossii s drevneishikh vremen*, Kniga VII (Toma 13–14), Moscow, Izd. sots-ekon. lit., 1962, p. 8.

[2] M. Rubel ed., *Marx/Engels: Die russische Kommune*, Munich, Carl Hanser Verlag, 1972.

the Russian autocracy was an essential ingredient in the success of the social movement in Western Europe.[3] Hence their enthusiasm for any revolutionary tendency which seemed capable of toppling the existing regime, regardless of its theoretical errors.[4] ('What matters is not so much their theoretical clarity as their practical energy.')[5] At no time, however, did Marx or Engels consider the possibility that a revolution against the autocracy might be a socialist one *ab initio*.[6] In spite of their 'Narodnik' sympathies, discussed in Chapter Two, the views of Marx and Engels gravitated around the proposition that the development of socialism in Russia, as in Asia, required the prior development of the 'material foundations of Western society';[7] i.e., the unfettered development of capitalism on the English model and the abolition of the state interventionism of the past in order that the contradictions of capitalism might freely work themselves out. According to Engels 'all these contradictions [including those existing between pre-capitalist and capitalist elements in Russian society] are violently held in check by an unexampled despotism [...]'[8] The allegedly imminent Russian revolution, therefore, would be a bourgeois democratic revolution, a 1789 and not a 1793, even if it would in all probability emerge from a 'Blanquist' *coup d'état*. As Engels wrote,

... the people who laid the spark to the mine will be swept away by the explosion, which will be a thousand times as strong as they themselves and which will seek its vent where it can, as the economic forces and resistances determine.'[9]

The revolution once initiated would bring to the top 'not the socialists

---

[3] In later years their interest received a further stimulus in the form of the relative success in Russia of *Capital*.

[4] Marx and Engels favoured the tactics of the terrorist (or 'Blanquist') *Narodnaia Volia* group, rather than the tactics of their own disciples. (E.g. Marx to Jenny Longuet, 11 April 1881, *Werke*, Vol. 35, p. 179; Engels to Vera Zasulich, 23 April 1885, *MESC*, pp. 383–385). Engels was very critical of Plekhanov's book *Nashi Raznoglasiia* (1884) which was a full-scale attack on Russian Blanquism, and on the idea of a 'quick' revolution as opposed to solidly-based working class participation in a bourgeois revolution. See for example the extract from Voden's memoirs reprinted in M. Rubel ed., *Marx/Engels: Die russische Kommune*, *op.cit.*, pp. 181–190.

[5] Engels, conversation with Kautsky, as reported by Kautsky in a letter to Bernstein, dated 30 June 1885, *ibid.*, p. 177.

[6] Although they did believe that if the revolution in Russia triggered off socialist revolutions in Western Europe these would influence the development of the Russian revolution in a socialist direction.

[7] Marx, 'The Future Results of British Rule in India', *N.Y.D.T.*, 8 Aug. 1853, *Karl Marx on Colonialism and Modernization*, p. 133. The original unity of the worker and the conditions of production, as found in the village communal system could be 're-established only on the material foundation which capital creates [...]' (Marx, *Theories of Surplus Value*, Part III, p. 423.)

[8] Engels to Vera Zasulich, 23 April 1885, *MESC*, p. 385.

[9] Engels to Vera Zasulich, 23 April 1885, *MESC*, p. 384.

but the liberals,'[10] an outcome determined by the level of Russian development[11] and the absence of the material foundations of socialism (which could be provided only by capitalism).

Behind all this was Marx's view that the historical categories which he extrapolated from Western history and applied to it did not necessarily appertain to Russia's historical development although they became relevant in the present situation of a world capitalist market, and in the socialist future. As we have noted, Marx and Engels followed the great tradition of Western European political thought in classifying the Russian state as an Oriental or at least a semi-Oriental despotism. Typical of this tradition was Astolphe de Custine's four volume *La Russie en 1839*, a book with which Marx and Engels almost certainly became acquainted in 1844, the year after its publication.[12] De Custine provided a vivid sketch of the Asiatic and despotic character of the Russian state,[13] emphasizing the failure of the nobility to serve as a check to the central power, the absence of a middle class of the Western European type, and the organisation of social classes from above, according to services performed for the state. Marx *could* have utilised de Custine's social analysis to his advantage, but the only direct reference to de Custine by Marx or Engels is one by Engels in the Russian section of his series of articles on European armies.[14]

Marx's writings on the Russian state, as Maximilien Rubel observes, can be divided into two major periods.[15] During the first period, lasting up till about 1858, Marx perceived Russia solely in terms of an internally immobile semi-Asiatic colossus, the bastion of European re-

---

[10] Engels, conversation reported in K. Kautsky to E. Bernstein, 30 June 1885, in M. Rubel ed., *Marx/Engels: Die russische Kommune, op.cit.*, p. 117.

[11] 'After studying his [Flerovsky's] book, one is firmly convinced that an appalling social revolution is unavoidable in Russia and is quite imminent – naturally a revolution in its lower forms corresponding to the present state of Muscovite development. That is good news. Russia and England are the two great pillars of the present European system.' (Marx to Laura and Paul Lafargue, 5 March 1870, *Werke*, Vol. 32, p. 659.)

[12] Numerous articles discussing de Custine's book appeared in the Paris journal *Vorwärts* during 1844, the year in which both Marx and Engels contributed articles to the journal. Rubel emphasises the parallels to be found between de Custine's dicta on Russia and some of the anti-Russian writing of Marx and Engels. (M. Rubel ed., *Marx/Engels: Die russische Kommune, op.cit.*, pp. 288–292.) The significance of such parallels should not, however, be exaggerated as similar parallels could be drawn between the writings of Marx and Engels and those of many other of the writers cited in Chapter One, such as von Haxthausen.

[13] De Custine wrote in a quotable aphoristic style, and his work on Russia included the now familiar epigram: 'The Russian government is an absolutism tempered by assassination.'

[14] Engels, 'The Armies of Europe' (Second Article), *Putnam's Monthly*, No. XXXIII, Sept. 1855, *Werke*, Vol. II, p. 451.

[15] M. Rubel ed., *Marx/Engels: Die russische Kommune, op.cit.*, p. 13.

action.[16] So, on the whole, did Engels. Both he and Marx agreed that the only way in which the character of the Russian state could be changed (in the absence of an internal social dialectic) was through the impact of external factors such as the victory of European democracy.[17]

Some of Marx's most sustained (and polemical) writing on the Russian state is to be found in his *Secret Diplomatic History of the Eighteenth Century*, which dates from the pre-1858 period.[18] The interpretation of events to be found in the *Secret History* is couched in purely 'political' terms, in fact in terms of 'great men', in this case a series of villains who by craft and cunning bring about Russia's expansion into a great empire.[19] The Muscovite princes, according to Marx, achieved their supremacy through absorbing and applying the political lessons to be learnt from the Tatars – i.e. on how to impose 'general slavery'.[20] Needless to say, this is not the kind of approach adopted by Marx in relation to Western European history where he keeps the trend of economic development very much in the foreground. It seemed to him natural to apply a different order of explanation of the Eastern form of

---

[16] Engels had anticipated the post-1858 position as early as 1853, when he wrote that: 'Also left out of account, of course, are any *internal* movements in Russia, and a noble-bourgeois revolution in Petersburg, with an ensuing civil war inside the country, is quite within the realm of possibility.' (Engels to J. Weydemeyer, 12 April 1853, *MESC*, p. 74.)

[17] E.g. Marx, 'The Real Issue in Turkey', *N.Y.D.T.*, 12 April 1853, *Karl Marx on Colonialism and Modernization*, p. 63. This attitude lingered on in Marx's work after 1858, particularly in association with the suppression of the Polish uprising in 1863. For example he declared in 1867 that: 'There is but one alternative for Europe. Either Asiatic barbarism under Muscovite direction will break over Europe like an avalanche, or Europe must re-establish Poland, thus protecting itself from Asia by a wall of twenty million heroes, and gaining time for the completion of its social transformation.' Marx, [Rede auf dem Polenmeeting in London am 22. Januar 1867], *Werke*, Vol. 16, p. 204.

[18] Marx, *Secret Diplomatic History of the Eighteenth Century* (first published in full as 'Revelations of the Diplomatic History of the Eighteenth Century' in David Urquhart's *Free Press*, London, Aug. 1856 – April 1857), ed. L. Hutchinson, London, Lawrence and Wishart, 1969. This work has been omitted from the official Soviet editions of the collected works of Marx and Engels (i.e. the two editions of the *Sochineniia*, and from the *Werke* edition).

[19] *Ibid.*, Ch. 5, pp. 108–121. The 'great man' approach is supplemented by a Russophobia in which the so-called Mongolian legacy of the Russians is the ultimate term of abuse: 'The bloody mire of Mongolian slavery, not the rude glory of the Norman epoch, forms the cradle of Muscovy, and modern Russia is but a metamorphosis of Muscovy.' (*Ibid.*, p. 111.) At a somewhat later date Marx was to praise the theories of the French geologist P. Trémaux ('a very important advance over Darwin'), and to note his point that physical terrain had led to the Tatarisation and Mongolisation of the Russian Slavs and to the contrast between the Russians and the Western Slavs and Lithuanians. (Marx to Engels, 7 Aug. 1866, *Werke*, Vol. 31, pp. 248–249.)

[20] Marx, *Secret Diplomatic History of the Eighteenth Century*, op.cit., pp. 112–121. 'At length Peter the Great coupled the political craft of the Mongol slave with the proud aspiration of the Mongol master, to whom Genghiz Khan had, by will, bequeathed his conquest of the earth.' (*Ibid.*, p. 121). This is one of the sources in Marx for Wittfogel's theory of the 'institutional time-bomb' left behind by the Mongols.

the state, here represented by the Tatar and Muscovite dynasties. (That is, assuming the underlying geographical and social conditions which made the area susceptible to this form of state in the first place.)

Although giving considerable weight to the autonomous role of political factors in his analysis of the Russian state, Marx drew back from some of the conclusions reached by the 'service-state' school of Russian history. For instance, the Russian neo-Hegelian historian B.N. Chicherin argued that *all* Russian social institutions owed their existence to the creative activity of the state, including the *obshchina* or *mir*. On Chicherin's account[21] the *mir* in its contemporary form was a comparatively recent institution, created by the state for fiscal purposes. In the controversy which was generated by this aspect of the service-state theory Marx took the side of those who, like von Haxthausen, regarded the *mir* as a vestigial remnant of the primitive clan organisation of society. Marx wrote, for example, that Schedo-Ferroti: 'is greatly mistaken – he is altogether quite a superficial fellow – when he says the Russian communal system originated as a consequence of prohibiting the peasant from leaving the land.'[22] On the same point Marx later wrote: 'How could this institution (communal property) have been introduced into Russia merely as a fiscal measure and as a corollary of serfdom, while everywhere else it arose naturally and formed a necessary phase of the development of free peoples?'[23]

Nevertheless Marx admitted that the commune and its collective responsibility for taxes was an efficient means of tying the peasant to the land and extracting a maximum proportion of the surplus for the benefit of the state. He wrote that:

... the more industrious a Russian peasant is, the more he is exploited by the state, not only for taxes but for the supply of produce, horses, etc., during the continual passage of bodies of troops, for government couriers, etc.[24]

It was in connection with the movement for the emancipation of the serfs that Marx first came to consider the possible sources of internal change in Russia. His new perspective on Russia was marked by a letter to Engels in which he wrote that:

[21] See Chicherin's influential essay, 'Obzor istoricheskogo razvitiia sel'skoi obshchiny v Rossii' in *Opyty po istorii russkogo prava*, Moscow, 1858.
[22] Marx to Engels, 7 Nov. 1868, *MESC*, p. 217.
[23] Marx to N.F. Danielson, 22 March 1873, *Werke*, Vol. 33, p. 577. (Marx's argument is here specifically directed against Chicherin.)
[24] Marx to Engels, 7 Nov. 1868, *loc.cit.*

... the movement for the emancipation of the serfs in Russia appears important to me in so far as it indicates the beginning of an internal history in the country, which may cut across the traditional foreign policy itself.[25]

The phrase 'beginning of an internal history' reveals to what extent Marx viewed the autocracy in terms of his model of Oriental despotism, a system which was historyless and static.

Russia had always differed from the classical Oriental despotism in so far as its propinquity to Europe had forced the autocracy into modernising programmes, in order to maintain a military superiority to its Western neighbours. However, in the period prior to the Crimean War such programmes had remained superficial in character in Marx's view, and had not affected the basic structure of the state. Peter the Great, for example, had obtained Western experts in order 'to drill Russians into that varnish of civilization that adapts them to the technical appliances of the Western peoples, without imbueing them with their ideas.'[26] At the same time Peter the Great had completed the old Muscovite (Asiatic) state system by generalising it.[27]

By the mid-nineteenth century however, in the wake of the Crimean débâcle, it was clear that a more thorough-going programme of economic and social modernisation was essential if the military machine was to be rendered capable of standing up to the Western powers. Russia's weakness, which had been manifested in the Crimean War, was aggravated in Marx's eyes, by Russia's dependence on the world market, which was predominantly capitalist.[28] As a consequence, the autocracy had itself been forced to take in hand the 'hot-house' development of the capitalist system in Russia.[29]

Because Marx's model of non-Western political economy specifically excluded the possibility of economic modernisation or industrialisation conducted from above by the state in a framework of structural continuity, he saw the policies inaugurated by the autocracy after the Crimean War as inimical to its survival in the long run.[30] In the short

[25] Marx to Engels, 29 April 1858, Werke, Vol. 29, p. 324. See also the article by Marx written later in the same year 'The Emancipation Question', N.Y.D.T., 17 Jan. 1859, given the title of 'Über die Bauernbefreiung in Russland' in Werke, Vol. 12, pp. 673–678.

[26] Marx, Secret Diplomatic History of the Eighteenth Century, op.cit., p. 125. Cf. de Custine: 'It is to Russia that we must go in order to see the results of the terrible combination of the mind and science of Europe with the genius of Asia [...]', Russia, abridged edn, London, Longmans, 1855, p. 144.

[27] Ibid., p. 121.

[28] First Draft of Marx's letter to Vera Zasulich, Werke, Vol. 19, p. 393.

[29] Ibid., pp. 393–394.

[30] The autocracy would be overthrown by the representatives of the rising class of capitalist entrepreneurs – unless, as Marx prognosticated in his 'Narodnik' phase discussed in Chapter Two, conditions arose in which the autocracy might be directly replaced by socialism.

run he saw advantages accruing to the autocracy, from, for example, the emancipation of the serfs. The emancipation effectively removed the checks to the central power which had been posed by the authority of the serf-owning landowners and of the village communities.[31] Thus in Russia the state power continued to tower above society even while, in Marx's view, it was undermining its own foundations by setting in train a more dynamic and individual form of economy.

MARX AND THE SERVICE-STATE THEORY OF RUSSIAN
HISTORY: A PARALLEL THEORY OF THE NON-EUROPEAN
CHARACTER OF RUSSIAN HISTORY

Many parallels may be drawn between Marx's conception of the Russian state and that of the nineteenth-century school of Russian historians loosely referred to as the 'service-state' school. This school of historical writing, which concerned itself with the 'special nature' of Russian development, was founded by S.M. Solov'ev, and its most outstanding representative was V.O. Kliuchevsky. The conceptual apparatus of this school consisted in a compound of elements drawn from Western historiography: i.e. elements of geographical determinism borrowed from, in particular, Hegel and Buckle; elements of economic determinism; and neo-Hegelian theories of the state as a creative entity.

Theories of geographic determinism had a particular appeal for these nineteenth-century Russian historians in their search for a scientific explanation of what they took to be the special character of Russian history.[32] Solov'ev, for example, wrote that the three conditions which exercised a special influence on the history of a nation were: 'the nature of the country in which the people settle; the nature of the tribe to which the people belong; and the course of external events and influences, stemming from the surrounding peoples.'[33]

[31] Marx, *Herr Vogt*, *Werke*, Vol. 14, pp. 497–498; [Rede auf dem Polen meeting in London am 22. Januar 1867], *Werke*, Vol. 16, p. 203.

[32] Sir Donald Mackenzie Wallace bore witness to the vast success in Russia of Buckle's *History of Civilization*, with its crude theories of geographical determinism. He wrote: 'In the course of a few years no less than four independent translations were published and sold. Everyone read or at least professed to have read, the wonderful book, and many believed that its author was the greatest genius of his time. During my first year of residence in Russia (1870) I rarely had a serious conversation without hearing Buckle's name mentioned. In books, periodicals, newspapers, and professional lectures, the name of Buckle was constantly cited [. . .] and the cheap translations of his work were sold in enormous quantities.' See Sir Donald MacKenzie Wallace, *Russia* (first published in 1877), 2 vols., London, Cassell, 1905, Vol. I, pp. 140–141.

[33] S.M. Solov'ev, *Nachalo russkoi zemli*, Sb. gos. znanii, Tom IV, St. Petersburg, 1877, p. 1. (Cf. Marx, *Grundrisse*, pp. 472; 486.)

Solov'ev saw Russian development as having been retarded by the natural environment specific to the East European plain. Western Europe enjoyed the advantage of being diversified by mountain ranges etc., which gave rise to diversified development. This in its turn accelerated the pace of economic growth.[34] Western Europe had the added advantage of long sea borders, which both sharply demarcated the territorial limits of states[35] and provided ease of communication between its diverse regions.

The East European plain, on the other hand, suffered both from a lack of internal diversity and from a lack of natural barriers to hostile incursions. The undiversified nature of the plain led to an absence of diversity in occupation and hence to a lack of diversity in customs, morals and beliefs. This in turn meant an absence of strongly developed regional loyalties.[36] As well as their homogenous nature and the absence of regionalism, there was a strong common bond between all the agricultural peoples inhabiting this plain *vis à vis* the nomadic plunderers from Asia who desired to live at their expense. This widely spread common bond was the basis for the development of a Russian state of corresponding proportions.[37] Moreover, the state organisation was not only territorially extensive, but necessarily took on an exaggerated form as a substitute for the defence provided elsewhere by natural barriers.

As seen in Chapter Two, the idea that in the East extensive geographical units gave rise naturally to co-extensive political units or land empires was given currency by Montesquieu in the eighteenth century. It has always been an idea very popular with Russian historians in connection with the East European or Eurasian plain. A modern, typically unselfconscious example of this reads as follows:

... With the annexation of the Amur Region and of Central Asia an important phase in Russian history came to an end. The possession of the entire Eurasian plain and of its geographical extensions had been secured, and the natural limits of greater Russia in every direction had been achieved.[38]

Solov'ev extended his account of the influence of geographical factors even further, into the sphere of *class relationships*. According to

[34] S.M. Solov'ev, *Istoriia Rossii s drevneishikh vremen*, Kniga VII (Toma 13–14), *op.cit.*, p. 7. (Cf. Marx, *Capital*, Vol. I, pp. 351–352.)

[35] *Ibid.*

[36] S.M. Solov'ev, *Istoriia Rossia s drevneishikh vremen*, Kniga I (Toma 1–2), Moscow, Izd. sots.-ekon. lit., 1959, p. 60.

[37] *Ibid.*, pp. 60–61.

[38] A. Lobanov-Rostovsky, *Russia and Asia*, (first published 1933), Michigan, Wahr, 1965, p. 193.

his rather facile argument, the mountain ranges of Western Europe not only provided the basis for diversified development and firm territorial demarcation, but they also provided material for the consolidation of feudalism. The mountains provided the stone necessary for the construction of castles, the bulwark of the power of the feudal lord over his serfs and *vis à vis* the king. In the East European plain, by contrast, the absence of stone meant that the nobility did not live separately and independently in their castles, but rather formed a company (*druzhina*) around the prince, and followed him through the wide unlimited spaces. The fact that the peasant built in wood also encouraged *their* wandering habits, and inhibited the spontaneous growth of serfdom from the local level upwards. Should a careless spark set fire to the collection of wooden huts (izbas) the village simply moved elsewhere.

The service-state theory of history which was foreshadowed in Solov'ev's work was more fully developed by the greatest of the nineteenth-century Russian historians, V.O. Kliuchevsky. Kliuchevsky employed the concept extensively for the first time in his lectures on 'The History of Estates in Russia', which were delivered at Moscow University in 1886. In his hands the basic element of the theory was the acknowledgement of the primacy of the state in the economic and social formation of Russia. Owing to geographical conditions – the nature of the East European plain, its vulnerability to nomadic raiders etc. – the state structure came to play a preponderant role in the life of the nation, unlike its more secondary role among the countries of Western Europe.[39]

For defence purposes, the state called into being a military/gentry class who were granted land for their support, in return for their service to the state. The rest of the population were obliged to provide agricultural labour on the estates of the gentry or on state land, and almost

[39] From a Bolshevik perspective Pokrovsky was later to describe the significance of the service-state theory as resting in its acknowledgement that the evolution of the 'State principle' was determined by *objective* causes. 'The acceptance of the scheme was thus a considerable, though quite unconscious, concession to historical materialism. The late J. [sic] V. Plekhanov was so fascinated by this step in the direction of Marxism that in the introduction to his *History of Russian Political* [sic] *Thought* he almost entirely endorsed the Chicherin-Gradovsky-Klyuchevsky scheme.' (M.N. Pokrovsky, *A Brief History of Russia*, 10th edn, 2 vols., tr. D.S. Mirsky, London, Martin Lawrence, 1933, Vol. I, p. 243.) Pokrovsky is of course scornful of the objective causes selected by the service-state historians – the struggle with the steppe, rather than domestic class struggle.

all categories of direct producers, whether agricultural or artisan, contributed in taxes and services to offset the needs of the state.[40]

In Kliuchevsky's view, the genesis of Muscovite social classes in the needs of the state differentiated them from the social corporations or estates of Western Europe. The Muscovite classes remained 'service divisions or grades, which were known, in the official jargon of Moscow as *tchini* ....'[41] Kliuchevsky summed up the social constitution of Muscovite Russia as follows:

> ... In general, Muscovite legislation was devoted, more or less, to the defining and apportioning of State obligations, and formulating or securing of rights, whether personal or corporate. In practice, the position in the State of the individual or class was defined by his or its duties to the State...[42]

According to Kliuchevsky's theoretical abstract, the Muscovite state had created an elaborate administrative and fiscal structure in order to ensure the service of all categories of the population, and to prevent any land, the chief economic resource of the state, from 'going out of service' – i.e. ceasing to contribute to the exchequer. From the end of the sixteenth century, owing to a number of circumstances, this gradually entailed the legal enserfment of the direct producers.

One of the major and most frequent criticisms made of Kliuchevsky is that although on the conceptual level he attributed the formation of the Russian class system to the initiative of the state, in his concrete historical description he showed feudal relationships and enserfment as arising out of the day-to-day struggle between landowners and peasants, and out of the indebtedness of the peasantry – i.e., he described this class relationship as developing in the same way in Russia as in Western Europe, as a consequence of particular conditions of rural production.[43]

Leaving aside the question of the consistency between Kliuchevsky's general conclusions and his more empirical work, one comes up against his rather narrow interpretation of Oriental despotism, according to which the Oriental system was characterised by the *absence* of social classes rather than by their particular genesis in the needs of the state for different kinds of service. This interpretation led Kliuchevsky to differentiate the Muscovite service state from Oriental despotism by reason of the existence of distinct classes within the Muscovite population, rather than by reason of some more cogent argument. He con-

[40] V.O. Kliuchevsky, *A History of Russia*, 5 vols., (this edition originally published 1911–1931), N.Y., Russell & Russell, 1960, esp. Vol. III, pp. 52–53.
[41] *Ibid.*, Vol. III, p. 52.
[42] *Ibid.*, Vol. III, p. 53.
[43] See especially Vol. IV of Kliuchevsky's *History of Russia*, *op.cit.*

trasted the Muscovite system with the 'case of Oriental despotism, where general equality rests upon a general lack of rights'.[44] As we have seen in previous chapters this belongs among the more polemical and unrealistic aspects of the Western concept of Oriental despotism.

One of the most systematic expositions of the service-state theory *qua* theory is to be found in P. Miliukov's *Ocherki po istorii russkoi kul'tury*, first published in 1896. According to Miliukov, the service-state system arose because at a certain stage of Russian history there occurred a major disparity between the external demands made on the state, in terms of defence and territorial consolidation, and the economic and social development of the nation.[45] In the absence of a monetary economy the state was obliged to have recourse to a service (military) class who were provided with support in the form of conditional land grants. Miliukov, like the sixteenth and seventeenth century English theoreticians of feudalism,[46] saw this process as analogous to the original land-grant system in medieval Europe.

Miliukov argued, however, that the consequences of the imposition of such a system in Russia were very different from the consequences in Western Europe. In moving East one found an absence of the strong local development of feudalism such as had developed in Western Europe out of tribal arrangements.[47] On Miliukov's account, the basis of feudalism *had* existed in the South of Russia, where there were strong tribal formations surviving in the agricultural settlements. But Miliukov accepted the thesis put forward by Pogodin and Solov'ev concerning the effects of the internal colonisation of Russia – i.e., that in the process of migration into the empty lands of the North-East, the tribal configurations were broken up, and it was relatively easy for the state in the form of the prince, to assume control over the land. And as the centre of gravity in Russian political life moved more and more from the South to the North, the more 'Eastern' development became inevitable.[48]

Hence, in Russia, as in the East generally, the military land-grant system gave rise to the service-state system rather than to feudalism as found in Western Europe, where the central state structure maintained

---

[44] V.O. Kliuchevsky, *A History of Russia, op.cit.*, Vol. III, p. 52.

[45] P. Miliukov, *Ocherki po istorii russkoi kul'tury*, Vol. I, 5th edn, St. Petersburg, Mir Bozhii, 1904, p. 144.

[46] See J.G.A. Pocock, *The Ancient Constitution and the Feudal Law*, Cambridge U.P., 1957 *passim*.

[47] P. Miliukov, *Ocherki po istorii russkoi kul'tury, op.cit.*, Vol. I, p. 42.

[48] *Ibid.*, pp. 132–140.

little weight in the political equation. In the service state, social classes or strata were essentially defined by the kind of service they rendered to the state, rather than by the original pattern of tribal subordination and superordination. Whether or not the functional elite in the service-state system succeeded in converting their conditional estates into unconditional holdings,[49] they remained a class dependent on the favour of the state and moulded by this dependence.

One version of the service-state theory, which anticipated some of the modifications made by Plekhanov when absorbing it into a specifically Marxist analysis, was provided by the foreign observer of nineteenth-century Russia, Mackenzie Wallace. He wrote as follows:

... Thus, we see, the oft-repeated assertion that the Russian social classes are simply artificial categories created by the legislature is to a certain extent true, but is by no means accurate.

What is peculiar in the historical development of Russia is this: until lately she remained an almost exclusively agricultural Empire with an abundance of unoccupied land. Her history presents, therefore, few of those conflicts which result from the variety of social conditions and the intensified struggle for existence. Certain social groups were, indeed, formed in the course of time, but they were never allowed to fight out their own battles. The irresistible autocratic power kept them always in check and fashioned them into whatever form it thought proper, defining minutely and carefully their obligations, their rights, their mutual relations, and their respective positions in the political organisation. Hence we find in the history of Russia almost no trace of those class hatreds which appear so conspicuously in the history of Western Europe.[50]

The parallels between the service-state concept evolved by the nineteenth-century Russian historians and Marx's concept of Oriental society are manifest, and reveal the similar ancestry of the concepts in the great tradition of European theorising about non-European polities. However, Russian Marxists were in general to ignore both Marx's model of an Asiatic mode of production and his qualified application of this model to Russia, and the service-state theory of the great Russian historians. Instead the Russian Marxists were to do what Marx had specifically warned against in 1877: that is, to 'metamorphose [his] historical sketch of the genesis of capitalism in Western Europe into an historico-philosophic theory of the general path every people is fated to tread ...'[51]

[49] Miliukov cites the two cases also cited by Marx – the British conquest of India and the French conquest of Algeria, in both of which service lands survived very late on a conditional basis, but were then converted by conquerors 'partly through misunderstanding' (Miliukov) into aristocratic forms of tenure. (See Miliukov, *ibid.*, p. 142, and Marx's conspectus of Kovalevsky cited in Chapter Two.)
[50] Sir Donald Mackenzie Wallace, *Russia, op.cit*, Vol.. I, pp. 455–56.
[51] Marx to the Editors of *Otechestvennye Zapiski, MESC*, p. 313.

RUSSIAN HISTORY IN EUROPEAN DRESS:
THE ORTHODOX MARXIST APPROACH

Much of Marx's analysis of the Russian state was both distasteful and inconvenient to the Russian Bolsheviks. Moreover, for reasons to be discussed, Bolshevik historiography came to enshrine the unilinear schema of history, and to abandon the suggestion by Marx that there existed alternative paths of historical development. Hence, 'orthodox' Russian Marxist historiography ignored Marx and endowed Russian history with a feudal stage, completely analogous to that of Western Europe, which was supposed to lead through the operation of its own internal laws to capitalism and hence to socialism.[52]

The most important single influence on the formation of the orthodox Marxist approach to Russian history was the work of N.P. Pavlov-Sil'vansky, published in the early years of the twentieth century.[53] Pavlov-Sil'vansky was the first important Russian historian completely to deny the prevailing nineteenth-century historical tradition of viewing Russia's development as idiosyncratic in comparison with the development of the Western European nations.

An impressive amount of evidence was marshalled by Pavlov-Sil'vansky in support of his contention that Russian feudalism was *essentially* of the same nature as the classic model extrapolated from French history.[54] On the basis of his evidence he was able to argue quite persuasively that feudalism had developed at approximately the same time and for the same reasons in Western Europe and in Russia – i.e., it arose out of the conflict between landowners and peasants, not out of the activity of the state. By inference Russia shared in the laws of social development found in Western Europe.

Pavlov-Sil'vansky's detailed rejection of the notion of the 'special

[52] There has been another tendency, represented in recent years by A.P. Pogrebinsky and Ia. I. Livshin, that has stressed Russia's semi-colonial status in the pre-Revolutionary years, and the 'anti-colonial' rather than purely anti-capitalist nature of Russia's socialist revolution. See John L.H. Keep, 'The Rehabilitation of M.N. Pokrovsky', in Alexander and Janet Rabinowitch, etc. ed. *Revolution and Politics in Russia*, Bloomington, Indiana U.P., 1972 p. 312.

[53] During the popularisation of his work after the Revolution Pavlov-Sil'vansky was even labelled a 'spontaneous Marxist'. See K.F. Shteppa, *Russian Historians and the Soviet State*, New Brunswick, Rutgers U.P., 1962, p. 256.

[54] Pavlov-Sil'vansky's major work was entitled *Feodalizm v drevnei Rusi*, St. Petersburg, Brockhaus-Efron', 1907, published the year before his death. His ideas to a certain extent had been foreshadowed by A.G. Presniakov, who was to continue to popularise them as a member of the Society of Marxist Historians after the Revolution.

nature' of Russian history was popularised by Soviet historians in the post-Revolutionary period. Most important among these Soviet historians was M.N. Pokrovsky, whose influence was pre-eminent in the period up to 1934. Pokrovsky was eager to be rigorous in the application of Marxist categories, as he understood them, to Russian history and to play down any 'special factors' such as territorial exigencies, international relations, the role of great men, or the possibility of the relatively autonomous role of the state *vis à vis* social classes.

Having eliminated such factors from his purview, Pokrovsky was confronted with the problem that Russian 'feudalism' looked rather odd in comparison with its European equivalent. Pokrovsky's solution to this problem was to juggle his periodisation. In order to explain away the Russian autocracy, which did not fit easily into the Marxist model of feudalism, Pokrovsky pushed back the rise of the Russian bourgeoisie to the sixteenth century. Thus the consolidation of the Russian autocracy was associated in his schema with the political requirements of merchant capital.

Because Pokrovsky was not aware of, or rejected, Marx's model of a non-Western political economy, the appearance of the centralised state and bureaucratic structures were associated in his mind only with the period of the primitive accumulation of capital. He believed that 'bureaucracy can only grow on a bourgeois soil',[55] and hence the principal support of the Russian bureaucratic monarchy must *ipso facto* have been merchant capital – the first important stage in the development of industrial capitalism, and a stage that was exceptionally prolonged in Russia, lasting about four centuries.[56]

Although Pokrovsky's approach to Russian history was to attract almost universal condemnation with the deliberate initiation of a more 'patriotic' historiography in 1934,[57] his formulations were symptomatic of the attempt to view Russian history in terms of Western Europe. An alternative formulation of the genesis of the Russian autocracy, equally designed to minimise the significance of any particularities, was

[55] M.N. Pokrovsky, Preface to the 10th edn of *A Brief History of Russia, op.cit.*, Vol. I, p. 13.

[56] This aspect of Pokrovsky's work never really gained wide acceptance and the official Soviet periodisation extended the feudal stage up to the middle of the nineteenth century, and pushed back its origins as far as possible.

[57] In the period from 1934 the 'class' nature of the tsars was often played down completely, in favour of their heroic role in protecting all classes from foreign aggressors. The rise of the centralised state was also associated with defence factors rather than with economic class interests. Pokrovsky's characterisation of the Tsarist Empire as a 'prison of peoples' fell right out of favour in this period.

that the centralised state was brought into existence to defend the interests of the feudal landowners. Local unrest had arisen in the train of creeping enserfment, and the strong hand of the state was needed by the feudal lords to enforce the extension of their control over the land.

One way of avoiding the rather unconvincing characterisation of the Russian autocracy as merely the instrument of class rule by feudal lords was to fasten onto Marx and Engels' explanation of the relative autonomy of the absolutist state in Western Europe – i.e., that there was an equilibrium between economic classes which was exploited by the state. However, in the Western context this equilibrium was portrayed as arising between the feudal landowners and the rising bourgeoisie, and in the Russian context this would mean a return to Pokrovsky in so far as it pushed back the rise of the political signifi- cance of the bourgeoisie. One solution was to depict the equilibrium as arising between two sections of the same class – the aristocratic boyars and the lower-grade serving gentry.[58] Once again such a solution had obvious problems – the serving gentry were very much the creature of the state, rather than enjoying independent economic power.

One area outside the autocracy itself which has presented special problems to those attempting to fit Russian history to the Western pattern has been the need to discover a structure comparable in nature and functions to the medieval city in Western Europe. Noticeable among the work done in this area is that of B.A. Rybakov. Rybakov claims that a craft-guild system analogous to that of the West devel- oped in Russia during the fourteenth and fifteenth centuries,[59] and that a third estate emerged in this period as a significant progressive force.

The unorthodox and ultimately 'heretical' Russian Marxists, such as Trotsky, were to stress on the contrary, the absence of craft-guild development in Russia, or the absence of craft-guild culture in the cities.[60]

The work of M.N. Tikhomirov has also given prominence to the

---

[58] See John Keep, 'The Current Scene in Soviet Historiography', *Survey*, Winter 1973, p. 9.

[59] See B.A. Rybakov, *Remeslo drevnei Rusi*, Moscow, 1948, pp. 766, 775, 782. For an analysis of Rybakov, see A. Gerschenkron, *Europe in the Russian Mirror*, Four Lectures in Economic History, Cambridge U.P., 1970, pp. 142–143.

[60] See particularly Trotsky's 'Reply to M.N. Pokrovsky' (first published in *Pravda*, 1st and 2nd July 1922), included in an abridged form as Appendix 1 to Trotsky's *The History of the Russian Revolution*, tr. Max Eastman, Vol. I, London, Gollancz, 1932, pp. 469–475. The unorthodox Marxist approach to Russian history will be discussed in greater depth in the next section.

alleged creation of a third estate or burgher class in Russia, according to his dating in the period between the eleventh and thirteenth centuries. Curiously, Tikhomirov not only equates the role of the city in Russian history with the role of the city in the development of Western feudalism, but *also* with the city's role in the development of so-called Eastern or Asiatic feudalism.[61]

Marx, and after him Weber, saw the Oriental and Occidental city as fundamentally differing, both in structure and functions. However, because Tikhomirov was working within the unilinear model of history, he needed to universalise the Western city, which provides the essential transition between feudalism and capitalism in the model. According to Tikhomirov the third estate was such a vital force in Russian history that not even the Tatar invasion could impede its rise and rise.[62]

The Soviet historians have been concerned not only to prove that a viable burgher class develops within Russian 'feudalism', but also, as will be discussed in the next chapter, that Russian feudalism emerged at least as early as Germanic feudalism, and in the same manner – directly from tribal communalism. During the period 1929 to 1934 a number of authoritative writings by A.G. Prigozhin[63] were published on the theme of the absence of a slave epoch in Russian history, though unfortunately the author described the process of feudalisation as beginning considerably later in Eastern Europe than in Western Europe (Prigozhin was to be purged in 1935). This chronological oversight was soon rectified, and from the middle of the 1930s the concept of the parallel development of Germanic and Slavic feudalism out of tribal communalism was strongly entrenched. Its most influential proponent was B.D. Grekov (1882–1953), the historian of Kievan Rus. Grekov set back the beginnings of feudalism among the Eastern Slavs to the period between the sixth and eighth centuries. During this period, in Grekov's account, the fortified tribal settlements of the Eastern Slavs were gradually replaced by the feudal configuration of unfortified

[61] M.N. Tikhomirov, *Drevnerusskie goroda*, Moscow, Gos. izd. pol. lit., 1956, p. 436.

[62] *Ibid.*, p. 437. An important challenge to such a 'Western' interpretation of Russian feudalism has come from one of the editors of *Voprosy istorii*, A.M. Sakharov. Sakharov has rejected the view that in Russia there was a development of a third estate or revolutionary urban-element analogous to that in Western feudalism. He has argued that in fact guilds were unable to develop in Russia as they did in Europe, and that the Grand Duke of Moscow destroyed whatever municipal autonomy there was previously. (A.M. Sakharov, *Gorody Severo-Vostochnoi Rusi XIV-XV Vekov*, Moscow, 1959, pp. 129, 138).

[63] See A.G. Prigozhin, *Karl Marks i problemy sotsio-ekonomicheskikh formatsii*, Moscow, 1933; the title essay in the collection *Karl Marks i problemy istorii dokapitalisticheskikh formatsii*, Moscow, 1934; and 'O nekotorykh svoeobraziiakh russkogo feodalizma', *Izvestiia Gosudarstvennoi Akademii Istorii Material'noi Kul'tury*, No. 72 (1934).

village and fortified manor.[64] Grekov claimed that the Kievan economy was basically agricultural (rather than hunting/trading) and that feudal relations were predominant in the period. They took the form of various types of labour service, which preceded the legal institutionalisation of serfdom from the end of the sixteenth century.

Hence Soviet historiography has basically restricted itself within the unilinear schema of history and the categories Marx extrapolated from his study of the origins of Western capitalism.[65] This is in spite of the deviations mentioned, such as the appeal to special (and glorious) features of the Russian past for nationalistic purposes on the one hand, and the attempt to identify with the historical experience of the third world countries on the other. In general, the attempt to interpret Russian history in Western European terms has served to identify Soviet socialism with Marx's concept of socialism (the logical outcome of Western European history), and to endow the Soviet example with universal validity.

PLEKHANOV ON RUSSIAN HISTORY: THE ALTERNATIVE MARXIST APPROACH

The only Russian Marxist so far who has systematically applied Marx's concept of multilinear development to Russia's own history has been G.V. Plekhanov. Plekhanov employed the multilinear approach in his much neglected work, *History of Russian Social Thought.* Owing to his belief that movements in the economic base provided the real key to movements in the ideological superstructure, his account of the development of Russian social thought (unfinished when he died in 1918) was accompanied by an extensive account of Russian history. This outline comprises Part One of the *History* and will be discussed in detail in this section. It draws on the service-state theory as well as on Marx's

---

[64] B.D. Grekov, *Kiev Rus*, tr. from the 1949 Russian edition by E. Sdobnikov, Moscow, Foreign Languages Publishing House, 1959, p. 150.

[65] There have been recurrent tendencies towards dividing 'feudalism' into Western and Eastern models, state ownership of the land and serfs being an important element in the latter. Under this camouflage, an approach to the multilinear conception of history could be made, even in relation to Russia. For example, A.M. Sakharov has written: 'It is thus necessary to study the problem of the centralised [Russian] state in wide terms of the analogous processes not only in the countries of the West, but also in the countries of the East [...] state ownership of the land was extremely significant in a series of centralised feudal states in the East.' (A.M. Sakharov, 'Problema obrazovaniia russkogo tsentralizovannogo gosudarstva v sovetskoi istoriografii' *Voprosy istorii*, 1961, No. 9, p. 88).

theory of the Asiatic mode of production, and adds new dimensions to both.[66]

A brief discussion of the theoretical importance of Plekhanov's *History*, which, however, completely misfires owing to the author's limitations in the field of Marxist theory, is to be found in Samuel H. Baron's *Plekhanov: The Father of Russian Marxism*.[67] Baron considers any departure from the unilinear schema of history in which class struggle is the inexorable engine of development as a departure from Marxism *per se* ('from a Marxist it represented a large concession'[68]).

A more relevant, though very brief, discussion of Plekhanov's work, relying on the French translation of Part One, is to be found in an article by Umberto Melotti in *Il Terzo Mondo*, Vol. 3 (1970–1971).[69] Melotti gives serious consideration to Plekhanov's attempt to work out the implications of the concept of the Asiatic mode of production in its relation to Russia, and in its relation to a Marxist theory of alternative forms of historical development.

Plekhanov begins his survey of Russian history with a discussion of the politically-oriented historiographical theories that postulated either Russia's complete peculiarity, or its complete adherence to the pattern of Western European development. In the first half of the nineteenth century, both the Slavophiles, such as Kireevsky, and the Westernisers, such as Belinsky, had stressed the special character of Russia's historical

[66] Considering the importance of Plekhanov's *History* in relation to Marxist historiography, it is unfortunate that this work has fallen into almost complete oblivion. The only place in which it has been published *in full* is in Volumes XX–XXII of Plekhanov's *Sochineniia* edited by David Riazanov and published in Moscow 1923–1927 – needless to say, a bibliographical rarity today. When the work was being originally published during Plekhanov's lifetime the overdue Volume III was snatched away from him by the publishing firm 'Mir' and printed at the end of 1916 without Chapters X–XII. These were published separately after his death, and the unfinished Chapter XIII was published by Lev Deutsch in the Sbornik No. 1 of the Gruppa 'Osvobozhdenie Truda'. However when a new three volume edition of the work appeared in Moscow, 1918, under the auspices of the People's Commissariat for Culture, it appeared without Chapters X–XIII of Part III. A second edition of this incomplete version appeared in Moscow, 1925. The only (partial) translations of the work which have been undertaken have been into French and English. Plekhanov's daughter, Mme Eugenia Batault-Plékhanova, translated Part One of the *History* into French, and this translation was published in Paris by Bossard in 1926. A mimeographed English translation (largely by Boris M. Bekkar) of one of the least interesting parts of the *History*, Chapters I, II and III of Part III, was published in 1938 as a joint project between Columbia University and the New York City Board of Education. This was reprinted in 1967 by Howard Fertig, N.Y.

[67] Samuel H. Baron, *Plekhanov: The Father of Russian Marxism*, London, Routledge and Kegan Paul, 1963, pp. 295–307.

[68] *Ibid.*, p. 298.

[69] Part Two of a series by Umberto Melotti entitled 'Marx e il Terzo Mondo,' *Il Terzo Mondo*, Vol. 3, No. 11 (1970–1971), pp. 7–32.

path – although their evaluations of this special character were dia-metrically opposed.[70]

Later in the nineteenth century the Narodniks provided another stream of political thought which stressed the unique character of Russia's historical path. The Narodniks in fact made some effort towards developing a *Marxist* conception of Russian history which fully acknowledged the peculiarities of Russia's historical and geo-graphical situation. The Narodniks foreshadowed Trotsky's theory of *combined development* both in their analysis of Russia's past and in the implications they drew for the future. V.P. Vorontsov in particular argued strongly that Russia could utilise the experience of the capitalist West in order to avoid a capitalist stage and move straight into social-ism – drawing on the traditional Russian village communalism.[71] The Narodnik approach to Russian history tended to lose credibility *pari passu* with the disintegration of the *mir*, the pivotal element of the Narodnik conception.

By contrast to the Narodniks, the Russian Social Democrats, as seen above, sought to accommodate Russian history completely within the paradigm of development abstracted from Western European history.[72]

Plekhanov rejected the theory of the complete peculiarity of Russian development as being unscientific, in that it overlooked the operation of certain sociological regularities in all human societies.[73] One such regularity specifically noted by Plekhanov was the universal occurrence of a feudal phase, both in the history of Western Europe and in Egypt, Chaldea, Assyria, Persia, Japan and China.[74] Plekhanov however makes it clear that in his view this sociological regularity was confined to the existence at a given period of a system of service land; the form assumed by 'feudalism' in the East was so different from that assumed

[70] G.V. Plekhanov, *Istorii russkoi obshchestvennoi mysli*, Vol. I, first published by 'Mir' 1914, *Sochineniia*, Vol. XX (1925) p. 9. Vol. I includes the very important 'Introduction: an outline of the development of Russian social relations' (comprising Part One of the *History*), and the very interesting 'Movement of social thought in pre-Petrine Russia' (comprising Part Two). In subsequent citations this volume and edition of Plekhanov's *Istoriia* will simply be referred to in the following manner: Plekhanov, *History*, p. 9.

[71] See Andrzej Walicki, *The Controversy over Capitalism*, Oxford, Clarendon Press, 1969, for an account of V.P. Vorontsov's *The Fates of Capitalism in Russia*, St. Petersburg, 1882.

[72] For Plekhanov's criticisms of Pavlov-Sil'vansky, the authority for the 'European' interpretation of Russian history, see Plekhanov, *History*, pp. 10–11.

[73] *Ibid.*, pp. 11–12. The existence of universal laws of social development was intrinsic to the theory of historical materialism which Plekhanov helped to establish through his syste-matising theoretical works.

[74] *Ibid.*, p. 11. Ernest Mandel has (wrongly) concluded from this isolated passage that: 'Plekhanov eventually rejected its [the concept of the Asiatic mode of production's] relevance to Russia, and even to history in general.' (E. Mandel, *The Formation of the Economic Thought of Karl Marx*, London, NLB, 1971, p. 117).

by Western feudalism that it constituted an alternative path of development. In the East the landholders, despite their efforts, did not succeed in converting their feoffs into heritable property: 'The seigneurs [despots] not only in principle preserved the highest right to the land, but in practice continually availed themselves of it.'[75]

The characterisation of Russian history adopted by Plekhanov consisted in a theory of the 'relative peculiarity' of Russian development, as compared with either Western Europe or the East. Plekhanov saw world history as being divided into two major streams, the European and the Asiatic, and he saw Russia as distinguished by its oscillation between the two.[76]

In analysing the reasons for Russia's singularity, Plekhanov first rejected the view, which he saw as epitomised in Kliuchevsky, that this singularity was due to the absence of tribal stratification. According to the view under attack, the impulse to the development of social classes in Western Europe had been supplied by intertribal conquest, i.e., the political factor [moment] took precedence over the economic factor in the creation of the social fabric. In Russia, on the contrary, according to Plekhanov's account of Kliuchevsky, there ruled a mixed process whereby the formation of classes was determined by political and economic factors in turn.[77]

Having rejected the conquest theory, Plekhanov turned to the theories of geographical determinism associated with the service-state historians, such theories being consonant with his own tendency to expand the geographical component of the Marxist conception of history. He drew upon Solov'ev in particular, and attempted to demonstrate the correctness of Solov'ev's thesis that:

... in our country, as everywhere, the course of events has always been subordinate to natural conditions. The relative peculiarity of the Russian historical process is indeed explained by the relative peculiarity of that geographical environment in which the Russian people came to live and work.[78]

Plekhanov, however, was critical of Solov'ev's more facile interpretations of the way in which the geographical environment exercised its influence, for example Solov'ev's belief in the direct influence of

[75] Plekhanov, *History*, p. 79.
[76] *Ibid.*, pp. 14, 77.
[77] *Ibid.*, p. 16.
[78] *Ibid.*, p. 99. V.A. Anuchin has cited this passage as an illustration of the tribute paid by Plekhanov to geographical determinism. As we have seen Anuchin believes that geographical determinism is a much less dangerous phenomenon in relation to Marxism than geographical indeterminism, which led to voluntarism. (V.A. Anuchin, *Teoreticheskie problemy geografii*, Moscow, Gos. izd. geog. lit., 1960, p. 157.)

geography on national character and on class relations (as in his stone and wood thesis outlined above).[79] The hypothesis which Plekhanov found suggestive and useful was the correlation drawn by Solov'ev between the undiversified character of the East European plain and the relative slowness and peculiarity of Russia's social development.

Plekhanov adopted this hypothesis, though with added emphasis on the consequences for the mode of production and *hence* for social development in general.[80] As seen in Chapter Three Marx had described diversity of natural conditions as a vital factor in the rise of the division of labour, the stimulation of diverse wants and needs, the development of exchange and so on.[81] The absence of such diversity and its stimulus meant, according to Plekhanov, that the level of economic development on the Russian plain remained very low.

In the sphere of social relations, the lack of diversity of natural conditions resulted in a constant repetition of the same basic social unit. Plekhanov described the colonisation[82] of the Russian plain in terms drawn from biology: when the land became overcrowded the basic production unit, the village commune, underwent binary fission and a new identical one was established in the surrounding unpopulated spaces. The kind of differentiation between these cells which would have enabled them to form parts of a complex social organisation did not take place, as the natural conditions of production in the new unit tended to be the same as in the old.[83]

Plekhanov's analysis of the agricultural commune as the self-reproducing foundation of Russian despotism appears to be somewhat at variance with his simultaneous espousal of the views of B.N. Chicherin and A. Efimenko on the active role of the state in creating the commune system. In agreement with Chicherin and Efimenko, Plekhanov wrote that with the migration of population to the North-East towards the end of the Kievan period, the new arrivals settled as free peasants on their own land. The *obshchina* was artificially revived by the government through fiscal measures, as the means of bonding the peasants to the state.[84]

---

[79] Plekhanov, *History*, pp. 28–34.

[80] *Ibid.*, pp. 34–38.

[81] Marx, *Capital*, Vol. I, pp. 351–352; Vol. III, p. 177. Plekhanov, *History*, p. 36. Plekhanov quotes *Capital*, Vol. I, only.

[82] The idea of the special significance of the colonisation process in Russian history stems, as previously mentioned, from Pogodin and Solov'ev. Plekhanov expressly says: 'The history of Russia was the history of a country in which the process of colonisation was dragged out over many centuries.' (Plekhanov, *History*, p. 90).

[83] *Ibid.*, p. 35. Thus what was brought into being was 'a certain aggregate of cells, living *tissue*, but no complex *organism*.'

[84] *Ibid.*, p. 71.

Plekhanov had earlier written at greater length on the derivation of the village commune in his polemic against the Narodnik, V.P. Vorontsov (V.V.). In the mature Asiatic system as found in Russia, ancient Egypt, Byzantium, China and India, the village structure was not the same as the kinship structure found in primitive society, nor even a modified form of this, but rather the historical product of the expropriation of the direct producers by the state and by the upper classes or strata supported by the state.[85] According to Plekhanov the village system, as perfected in eighteenth-century Russia, for example, represented a form of the expropriation of the direct producers – the expropriation not only of their land, but also of their personal freedom.[86] In this area Plekhanov was substantially modifying Marx's account of Oriental society by adding to it those elements of the service-state theory which appeared to fit the empirical evidence more closely. As we have seen earlier, Marx was reluctant to acknowledge the 'Asiatic' village system as part of the infrastructure created by the state even where the state was inextricably involved in the process of social production.[87]

The other geographical factor which Plekhanov viewed as playing a vital role in the shaping of the mode of production and the development of social relations on the East European plain was the *extensiveness* of the arable land. This factor, together with the lack of diversity of the natural environment militated against the development of a complex social division of labour. Whereas the absence of diversity inhibited horizontal division, the availability of land inhibited vertical class division based on access to the means of production. Overcrowding on the Russian plain tended to lead to the colonisation of new areas rather than to the development of exploitative class relations and class struggle.[88]

According to Plekhanov it was only during periods when the possibility of migration was restricted, as during the period of the Tatar yoke, that the boyars were able to establish an independent grip over

---

[85] G.V. Plekhanov, *Obosnovanie narodnichestva v trudakh g. Vorontsova (V.V.), Sochineniia,* Vol. IX, pp. 135–138.

[86] *Ibid.*

[87] Jean Suret-Canale has recently criticised Marx's account of the genesis of the 'Asiatic' village system in terms similar to Plekhanov's. For example, 'In Africa, we can verify that it is precisely the appearance of class society which has generalised the village form as a convenient framework for class exploitation.' (Jean Suret-Canale, 'Problèmes théoriques de l'étude des premières sociétés de classes', *Recherches internationales à la lumière du marxisme* No. 57–58 (Jan.–April 1967), p. 15.)

[88] Plekhanov, *History,* p. 84.

the population, and become an important economic class. With the rise of the Muscovite state however, and with the conquest of Kazan and Astrakhan, the possibility of migration was again opened up, and only the state had the power to achieve the eventual bonding of the peasants to the land.[89]

The extensiveness of the Russian plain also neutralised the effects of the emergence of disaffected elements in the population. In Western Europe, according to Plekhanov, the disaffected elements on leaving the villages had congregated in the cities because there was nowhere else for them to go. Once congregated in the cities they had played a vital role in the creation of the new economic relations which eventually led to a monetary economy.[90] In Russia, on the other hand, the dissatisfied elements fled to the steppe where economic relations were even more backward than in the central regions of the state.[91]

The steppe in fact came to act as a safety-valve, preserving the old order from explosion. The Cossack revolts were themselves fruitless, in that they did not reflect the emergence of a new mode of production.[92] As in all 'Asiatic' systems, peasant rebellions provided superficial historical movement, without effecting any real social change.[93]

Thus Plekhanov followed Solov'ev in viewing the extensiveness and lack of diversity of the East European plain as the factors primarily responsible for the *retardation* of Russia's historical growth and the weak development of Russian feudalism. We have seen how on Plekhanov's account these factors inhibited the emergence of feudal relations between landowners and peasants. Because the *druzhinniki* tended to receive their income directly from the prince, or from trading operations carried out under his aegis, rather than from independent manorial land-holding, their position was much weaker than that of the equivalent military servitor class in feudal Europe.[94] Although the *druzhinniki* retained the right during the Kievan period to transfer their allegiance to another prince, Plekhanov interpreted such transfers as a sign of the weakness rather than of the strength of their position;

[89] *Ibid.*

[90] *Ibid.*, pp. 104–105.

[91] *Ibid.*, Cf. Leon Trotsky, *The History of the Russian Revolution, op.cit.*, Vol. I, p. 23. Trotsky sums up the historical consequences of the extensiveness of the Russian plain as follows: 'The process of social differentiation, intensive in the west, was delayed in the east and diluted by the process of expansion.' *(Ibid.)*

[92] Plekhanov, *History*, p. 105.

[93] See Trotsky's analysis of the role of peasant rebellions within Asiatic society, discussed in the next section.

[94] Plekhanov, *History*, pp. 51, 58.

they had no personal base from which to conduct a struggle with the prince for the satisfaction of their demands.[95]

In spite of these peculiarities, Russia was closer to the West (according to Plekhanov's pendulum view of Russian history) during the Kievan period than during the subsequent Muscovite period.[96] During the Kievan period Russia had participated more fully in international exchange with the West and the prince had been able to pay the expenses of the state from the proceeds of foreign trade.[97] There was as yet no need for the state to exercise control over the dominant mode of production (agriculture) or over the direct producers in order to fulfil the public function of defence.

Another geographical factor associated with the East European plain was largely responsible for the turn away from the West at the end of the Kievan period. This factor was the openness of the plain to the South-East and its contiguity with the steppes of central Asia, the home of the nomadic hordes whose incursions were becoming more and more serious towards the close of the Kievan period.[98] Such incursions resulted in a major shift of the Russian population away from the South-West towards the North-East in the second half of the twelfth century.

The geographical environment in the North was in general even more unfavourable to Western-style economic development than that of the South. There was no ready access from the North to markets for the luxury items (furs, wax, honey etc.) which had been the chief trade-commodities of Kievan Rus.[99] Furthermore, existing trade routes were cut off by the Tatar invaders. Deprived of foreign trade, the state had to meet its expenses from the agricultural labour of the people (rather than from their auxiliary industries, such as hunting). Agricultural labour, in turn, was less productive in the North and the state demands were correspondingly more oppressive. 'In order to ensure the fulfilment of these demands it was necessary [for the state] to increase the extent of its direct power over the rural population. The history of the population of the Volga basin consists in the process of their gradual enserfment [zakreposhchenie] to the state.'[100]

[95] *Ibid.*, p. 51.
[96] *Ibid.*, pp. 12, 52.
[97] *Ibid.*, pp. 58–59.
[98] *Ibid.*, p. 36. Plekhanov is here commenting on Solov'ev, who included the openness to nomadic invaders as one of the geographical factors influencing Russian history, but in Plekhanov's view underestimated the importance of the struggle with the nomads.
[99] *Ibid.*, p. 75.
[100] *Ibid.*, p. 64.

The extension of state power over primary production meant that a despotic system similar to that of the Asiatic empires came into being; and as in Asiatic societies, centralisation flourished in the absence of a complex social division of labour or social stratification. Plekhanov completely rejected the view that Muscovite absolutism was merely the political instrument of a feudal ruling class of the Western type. He pointed out that if the feudal class in Russia had enjoyed sufficient power to translate their aspirations into political terms, they would have brought into being the kind of aristocratic constitution found in Lithuania and Poland, rather than a despotism which severely curtailed their rights.[101]

The major difference between post-Kievan Russia and the classic Asiatic despotisms, as described by Plekhanov, was that in Russia it was not the need to provide economic preconditions of production such as the irrigation and flood-control systems of the East which brought the despotic state into being, but rather the need for defence against nomadic raiders.[102]

The nomadic peoples, because of their particular mode of production, (i.e. herding) were militarily stronger than the settled agricultural peoples of the Russian plain. The development of agriculture meant a division of labour between direct producer and warrior; the vast majority of the population became tied to the soil, while the military function devolved on a comparatively small group (i.e. the prince and his *druzhina*) who retained their mobility. Hence the weakness of the sedentary agricultural peoples of the East European plain *vis à vis* the nomadic raiders, and their need to compensate for this weakness by 'uniting in one great political union',[103] thus combining all their military resources. This in turn brought about the expansion of the power of the prince as the 'military watchman of the Russian soil'.[104]

According to Plekhanov the Russian situation was paralleled in Asia where it also happened that agricultural peoples were only able to prove themselves stronger than the nomads after they had succeeded in forming great despotic states.[105] This parallel had earlier been noted by Parvus, who had written:

---

[101] *Ibid.*, p. 96.
[102] *Ibid.*, pp. 53–54.
[103] *Ibid.*, p. 47.
[104] *Ibid.*, pp. 53–54, 57. The appellation *'voennyi storozh'* derives from Kliuchevsky.
[105] *Ibid.*, p. 100.

... Russia [...] was on the way to becoming an Asiatic despotism. She even surrounded herself with a Chinese wall. To convince oneself of this, it is sufficient to cast a glance at the line of fortresses of the Moscow state, built by the way, like the Chinese wall, as a defence against the attacks of the nomadic Mongols.[106]

The Chinese wall and its equivalents were symbolic of the type of centralised political organisation and state-directed corvée labour required to protect these agricultural states from the constant threat of invasion.

Although Plekhanov acknowledged parallels between the kind of defence function fulfilled by the Russian state and that fulfilled by Eastern states, he still awarded primacy in the emergence of the classical Asiatic despotism to the irrigation function. The defence burden was less onerous in the latter than in Russia, because Russia was confronted not only by barbarian nomads, but also by neighbours to the West who had achieved a much higher level of development.[107]

In discussing the military superiority of the nomads and the defeat of Kievan Rus, Plekhanov was at pains to argue that these facts by no means disproved the theory of historical materialism. The reason they might be thought to do so was that according to the materialist conception of history, military victory was ultimately determined by the comparative level of economic development of the combatants; and pastoral activity represented a lower stage of economic development than agriculture.[108]

Plekhanov's method of saving the theory was to advance another theoretical point, which could also be found in Marx. That is, that progress does not occur simultaneously in all spheres of society. The illustration used by Plekhanov was the superiority of hunting tribes over people of more 'advanced' stages of social development in the sphere of the plastic arts.[109] The same kind of asymmetrical development was the cause of the military superiority of the nomads. Nomadic herding, with its constant mobilisation to seek new pastures, gave rise to a warlike disposition and capacity, and the eventual military

[106] Parvus, *Rossiia i revoliutsiia*, St. Petersburg, izd. N. Glagoleva, 1906, p. 96.
[107] Plekhanov, *History*, p. 87.
[108] The question of the chronological priority of herding over agriculture is one in which Marx's assumptions appear to have been superseded by the recent growth of anthropological knowledge. See my Note on the Population Factor and also M. Godelier, 'La notion de "mode de production asiatique" et les schémas marxistes d'évolution des sociétés', *Sur le 'mode de production asiatique'*, C.E.R.M., Paris, Éditions sociales, 1969, p. 53.
[109] *Ibid.*, p. 44. Cf. Marx, *Grundrisse*, Introduction, p. 109. The examples given by Marx of the 'uneven development of material production' include the development of Greek art and of Roman private law. Marx warned that the 'concept of progress' should not be conceived in the usual abstractness'. *(Ibid.)*

advantage of societies based on agricultural production emerged only very slowly.[110]

An alternative attempt to bridge the apparent gap between the materialist conception of history and the 'facts' of Russian history consisted in the argument that Kiev Rus was in reality at a lower level of development of productive forces than the nomadic raiders. The argument involved the claim that the basic mode of production in Kiev Rus was hunting combined with trade,[111] hunting ranking below pastoral activity in any Marxist schema of history. Plekhanov completely rejected this argument, citing the historical evidence for his own view that the mode of production of Kiev Rus was basically agricultural, although the collection of furs and other forest products constituted an auxiliary industry which corresponded to the demands of the international (particularly the 'Greek') market.

The general functions of the centuries-long onslaught of nomadic invaders were, as Plekhanov stated them, the shifting of the centre of gravity of Russian history Northwards; the retardation of economic development both through devastation and through the cutting of trade links with Europe; and the strengthening of the princely power to meet the constant military emergencies. The period of actual Tatar rule witnessed the further strengthening of the grip of the princes over the land and its inhabitants in order to fulfil the payments due to the Khan, the princes being answerable for these payments.

However although the Tatar invasions functioned to push Russian socio-political relations into an ever more 'Eastern' framework, Plekhanov denied that this indicated in any way the so-called 'Tatarisation' of Russia. The actual borrowings were superficial, and could not be otherwise considering the relatively higher mode of production and greater complexity of social relations to be found among the Russians.[112] In Plekhanov's words:

---

[110] Plekhanov, *History*, p. 44. Plekhanov had earlier made this point in his *Fundamental Problems of Marxism* (1908), where he wrote that: 'advance in economic development, which exerts a considerable influence on the character of a given people, sometimes reduces its warlikeness to such a degree that it proves incapable of resisting an enemy economically more backward but more accustomed to warfare [. . .] it should, however, be remembered that even in such cases (China is a good example) economically backward *conquerors* gradually find themselves completely subjected to the influence of a *conquered* but economically more advanced people.' (*Fundamental Problems of Marxism*, tr. J. Katzer. Moscow, n.d., pp. 33–54.)

[111] Plekhanov criticises this argument specifically as it appears in the work of V.A. Keltuiala, *Kurs istorii russkoi literatury*, Part I, Book 2, St. Petersburg, 1911. (Plekhanov, *History*, pp. 38–44.)

[112] In an earlier part of his work Plekhanov had outlined the conditions of cultural borrowing as follows: 'the influence of one country on the configuration of inner relations of another is possible only when in the latter there are already social elements at hand, for

... The inner mode of life of the Russian state did not become like the mode of life of the nomads, but rather, like the mode of life of the great agricultural despotisms of the East. These despotisms also suffered from the steppe horsemen and even borrowed from them a certain amount in the way of culture.[113]

Plekhanov's criticisms of the concept of Tatarisation were directed against the German historian A. Brückner, and against the latter's 'idealist' account of the influence of Tatar political ideas and methods on Russian development.[114]

Brückner's approach to Russian history has still been very much alive in the twentieth century. The following is from Vernadsky's *A History of Russia*:

... The Mongolian state was built upon the principle of unquestioning submission of the individual to the group, first to the clan and through the clan to the whole state. This *principle** was in the course of time impressed thorougnly upon the Russian people. It led to the system of universal service to the state which all without differentiation were forced to give. Under the influence of Mongolian *ideas**, the Russian state developed on the basis of universal service. All classes of society were made a definite part of the state organization. Taken altogether, these *ideas** amount to a peculiar system of state socialism [sic]. The political *theory** developed into a finished *plan** later, in the Moscow Kingdom and the Russian Empire; but the basis of the *idea** of state service was laid down during the period of Tartar domination.[115]

Even K.A. Wittfogel, because of his very desire to correlate despotism and hydraulic agriculture,[116] has to some extent provided a similarly 'idealist' account of the impact of the Tatars on Russia. As the hydraulic mode of production did not exist in Russia, Wittfogel has portrayed the Tatars as a transmission belt, importing the despotic system of government from China to Russia. Once infected by these political ideas ('the Mongol bacillus'), the Russians developed their own system based on them.

Although disagreeing with the Tatarisation thesis, and viewing the socio-political changes in Russia as a *response* to Tatar pressure rather

whom it is advantageous to assume the role of bearer [of this influence].' Thus, for example, proto-feudal elements in the Lithuanian borderlands of Russia assumed the role of bearer of influence from Poland, where the rights and privileges of the feudal nobility had developed a more advanced form in accordance with the comparatively advanced economic and social condition of the country. *(Ibid.,* p. 33.)

[113] *Ibid.,* fn. pp. 247–248.

[114] Baron, in his biography, mistakenly writes that: 'clearly recognizable in Plekhanov's history are the ideas [. . .] of Brückner on the influence of the Mongols'. What is actually present in Plekhanov's work is a *refutation* of Brückner's views. (See Samuel H. Baron, *Plekhanov . . . , op.cit.,* p. 296.)

[115] George Vernadsky, *A History of Russia*, 3rd rev. edn, New Haven, Yale U.P., 1951, p. 56.

* My emphasis.

[116] Wittfogel's geographical determinism is closely related to that of Plekhanov.

than as cultural borrowing, Plekhanov agreed that at the end of the period of the Tatar yoke the newly emergent Muscovite state was quite different in character from the absolute monarchies developing in Western Europe. In France, for example, the rise of a monetary economy meant that kings as early as Philip the Fair were able to begin liberating themselves from dependence on a noble militia. On the other hand, the French kings were compelled to leave sacrosanct the rights of the nobles over their land.[117] The reverse of these two circumstances held true in Muscovy; the persistence of natural economy meant continued reliance on a gentry army, and on the other hand, there was a steady retreat of allodial aristocratic forms of landholding (*votchina*) in favour of service land (*pomest'e*).

As sketched out above in reference to the changes between Kievan and post-Kievan Rus, there took place a gradual transformation of all land into a 'state fund forming the economic basis of a system of national defence'.[118] The population became bound to the state either as stipendiary civil and military servitors (the upper classes) or as producers of the goods necessary for the support of these echelons (the townspeople and peasantry).

To illustrate the differences between the Muscovite and Western political systems, as perceived by contemporaries, Plekhanov drew on the accounts of the sixteenth-century travellers, Fletcher and von Herberstein. Dr Giles Fletcher, an ambassador from Elizabeth I to the Tsar Fedor in 1588, had written, for example:

> ... The Manner of their government is much after the Turkish fashion: which they seem to imitate as neare as the countrie, and reach of their capacities in pollitique affayres, will give them leave to doo.[119]

Von Herberstein had summed up the situation of all ranks of society in relation to the princes as follows: 'All confess themselves to be Chlopos [*kholopy*], that is, serfs of the prince.'[120]

In Plekhanov's interpretation, the bondage of the Russian population to the state recounted by the travellers was 'the necessary consequence

---

[117] Plekhanov, *History*, p. 83.

[118] *Ibid.*

[119] G. Fletcher, *Of the Russe Common Wealth* (first pub. London, 1591), London, Hakluyt Society, 1856 (First Series, No. XX), p. 26. Quoted by Plekhanov from a Russian edition, *History*, p. 79.

[120] Freiherr Sigmund von Herberstein, *Rerum Moscoviticarum Commentarii* (first published Vienna, 1549), translated as *Notes Upon Russia* by Sigismund von Herberstein, Hakluyt Society, 1851, (First Series, No. X), reprinted Burt Franklin, N.Y., n.d., Vol. I, p. 95. This description was taken up by Jean Bodin in Book Two, Chapter Two of the *Six Books of the Republic* when he included Muscovy in the list of countries approximating to Aristotle's category of despotic government.

of those conditions in which the Russian people had to struggle for their historical existence once they had settled in the Upper Volga area and had been gradually united by Moscow. Once having arisen, this consequence became a cause – a powerful hindrance to the further economic and cultural progress of Greater Russia.'[121]

One way in which the consequence of natural conditions became transmuted into an active cause was through the influence of ideology. The ideologist *par excellence* of Muscovite absolutism was, in Plekhanov's view, S. Peresvetov.[122] Peresvetov was the contemporary of Jean Bodin, and the differences in approach of these two ideologists reflected the different courses which the history of their countries were taking.[123]

Bodin's work expressed the interests of the third estate in the period when they joined forces with the French monarchs for the purpose of the struggle against the feudal nobility. For this reason, Bodin supported the concept of an absolutism which would clear away feudal anachronisms, but would at the same time respect personal and civil freedoms and property rights.[124]

Peresvetov, on the other hand, reflected the outlook of the lower echelons of the service class (the *dvorianstvo*), who in Muscovy replaced the third estate as the chief support of absolutism in its struggle with the feudal classes (the boyars).[125] Peresvetov, like indeed Bodin, held up the Turkish system of non-heritable service lands as a model to be preferred to the existing forms of noble land tenure.[126] However Peresvetov's

[121] Plekhanov, *History*, p. 94.
[122] Peresvetov's writings had been republished shortly before Plekhanov began work on his history, in the addenda to V.F. Rzhiga, *I.S. Peresvetov, publitsist XVI veka*, 2 vols., Moscow, 1908.
[123] Plekhanov, *History*, pp. 150–169.
[124] As seen in Chapter One, Bodin favoured what he called Royal (constitutional) Monarchy but not Seigneurial Monarchy (Aristotle's despotic government) which Bodin described as still existing in Asia, Ethiopia, Turkey, Tartary and Muscovy.
[125] Cf. a recent Soviet history in which an account (by A.I. Pashkov) of Peresvetov appears under the rubric 'The Spokesmen of the Landed Nobility'. While acknowledging Peresvetov's hostility to the 'boyars and big feudalists' Pashkov claims that: 'Peresvetov clearly expresses in his works the ideology and interests of the nobility, as well as its political and economic demands, during the period of the formation of the centralised state.' (*A History of Russian Economic Thought: Ninth through Eighteenth Centuries*, ed. John M. Letiche, University of California Press, 1964, p. 129). Because orthodox Soviet historiography views the autocracy as the instrument of the feudal ruling class, the ideologists of the autocracy must *ipso facto* also represent the interests of that class. Accordingly, Pashkov describes Peresvetov's attacks on allodial land-holding, on the system of *kormlenie*, and on centrifugal feudal tendencies, as the work of a feudal spokesman.
[126] Although Peresvetov also recommended monetary payment as the preferable form of reimbursement for service – one which would enforce the dependence of those in the state service on the central treasury. (*Ibid.*, p. 160). Cf. Max Weber, according to whom 'the

admiration for the Turkish system was more thorough-going than that of Bodin, whose main interest was in how the system held in check its class of military servitors. Peresvetov praised, for example, the organisation of janissaries, which he viewed as the Turkish equivalent of the *oprichnina* – an elite chosen for their qualities rather than for their birth. He also supported the pretensions of the Tsar to unlimited power and god-like authority. He did not demand, as Bodin did, that the monarch should obey natural law and protect property rights.

Ivan IV, Peresvetov's master, fully endorsed the interpretation of his role as seigneur or despot, both in practice and in his correspondence with Prince Kurbsky. 'Everything that belonged to the state or to the individual inhabitants of the state, was according to his firm conviction, the property of the state. [...] He was convinced that the boyars ate his bread.'[127]

Plekhanov described the historical significance of Ivan the Terrible as resting on the fact that he more or less completed the conversion of the Muscovite state into a 'monarchy of the Eastern type'.[128] As we have seen, Plekhanov believed that once this system was imposed, it had the same effect as it did in Asia proper, of contributing to a general socio-economic stagnation. The system of state control over the land and population (i.e., control over the production and allocation of surplus value) was, by the Marxist criteria discussed earlier, inevitably non-progressive, being inimical to the emergence of potentially dynamic class from within itself.

Into such a system, the dialectic of social development could only be reintroduced through the impact of external factors. Both Marx and Plekhanov believed that in Russia these were provided by the presence of neighbouring countries to the West which possessed more dynamic economies and which posed a military threat to Russia.

Due to the threat from the West, the very consolidation of the Muscovite state under Ivan III and Vasily III was accompanied by the first seeds of the eventual transformation of the system – the attempts to introduce Western military techniques. The gradual modernisation of the army over the centuries was to bring in its train changes in other spheres – the introduction to a certain extent of a monetary economy, the release of the upper classes from service, etc. The last area to be

development of a money economy [...] is the primary social and economic condition of bureaucracy in its modern form [...]' Otherwise there is a constant tendency by officials towards the 'appropriation of prebends' and refeudalisation.

[127] *Ibid.*, p. 193.
[128] *Ibid.*

affected by these changes was the peasantry, the human resource on which the whole economy rested.

The simultaneous process of consolidation and transformation of the Asiatic system was illustrated by the reign of Peter the Great. Under Peter, in connection with the modernisation of the army, the nobility were to some extent emancipated from their service role, gained increased control over their land, and in general became more like the nobility of the Western absolutisms. In contrast, the service that the peasantry owed to the state and to the *pomeshchiki* became ever more onerous. 'Consequently the social position of the "well-born" was changing in one direction – in the direction of the West – at the same time that the social position of the "base-born" was continuing to change in the completely opposite direction – in the direction of the *East*.'[129]

Plekhanov's characterisation of Petrine Russia was very close to that of Marx – they both rejected the notion that Peter's reforms involved the genuine Westernisation of society. Plekhanov found great historical significance, though doubtful authenticity, in the saying attributed to Peter that: 'We need Europe for a few decades – but then we must turn our backs on it.'[130]

The question of the role of external military and financial pressure on internal development has always been a difficult one for Marxist historiography. To grant a determining role to external contingencies (the 'legitimation of chance'), has seemed a derogation of the laws of development intrinsic to the process of social production. Somewhat more elasticity has been shown in demonstrating the *retarding* role of some external contingencies – as in the Leninist theory of imperialism.

Pokrovsky, in his influential *History of Russia*, specifically rejected the influence of external military and financial pressure as an explanation of Russia's 'turn to the West'. This explanation had been put forward by Solov'ev and Kliuchevsky, and Plekhanov argued that, *pace* Pokrovsky, there was no need for a Marxist to deny their findings. According to Plekhanov it was by no means *metaphysical*, as Pokrovsky suggested, to claim that the Asiatic form of state, holding as it did a monopoly over economic and social initiative, might itself introduce changes into the social structure as conscious policy.[131] In the case of

[129] *Ibid.*, p. 118.
[130] *Ibid.*, p. 116.
[131] *Ibid.*, pp. 246–263.

Russia this policy arose from the very real threat from without to the existence of the state, which might be called *external* necessity.

Moreover, although only those associated with the state apparatus were in a position to be continually aware of the external threat and to draw up long-term policies to meet it, there was also a direct response from the rest of the population to any situation of national danger.[132] Thus Plekhanov argued that *co-operation* between social classes in the face of external threat had been more important as a factor in the development of social relations in Russia than the *struggle* between social classes.[133] Hence the general acquiescence of the peasantry in their service to the gentry class while the latter were themselves visibly providing service to the state in military and other forms.[134]

The editor of Plekhanov's *Sochineniia*, David Riazanov, in an uncharacteristically inept introduction to the *History*, refers, as his only comment on the theoretical content, to the criticism of the class co-operation thesis made by Pokrovsky.[135] For Pokrovsky, the proposition that under certain historical circumstances internal class struggle might be only of secondary importance betokened a direct betrayal of the working class; for example, it provided the theoretical basis for the 'defencist' attitude adopted by Plekhanov during the First World War. Riazanov modified what he termed Pokrovsky's 'polemical historiography' to the extent of describing Plekhanov's propositions as the logical outcome of the concrete political situation of the 1890's, when there was a need for the tactic of coalition with the liberal bourgeoisie. I.e., Plekhanov's theoretical ideas corresponded to a phase of the workers' struggle that was past history, rather than constituting a deliberate betrayal of the working class.

Needless to say, neither Pokrovsky nor Riazanov were to discuss Plekhanov's *History* in the light of its employment of Marx's concept of the Asiatic mode of production. The political implications of systematising Marx's own comments on Russian history have remained until this day an effective deterrent to a serious Marxist analysis of Plekhanov's *History*.

Plekhanov's own political perspective was in fact very closely tied to his mature interpretation of Russian history, and to his belief in the possibility of alternative forms of historical development – the belief

---

[132] *Ibid.*, p. 251.
[133] *Ibid.*, p. 13.
[134] *Ibid.*, p. 110.
[135] *Ibid.*, Editor's Preface, pp. xiii–xiv.

expressed theoretically in his adoption of Marx's concept of Asiatic society. Although Plekhanov saw the swing to the West as being well under way in Russia, with Russian capitalism developing along similar lines to Western capitalism, he was always hypersensitive to any tendencies which he felt might serve to reverse this swing. Thus while he had claimed that any description of post-1861 Russia as a 'kind of European China' was utterly false,[136] he was still to speak out against the possibility of a restoration of 'our politico-economic Chineseness',[137] a possibility Plekhanov associated with the Bolshevik policies of nationalisation of land.

With Russia's 'Asiatic' past always in mind, Plekhanov was opposed to any political programme that might tend to strengthen the central power and retard the devolution of social initiative from the state to Western-style political classes. Thus already in his polemics with the Narodniks, Plekhanov was warning against the dangers of a would-be socialist revolution brought about when the economic and social conditions were not yet ripe for it. Should such a revolution take place when the masses were still incapable of bringing socialism into being on their own initiative:

it [Narodnaia Volia] will have to seek salvation in the ideals of 'patriarchal and authoritarian communism', only modifying those ideals so that the national production is managed not by the Peruvian 'sons of the sun' and their officials but by a socialist caste.[138]

Apropos of another Narodnik, Plekhanov wrote:

Let us suppose that the peasant commune is really our anchor of salvation. But who will carry out the reforms postulated by Nikolai-on? Tsarist government? Pestilence is better than such reformers and their reforms! Socialism being introduced by Russian policemen – what a chimera![139]

According to Plekhanov, the absolute prerequisite of a true socialist revolution in Russia was a period of development under a democratic constitution, which would 'guarantee the workers the "rights of citizens" as well as the "rights of man" and give them by universal suffrage, the possibility to take an active part in the political life of the country.'[140]

---

[136] G.V. Plekhanov, *Sochineniia*, Vol. XXIV, p. 320.

[137] G.V. Plekhanov, 'K agrarnomu voprosu v Rossii', *Dnevnik sotsial-demokrata*, No. 5, March 1906, *Sochineniia*, Vol. XV, p. 37.

[138] G.V. Plekhanov, *Socialism and the Political Struggle* (Geneva, 1883), *Selected Philosophical Works*, London, Lawrence and Wishart, Vol. I, 1961, p. 114.

[139] Plekhanov to Engels, *Perepiska K. Marksa i F. Engel'sa s russkimi politicheskimi deiateliami*, 2nd edn, Moscow, 1951, p. 334. Cited in A. Walicki, *The Controversy over Capitalism, op.cit.*, p. 127.

[140] G.V. Plekhanov, *Socialism and Political Struggle, loc.cit.*, p. 116.

Once having committed himself to Marxism, in the early 1880's, Plekhanov became deeply suspicious of any political programme that depended on the revolutionary activity or participation of the peasantry. The peasantry were categorised in Plekhanov's Marxist historiography as the bulwark of the old order. They were revolutionary only in so far as they wished to dispossess the gentry – whom they saw as usurping land which had once been theirs by right of service, but to which they now had no legitimate claim.[141]

The peasantry instinctively sided with the autocracy against any attempt on the part of the gentry class to increase their privileges; they were also the staunch enemies of 'Westernisation', which they identified with oppression by the upper classes.[142] The Russian peasantry, like the peasantry of the Asiatic despotisms (and under the influence of the same mode of production with its social isolation and narrow horizons) regarded the head of state as semi-divine, although occasionally misled by evil advisers.[143] The ultimate demand of the peasantry was for a redivision of all land, a demand that Plekhanov saw as an atavism reflecting the belief that all land belonged to the Tsar, who had a duty to keep it all in *tiaglo* by means of periodic redivisions.

The general function of revolutionary peasant movements within Asiatic systems was simply to renew and revitalise the system on the old basis – through a change of dynasty etc.

... Chinese social revolutions consisted in the confiscation of land from the 'retainers' [of the old regime] and returning it to the Leviathan-State, after which the old history began again, engendering new 'retainers', giving rise to new revolutions, restoring the old 'Chineseness' [Kitaishchina].

We do not need Chineseness. Therefore we support the peasant movement *only* to the extent that it destroys the old order, but not to the extent that it strives to restore something in comparison with which this old order is itself a new and progressive phenomenon.[144]

The differing Marxist schemas of Russian history outlined in this chapter, that stressing the Western (universal) character of Russian history, and that stressing its non-Western (particularistic) character, were to become an integral feature of the clash between the Bolshevik

[141] Plekhanov, *History*, p. 112.
[142] *Ibid.*, pp. 116–119.
[143] Cf. the Russian saying quoted by Marx: 'The tsar is great, God is greater still, but the tsar is *still young*.' (Marx, *Die Neue Rheinische Zeitung*, No. 129, 29 Oct. 1848, *Werke*, Vol. 5, p. 442).
[144] Plekhanov, 'K agrarnomu voprosu v Rossii', *loc.cit.*, p. 36. Cf. Trotsky, and also the *Aziatchiki* of the 1925–1931 discussions cited in Chapter Two.

and Menshevik factions of Russian Social Democracy, and on a personal level of the clash between Lenin and Plekhanov. Lenin's first meeting with Plekhanov in 1895, was marked by an argument in which Lenin, as Plekhanov recalled:

> ... tried to convince me that feudalism in Russia was of the same kind as in the West. I replied that the similarity in this instance was no greater than that between the 'Russian Voltaire' – Sumarokov – and the genuine French Voltaire; but my arguments scarcely convinced my companion.[145]

Plekhanov is here more realistic than either K.A. Wittfogel or those past or present Soviet supporters of the AMP concept who have tended to exaggerate Lenin's understanding and acceptance of it in order to borrow his mantel. Although Lenin had excerpted passages from Marx and Engels' correspondence on the subject, he never himself used the concept for analytic purposes. He did however frequently use the term 'semi-Asiatic' as a rhetorical flourish to convey his despair at the 'backwardness' or 'barbarism' of Russia. It can be seen from the much-quoted passages in, for example, 'The right of Nations to self-determination' (1914) that where Lenin actually uses the term 'Asiatic despotism' it is only as a synonym for a patriarchal pre-capitalist social and political system.

The argument from history reached a peak at the Fourth Congress of the R.S.D.L.P. in 1906. The controversy over the proposals for nationalisation of land which came to a head at the Congress, was essentially an argument between those who viewed Russian history in terms of West European categories and those who viewed it at least partly in terms of the Asiatic mode of production. The former, such as Lenin, drew the conclusion that feudal vestiges were the main enemy and that nationalisation was the means of eliminating these once and for all. The latter, including Plekhanov, Martov and Martynov, saw the centralised autocratic character of the Russian state as the main enemy, and regarded nationalisation as the revival of the old state monopoly over the land, the cornerstone of the whole despotic system Russia had suffered under.

The political significance of the historiographical debate was later summarised by a Soviet spokesman as follows:

> ... At the Fourth (Unity) Congress in Stockholm, Lenin raised precisely the objection that Plekhanov was attempting to construct the Menshevik conception of the Russian revolution out of his analysis of the 'Asiatic character of Russian

[145] Em. Gazganov, 'Istoricheskie vzgliady G.V. Plekhanova', *Istorik-Marksist*, Vol. 7, 1928, p. 110.

despotism' and of the Russian commune. If Marx and Engels really took the viewpoint of acknowledging an 'Asiatic' mode of production in Russia, then it was not Lenin who was right as we have thought and believed up till now, but Plekhanov: it was Menshevism that was right, and not Bolshevism![146]

An extremely damaging admission as we have seen in this chapter.

At the congress, Plekhanov described the nationalisation of land so energetically advocated by the Bolsheviks as the economic characteristic which Russia had, for much of its history, shared in common with Asia:

... The agrarian history of Russia is more like the history of India, Egypt, China and other Eastern despotisms than it is like the history of Western Europe. There is nothing surprising in this, because the economic development of every nation takes place under distinctive historical conditions. With us the situation consisted in the fact that the land together with its cultivators was bound to the state, and on the basis of this bondage there developed Russian despotism. In order to shatter despotism, it is necessary to eliminate its economic foundation.[147]

The Menshevik faction at the Congress favoured the programme drawn up by P.P. Maslov for putting the distribution of land under the control of municipal committees. These municipal committees would serve as a concrete form in which to build up democracy from below and provide a bulwark against the danger of restoration of the old order.[148]

The possibility of a restoration, such as that which occurred after the French Revolution, was one that was heavily stressed by Plekhanov and constituted an important element in the justification of the Menshevik programme. The Bolsheviks argued that in fact the restoration in France did not involve the restoration of feudalism – any attempt to confiscate the land from the peasants and return it to the nobility would only have succeeded in transforming the peasants once more from a reactionary into a revolutionary force and would hence have been self-defeating.[149]

Martynov attempted to answer this argument of the Bolsheviks, albeit in a manner which is rendered confusing by his rather loose employment of the term 'feudal'. According to Martynov:

[146] A. Prigozhin, 'Problema obshchestvennykh formatsii', *Pod znamenem marksizma*, 1930, No. 7–8, p. 165.

[147] G.V. Plekhanov, Speech in support of Maslov's agrarian programme, delivered at the Fourth Congress of the R.S.D.L.P., in *Chetvertyi (ob"edinitel'nyi) s"ezd RSDRP: Protokoly*, Moscow, Gos. izd. pol. lit., 1969, p. 59.

[148] See for example P.P. Maslov, (using the pseudonym John), Speech at the Fourth Congress, *Protokoly, op.cit.*, p. 57.

[149] Matveev (Bazarov-Rudnev), Speech attacking Maslov's agrarian programme and Plekhanov's defence of it, *Protokoly, op.cit.*, pp. 92–93.

... The restoration of feudalism in our country would be impossible after the expropriation of *pomeshchik* land, if the basis of our feudalism consisted in *pomeshchik* agriculture. But the fact is that Russian feudalism is first and foremost state feudalism [sic]. It is formed on the basis of the enslavement of the nation by the state. And our *pomeshchik* landownership itself did not evolve out of a *votchinnik* [patrimonial] form of agriculture, but out of the service relationship of the *pomeshchiki* to the state. Therefore Plekhanov is right when he affirms that the principle of nationalisation would in no way change those economic relationships on the basis of which our Asiatic despotic structure grew up [...][150]

Plekhanov's own defence of his propositions concerning the possibility of restoration and the consequent dangers of nationalisation was considerably more fluent:

... One comrade in answer to me has said: 'but in France the restoration did not bring back the old order'. To this Comrade Martynov has already replied, to the effect that such an argument is untenable. The restoration did not bring back the vestiges of feudalism, so much is true. But that which corresponds to these vestiges in our country is our old bondage of the land and its cultivators to the state, our old peculiar nationalisation of the land. In the event of a restoration here, it would be that much easier to bring back this nationalisation as you yourselves demand the nationalisation of land, and as you remain unconcerned that this is a legacy of our old half-Asiatic order. Besides which, it is generally known that the land belonging to the aristocrats which was not distributed in France during the revolutionary period, the land which remained in the hands of the state, was returned to its old owners. Do you really want the same thing to happen in our country?[151]

Lenin's sole concession to Plekhanov on this issue was to admit that the only guarantee against restoration, whether nationalisation, municipalisation or distribution of the land were attempted, was the success of the socialist revolution in the West. The petit-bourgeoisie (peasantry), he argued, would inevitably desert the revolution once they had achieved their limited goals, and small commodity production was the dominant mode of production in Russia. However, such a restoration taking place in the unlikely event of the failure of the socialist revolution in Europe, would constitute not an Asiatic restoration ('A sheer absurdity in the epoch of capitalism') but a restoration of capitalism.[152]

The debate between the Mensheviks and the Bolsheviks over nationalisation consisted largely in the participants firing right past

---

[150] A. Martynov, Speech on the agrarian question, *Protokoly, op.cit.*, p. 111.

[151] G.V. Plekhanov, Concluding speech on the agrarian question, *Protokoly, op.cit.*, pp. 140–141.

[152] Lenin, Concluding speech on the agrarian question, *Protokoly, op.cit.*, p. 127; *Report on the Unity Congress of the RSDLP* (A letter to the St. Petersburg Workers) (first pub. 1906), *Collected Works*, Vol. 10. pp. 331–335.

each other's heads. As seen, this was because their assumptions about Russian history and its political lessons were diametrically opposed.

The Mensheviks feared that, as before, revolution would come from above, the state would continue to monopolise political and economic initiative, and socialism in the Western sense of the word would disappear over the horizon. They believed that the consolidation of Westernisation was the essential prelude to socialism – a period of bourgeois liberalism during which the devolution of initiative from the state apparatus to the masses would become possible.

Plekhanov's concept of Asiatic restoration was to be taken up in 1918 by Martov, in his critique of Bolshevik policies. Martov wrote that the Bolshevik regime was merely continuing a bureaucratic dictatorship based on the 'atomisation of the masses', and that it was acting to intensify and strengthen that atomisation – or 'incapacity for organised collective self-activity'.[153] Instead of socialism the Bolsheviks had brought about a renewal of Russia's 'monstrous system of Asiatic government.'[154]

For Plekhanov, and the Mensheviks in general, the only way forward appeared to be through acquiring at least the latter phases of West European development. Plekhanov, like Marx, believed that non-Western forms of development were in themselves static, and incapable of giving rise to higher stages of development. Hence the historical convergence of paths of development under the standardising influence of world capitalism was the necessary prerequisite of socialism, which would similarly be of a both Western and universal nature.

MODERNISATION IN A NON-WESTERN MILIEU:
TROTSKY ON RUSSIA'S PAST AND PRESENT

Although no-one but Plekhanov has applied Marx's concept of the Asiatic mode of production to Russian history systematically, other Marxists have concerned themselves with the special character of Russia's historical development and the so-called 'Asiatic' features of this development. One such Marxist was L.D. Trotsky, who never wrote a full-length account of pre-Revolutionary Russia, but provided

---

[153] Iu. Martov, 'Diktatura i demokratiia,' *Za god*, p. 30, quoted in I. Getzler, *Martov*, Melbourne U.P., 1967, p. 186.
[154] Iu. Martov to A.N. Stein, 26 June 1920, quoted in I. Getzler, *Martov, op.cit.*, p. 195.

a number of sketches intended to throw light on the way the revolution might develop there.

Trotsky, like Plekhanov, borrowed a great deal from the service-state historians. Unlike Plekhanov, Trotsky never directly referred to Marx's concept of the Asiatic mode of production, although he echoed it very closely at times. He commented, for example, on the effects of the state appropriation of surplus value in hampering the process of social crystallisation and the development of privileged classes.[155] He did not go on from there, however, to a theory of the non-dynamic nature of such a system of state appropriation, as did Marx and Engels. In part this might be expected, as Trotsky by contrast with Marx and Plekhanov, viewed the peculiarities of non-Western history as giving rise to non-Western forms of revolutionary *development*.

The peculiarities of Russian history Trotsky attributed to the same kind of geographical and external factors as had seemed operative to Plekhanov. Indeed Trotsky brought into his explanation an additional geographical factor – the climate – which Plekhanov did not use except to explain the low level of productivity in the North-East. According to Trotsky, the long Russian winter, with its enforced respite from agricultural labour, meant that manufacturing industry remained in the status of an auxiliary to agricultural labour for far longer than in the West, where it became concentrated in the towns and more specialised in character.[156] Hence the climate was at least partially responsible for the underdeveloped character of the division of labour in this basic sphere of social life.

Trotsky also shared with Plekhanov an awareness of the problems raised for Marxist historiography by the large role they both attributed to external factors in the development of the Russian state. Trotsky wrote:

... It is difficult to say what shape Russian social development would have taken if it had remained isolated and under the influence of inner tendencies only. It is enough to say that this did not happen. Russian social life, built up on a certain internal economic foundation, has all the time been under the influence, even under the pressure of its external social-historical milieu.[157]

As we have seen, Plekhanov argued that external factors had been a formative influence on Russian history. The constant pressure from the

[155] Leon Trotsky, *Results and Prospects* in *The Permanent Revolution and Results and Prospects*, N.Y., Pioneer Publishers, 1965, p. 171.
[156] *Ibid.*, 179–180.
[157] *Ibid.*, p. 170.

Tatars, in combination with the (geographically determined) low level of internal development, resulted in the defensive creation of a despotic system in Russia. As pointed out before, Plekhanov employed a theory of uneven development to account for the military superiority of the Tatars over an economically more advanced nation, and their corresponding large impact.

Plekhanov had then gone on to argue that external factors had played an even greater role in Russia than in other countries subject to the threat of nomadic incursions, because of the simultaneous threat from neighbours to the West who were at a higher level of development. However, external pressure not only gave rise to the 'Asiatic' system of centralised control over economic resources within Russia, but also, in the form of the threat from the West, provided the stimulus for the eventual development beyond this system. The Russian government had beeen forced to set in train the development of a more dynamic economic system in order to compete with the economic and military might of the West.

Trotsky's exposition of the role of external factors in Russian history bypassed the problem (for Marxist historiography) tackled by Plekhanov, the problem how a nation at a lower level of economic development could influence the internal evolution of a nation at a higher level of economic development. Trotsky explained the apparently large role played by external factors in the inner development of Russia as follows: external factors were of greater importance in Russia than in Marx's general model of social development because the latter was extrapolated from the development of the Western European nations. The countries of Western Europe, in their mutual struggle for existence, depended on more or less identical economic bases. Russia, however, in its struggle for existence, had to contend with nations on a much higher level of development than its own.[158] For this reason the 'normal' tendencies of internal economic and social development were to a large degree superseded by the need for the state to appropriate a disproportionately large part of the surplus product.[159]

Not only did the Russian state, under external pressure, consume a comparatively large share of the surplus value, but it also attempted to accelerate economic development from above, and to force the development of social differentiation on a primitive economic foundation.[160]

[158] *Ibid.*, p. 171.
[159] *Ibid.*
[160] *Ibid.*, p. 173.

Thus while, as a result of extreme pressures, the state structure in Russia was quite different from the state structures found in the West, it was also the agent which imported aspects of Western economic development into Russia.

Trotsky not only accepted Plekhanov's general thesis, that with Russia geography was destiny, but he also followed Plekhanov's morphology of Russian history. He wrote that:

... She [Russia] was marked off from the European West, but also from the Asiatic East, approaching at different periods and in different features now one, now the other [. . .]. Russia was unable to settle in the forms of the East because she was continually having to adapt herself to military and economic pressure from the West.[161]

Elsewhere Trotsky described Russia's class system as being somewhere between the European situation where economic classes were strongly developed and the Asiatic system where they were extremely weakly developed, if at all (cf. Kliuchevsky).

It was not the equilibrium of the economically dominant classes, as in the West, but their weakness which made Russian bureaucratic autocracy a self-contained organization. In this respect Tsarism represents an intermediate form between European absolutism and Asian despotism, being, possibly, closer to the latter of these two.[162]

Both Trotsky and Plekhanov paid lip-service to the notion that Russia had gone through a feudal stage. For Plekhanov, Kievan Rus was in many respects a feudal society, although he pointed to the underlying features which distinguished it from Western European feudalism and which paved the way for the subsequent emergence of an 'Asiatic' socio-economic formation under Muscovite direction. Trotsky applied the term 'feudalism' also to the post-Kievan period of Russian history – he was never to acknowledge the Asiatic system as an autonomous socio-economic formation – but he admitted that certain features which made feudalism a dynamic system in the West were absent in Russia. He wrote that:

... The existence of feudal relations in Russia, denied by former historians, may be considered unconditionally established by later investigation.[163] Furthermore, the fundamental elements of Russian feudalism were the same as in the West. But the mere fact that the existence of the feudal epoch had to be estab-

---

[161] Leon Trotsky, *The History of the Russian Revolution, op.cit.*, Vol. I, p. 24.
[162] Leon Trotsky, *1905*, tr. from the July 1922 Russian ed. by Anya Bostok, London, Allen Lane, 1972, p. 8.
[163] See the section 'Russian History in European Dress' above.

lished by means of extended scientific arguments sufficiently testifies to the in-completeness of Russian feudalism, its formlessness, its poverty of cultural monuments.[164]

Trotsky came to view the absence of the Occidental city as the most important single feature distinguishing Russian 'feudalism' from Western European feudalism. Plekhanov had somewhat neglected this subject in his otherwise much more comprehensive historical survey. While he had commented on the general political inertness of the Russian cities under Muscovite rule, and the absence of anything approaching the Western European urban corporations, his remarks were largely directed against those who argued that 'the social role of the urban population of the North-East Rus is close to nil.'[165] This was one area in which Plekhanov played down the specificity of the Russian historical process.

Trotsky, on the other hand, saw the non-Western nature of the old Russian city as the key to Russia's distinctive history. Indeed the non-Western character of the Russian city was an intrinsic element in the theory of permanent revolution developed by Trotsky and Parvus in 1905. According to this theory, the democratic revolutions which had occurred in Europe had been inspired by the most radical class of the period, the urban petty-bourgeoisie. In Russia the urban environment which might have nurtured such a class had been lacking ('Our cities are mere government fantasies' Ogarev had written in *Kolokol*). There-fore the task of accomplishing the belated democratic revolution, as well as the socialist revolution, had devolved upon the proletariat.

It was Parvus (Alexander Helphand) who first enunciated the signifi-cance of the absence of the Occidental type of city for the development of the Russian revolution, and he did so in his preface to Trotsky's pamphlet 'Until the Ninth of January', written in January 1905. As Trotsky was later to write:

... The preface Parvus then wrote to the pamphlet entered permanently into the history of the Russian Revolution. In a few pages he shed light on these social peculiarities of backward Russia which, true enough, were already well known, but from which no-one before him had drawn all the necessary in-ferences.[166]

What Parvus had said in his preface was as follows:

---

[164] Leon Trotsky, *The History of the Russian Revolution, op.cit.*, Vol. I, p. 24.
[165] Plekhanov, *History*, p. 88.
[166] Leon Trotski (sic), *Stalin*, tr. and ed. Charles Malamuth, London, Hollis and Carter, 1947, Appendix: 'Three Concepts of the Russian Revolution', p. 430.

... In Russia, the cities in the pre-capitalist period developed more according to the Chinese than the European model. Thus they were administrative centres, bearing a purely official character and without the least political significance,[167] while in the economic sense they were trade bazaars for the surrounding landlord and peasant environment. Their development was still very insignificant when it was terminated by the capitalist process which began to create large cities after its own pattern, i.e., factory towns and centres of world trade. As a result in Russia there was a capitalist bourgeoisie, but there was not that petty-bourgeoisie, which provided the source and support for the revival of political democracy in Western Europe.[168]

The Trotsky/Parvus theory of permanent revolution indeed appears to give even more weight to the political role of the urban petty-bourgeoisie in the democratic revolutions of Western Europe than did Marx, who tended to talk in more general terms of the bourgeois character of these revolutions.[169] Trotsky wrote that 'It was precisely the craftsman class that constituted the bulk of the population in the most revolutionary quarters of Paris during the Great Revolution.'[170] It was also the 'sturdy artisans and independent peasants' who provided the bulk of Cromwell's army.[171]

The immediate reason for this stress on the role of the petty-bourgeoisie was that Trotsky and Parvus were seeking a sociological explanation of why the liberal democratic revolution as such had not succeeded and could not succeed in Russia, despite the development of a capitalist bourgeoisie. They wished to relate this failure (particularly evident in the aftermath of 1905) to the internal development of Russian society, as well as to the unfavourable international environment.

On the international level the failure of the democratic revolution in Russia could be explained by the 'fact' that the bourgeoisie in general had become a reactionary element supporting 'law and order'. According to Parvus' interpretation, the Russian autocracy had only fostered the development of a native capitalist bourgeoisie when this

---

[167] Cf. Trotsky: 'The majority of our old towns played hardly any economic role; they were military and administrative centres or fortresses, their inhabitants were employed in one or another form of State service and lived at the expense of the exchequer, and in general the city was an administrative, military and tax-collecting centre. [...] Thus, the Russian towns, like the towns under the Asiatic despotisms, and in contrast to the craft and trading towns of the European Middle Ages, played only the role of *consumers.*' (*Results and Prospects*, in *The Permanent Revolution and Results and Prospects, op.cit.*, p. 179.)

[168] Parvus, preface to N. Trotsky, *Do deviatogo ianvaria*, Geneva, R.S.D.L.P., 1905, pp. v–vi.

[169] Trotsky and Parvus drew chiefly on Marx's analysis of the petty-bourgeois base of the democratic parties of 1848 for their authority (Marx and Engels, *Address of the Central Committee to the Communist League*, March 1850, *MESW*, Vol. I, pp. 98–108.)

[170] Leon Trotsky, *Results and Prospects* in *The Permanent Revolution and Results and Prospects, op.cit.*, p. 180.

[171] Leon Trotsky, *The History of the Russian Revolution, op.cit.*, Vol. I, p. 32.

class had long since ceased to be in any sense a radical force in Europe, and had become as a class the conservative defender of centralisation and of the strengthening of government powers.[172] The Russian capitalist bourgeoisie, as the cadet branch of an international bourgeoisie already embattled by the rise of the proletariat as a political force, was itself drained of any revolutionary potential.

Trotsky in his writings was to confirm and expand Parvus' analysis of why the democratic revolution in its classical form was doomed to fail in Russia. In particular, as mentioned, he took up Parvus' ideas on the significance of the historical peculiarities of the Russian town and the absence of a radical urban third estate. For example, he wrote that:

... The meagreness not only of Russian feudalism, but of all the old Russian history, finds its most depressing expression in the absence of real mediavel cities as centres of commerce and craft. Handicraft did not succeed in Russia in separating itself from agriculture, but preserved its character of home industry. The old Russian cities were commercial, administrative, military and manorial – centres of consumption, consequently, not of production.[173]

He described the lack of differentiation of industry as bringing Russia 'nearer to India than to Europe, just as our medieval cities were nearer to the Asiatic than the European type, and as our autocracy, standing between the European absolutism and the Asiatic despotism, in many features approached the latter.'[174]

According to Trotsky, contemporary Russian history could largely be understood in terms of the cultural-political consequences of the lack of development of urban craft industry, and craft guilds. In Western Europe:

... guild craft was the basis of the medieval city culture, which radiated also into the village. Medieval science, scholasticism, religious reformation, grew out of a craft-guild soil. We did not have these things. Of course the embryo symptoms, the signs can be found, but in the West these things were not signs but powerful cultural economic formations with a craft-guild base.[175]

In the absence of such a craft-guild base, industrial democracy was unable to establish itself in Russian cities and spill over into political revolution. Trotsky compared the Pugachev rebellion with the French revolution which took place fifteen years later. The Pugachev rebellion was unable to transcend its character as a popular uprising and become

[172] Parvus, *Rossiia i revoliutsiia, op.cit.*, p. 109.
[173] Leon Trotsky, *The History of the Russian Revolution, op.cit.*, Vol. I, p. 27.
[174] *Ibid.*, Appendix I, p. 472.
[175] *Ibid.*, p. 473.

a revolution because of the fatal lack of a third estate. 'Without the industrial democracy of the cities a peasant war could not develop into a revolution, just as the peasant sects could not rise to the height of a Reformation.'[176]

In Trotsky's eyes, the absence of the Occidental form of city in Asia and 'Ancient Russia' meant that history there took on a cyclical pattern rather than the progressive pattern found in Western Europe. Peasant revolts which took place without the benefit of a radical urban element only succeeded in establishing a new cycle of the old order. The peasantry on their own were incapable of initiating a new political order because they did not represent a new form of production and culture.

On the other hand, in Europe peasant revolts did contribute to social progress because 'beginning with the emergence of the Middle Ages, each victorious peasant uprising did not place a peasant government in power but a Leftist burgher party. More precisely, a peasant uprising proved victorious only to the extent that it managed to establish the position of the city population's revolutionary sector.'[177] For Trotsky, it was the fact that a radical urban class had at last been formed in Russia, i.e. the proletariat, that made it possible for peasant Russia to break out of its old circularity and take a leap forward into socialism.

From his analysis of the peculiarities of Russian history, which in many respects resembled Plekhanov's analysis, Trotsky drew conclusions which were diametrically opposed to those of Plekhanov. Whereas Plekhanov stressed the need for Russia to turn her back on her non-Western past, Trotsky in effect argued that it could be utilised for a non-Western development into socialism. Plekhanov was a 'Westerner' who believed that socialism was the logical culmination of Western civilisation, and that the precondition of socialism was the acquisition of socio-political forms already existing in Western society. This included the need for a bourgeois-democratic period and the rise of a mass workers' movement to political maturity within it.

The contrast in positions was brought out sharply by Trotsky himself: 'While the traditional view [e.g., that of Plekhanov] was that the road to the dictatorship of the proletariat led through a long period of democracy, the theory of the permanent revolution [e.g. Trotsky's theory] established the fact that for backward countries the road to democracy passed through the dictatorship of the proletariat.'[178]

[176] *Ibid.*, p. 28.
[177] Leon Trotski, *Stalin, op.cit.*, Appendix: 'Three Concepts of the Russian Revolution' p. 425.
[178] Leon Trotsky, *The Permanent Revolution and Results and Prospects, op.cit.*, p. 8.

However, in spite of his radically different political stance, Trotsky was to defend Plekhanov's historiography from those such as Pokrovsky who attacked it in the name of orthodoxy, and who attempted to derive Plekhanov's political 'errors' from his theoretical heterodoxy. Pokrovsky, guided by his principle that 'history is the politics of the past', claimed, as we have seen, that Plekhanov's historical analysis reflected an erroneous political analysis of the contemporary Russian situation. And Pokrovsky argued that conversely, because Plekhanov under-emphasised the role of class struggle in Russian history, he was led into advocating co-operation with the liberal bourgeoisie, and eventually into supporting 'defencist' policies.[179] Trotsky's reply to Pokrovsky (who had correctly associated Trotsky's historiography with that of Plekhanov[180]) was as follows:

... Plekhanov quite rightly dismisses the schematic theories of both the doctrinaire 'Westernisers' and the Slavophil Narodniks on this subject, and instead, reduces Russia's 'special nature' to the concrete, materially determined peculiarities of her historical development. It is radically false to claim that Plekhanov drew any compromising conclusions from this (in the sense of forming a bloc with the Kadets, etc.), or that he could have done so with any semblance of logic.[181]

Trotsky was convinced that Plekhanov's historical propositions were correct, even if Plekhanov had failed to see that the peculiarities of Russian history would be carried forward into the socialist revolution, rather than being eliminated in a lengthy period of bourgeois democracy.

In fact socialism in Russia would be achieved in circumstances quite different from those prevailing in the West, because Russia possessed the 'advantages of backwardness.' Among such advantages Trotsky listed 'the absence of accumulated bourgeois-individualistic traditions and anti-proletarian prejudice among the peasants and intellectuals', although at the same time he added the provision that 'this absence of prejudices is not due to political consciousness but to political barbarism, social formlessness, primitiveness and lack of character.'[182]

---

[179] E.g. M.N. Pokrovsky, 'G.V. Plekhanov kak istorik Rossii', *Pod znamenem marksizma*, 1923, No. 6–7, pp. 5–18.

[180] Pokrovsky's attack on Trotsky's historiography appeared in *Krasnaia Nov'*, May–June, 1922.

[181] Leon Trotsky, 'On the Special Features of Russia's Historical Development: A Reply to M.N. Pokrovsky', *1905*, *op.cit.*, pp. 331–332. This chapter is a more complete version of Trotsky's answer to Pokrovsky than the version already cited which is attached as Appendix I to Trotsky's *The History of the Russian Revolution*, *op.cit.*, Vol. I.

[182] Leon Trotsky, *Results and Prospects*, in *The Permanent Revolution and Results and Prospects*, *op.cit.*, p. 208.

Trotsky was utterly opposed to the notion put forward by Marx in his preface to the first edition of *Capital* – the notion that: 'The country that is more developed industrially only shows, to the less developed, the image of its own future.'[183] On the contrary, Trotsky argued, the countries which stood outside the charmed circle in which industrialism had first flowered in Western Europe were destined to follow a very different pattern of industrial development. This was the pattern of 'combined development' both in the economic and socio-political spheres. The non-Western countries would skip over the intervening stages of development which had taken place in Western Europe and which in turn had become obstacles to the development of the socialist revolution in those countries. As Kautsky had said, the less advanced countries would quite likely take their place in the forefront of development, 'because they are not burdened with the ballast of tradition which the older countries have to drag along [...]'[184]

The peculiarities of Russia's history already provided the clues for Trotsky as to how the socialist revolution might develop there – i.e., the form appropriate to the special conditions prevailing. The 'immensely important' role played by the state in Russia in introducing capitalist relations foreshadowed the kind of role the state might play there in introducing a socialist economy.[185]

Trotsky's analysis of how non-Western types of historical development give rise to non-Western forms of the industrialisation process has been amply confirmed by events. His ideas on how the integrative force of the world economy would eventually bring about, though by different paths, a universal type of socialism based on the Western European conception of it, have not been confirmed in the same way.

---

[183] Marx, *Capital*, Vol. I, pp. 8–9. Trotsky's respectful criticism was that 'Under no circumstances can this thought be taken literally.' See Leon Trotsky, *Karl Marx*, 3rd edn, London, Cassell, 1946, p. 40.

[184] K. Kautsky, *American and Russian Workers*, quoted without specific reference in Leon Trotsky, *Results and Prospects*, in *The Permanent Revolution and Results and Prospects, op.cit.*, p. 237.

[185] Leon Trotsky, *1905, op.cit.*, p. 9.

CHAPTER V

THE ASIATIC MODE OF PRODUCTION IN RELATION TO THE MARXIST ANALYSIS OF PROGRESS AND MODERNISATION

> ... the Savage, Patriarchal, Barbarous, and Civilised forms of society are but the thorny paths, the ladders which are to lead us up to the social state which is the destiny of Man, and outside of which all the efforts of the best rulers are unable in any way to remedy the ills of mankind.
>
> CHARLES FOURIER

The theoretical crux of the concept of the Asiatic mode of production lies in its implications for the so-called 'stage theory' embedded in orthodox historical materialism. These subversive implications have only gradually been acknowledged within Marxist historiography.

THE UNILINEAR SCHEMA OF SOCIAL DEVELOPMENT

Before 1964 historical materialism was generally interpreted to mean that history displayed a single sequence of universally occurring stages of social development, each of them corresponding to a different stage in the development of productive forces.[1] The immanent logic of the development of material production was taken to be such that each stage of the succession would appear, unveil its inner contradictions, and give rise to the next, higher phase of economic production and social development. According to this law of social development, the same pattern or sequence of stages would be found in the history of any given society.

This interpretation of historical materialism, which never fitted at all well with the *details* of Marx's examination of history, stemmed

---

[1] This interpretation is to be found in the 'classics' referred to in Chapter Three – Lenin, Stalin, Bukharin *et al.* It is a corollary of the 'hard' technological version of Marxism; that is, where the tools of production rather than the organisation of production are awarded primacy as an explanatory factor (up to the socialist era).

largely from two of Marx's more programmatic pieces of writing. The first of these is the *Communist Manifesto*, which like the *German Ideology*, bears witness to the influence of Fourier's stadial analysis of human history. The second is the Preface to the *Contribution to the Critique of Political Economy*. In his Preface Marx wrote:

... In broad outline, the Asiatic, ancient, feudal and modern bourgeois modes of production may be designated as epochs marking progress in the economic development of society.[2]

This passage has been the subject of some controversy, particularly in recent years,[3] but it has also served as the primary authority for the unilinear conception of human history.

Apart from these sources, the works of Engels, particularly in the period after he wrote *Anti-Dühring*, contributed much towards the establishment of the unilinear schema as dogma. Statements such as the following assisted in the process: 'Without the slavery of antiquity, no modern socialism.'[4] Engels also believed, with Marx, that:

... to accomplish this [modern socialism] we need not only the proletariat, which carries out the revolution, but also a bourgeoisie in whose hands the productive forces of society have developed to such a stage that they permit the final elimination of all class distinctions [. . .] The bourgeoisie is consequently equally as necessary a precondition of the socialist revolution as the proletariat itself.[5]

The tendency was to take this to mean that a full sequence of Western social stages was necessary for the eventual creation of socialism, and that there were no alternative routes.

Engels was also largely responsible for the adoption into Marxist theory of Morgan's anthropological system. Morgan's system minimised the significance of external influence on the internal development of human societies, and hence reinforced the notion that social development progressed according to certain iron laws of its own, through a given sequence of necessary stages up to the socialist one.

The tendency to promulgate fixed laws of social development was linked with the more general tendency, also begun under the aegis of Engels, to transform Marxism into a 'science of society'. In its guise

[2] Marx, Preface to *A Contribution to the Critique of Political Economy*, tr. S.W. Ryazanskaya, Moscow, Progress, 1970, p. 21.

[3] See the section below entitled 'Chronological and Logical Problems Presented by the Stadial Analysis of World History'.

[4] Engels, *Anti-Dühring*, tr. E. Burns, London, Lawrence and Wishart, n.d. (reprinted with minor revisions from the 1934 edn), p. 203.

[5] Engels, 'Russia and the Social Revolution', (originally published as 'Soziales aus Russland', in *Der Volksstaat*, Leipzig, 21 April 1875), *The Russian Menace to Europe*, p. 205.

as a science of society, historical materialism was of great symbolic value to the European labour movement in the last quarter of the nineteenth century.[6] It was the ideological buttress of the socialist parties, in so far as it demonstrated the 'objective necessity' of their cause; it had the further function, however, of assisting in the substitution of the party for the masses, as the repository of socialist consciousness. If historical materialism was a science it was more likely to be mastered by the scientists (i.e. the party theorists) than by the masses. The implication was drawn that the masses could never achieve class-consciousness spontaneously, even in the course of bitter class struggle; rather, they required the mediation of the party.

The diagram repeated below from Chapter Three represents the stage theory to be found within the Marxism of both the Second and the Third International; it is largely derived from the Preface to the *Contribution to the Critique of Political Economy.*

THE UNILINEAR SCHEMA

Primitive Agricultural Community

↓

Asiatic Mode of Production*

↓

Slavery

↓

Feudalism

↓

Capitalism

↓

Socialism

* Frequently omitted

[6] As recognised for example by Karl Kautsky in his *Der Weg Zur Macht*, Berlin, Buch-handlung Vorwärts, 1909, *passim*. This organisational function of Marxist theory differed from the symbolic functions attributed by Georges Sorel to Marx's formulae of class struggle and revolutionary apocalypse. For Sorel the latter formulae were the kernel of Marxism, in so far as they served to insulate the proletarian movement and its revolutionary purity from the corrupting influences of bourgeois society. (See Georges Sorel, *Reflections on Violence* and the *Decomposition of Marxism*.)

The difficulties incurred in trying to fit what Marx conceived of as a geographically-specific mode of production, i.e., the Asiatic, into a universal schema of social development have been so formidable that they have frequently been resolved *modo tatarico*, as Wittfogel puts it, by simply cutting this socio-economic formation out of the schema. It was quite logical for this to happen in Lenin's influential lecture on *The State*, published for the first time in 1929, as Lenin was following closely Engels' *Origin of the Family, Private Property and the State*. A more glaring example of deliberate extrusion may be found in the 1938 *History of the Communist Party of the Soviet Union, Short Course*, where the unilinear schema from Marx's Preface is reproduced exactly, with the single omission of the reference to the AMP.[7]

The concept of the Asiatic mode of production as a socio-economic formation was, as we have seen in Chapter Two, virtually banned in the Soviet Union in 1931, for a variety of political reasons. In 1933 the view then held by V. V. Struve (after some vacillations), that the ancient Eastern civilisations belonged to the slavery formation, was officially adopted, and is still influential today. Struve *has* strongly supported the unilinear schema, and eliminated Marx's notion of an endlessly self-perpetuating Asiatic mode of production by ascribing a slave stage to the ancient East, and a feudal stage to the medieval East.

Struve does admit that the slave stage in the ancient East was marked by some peculiarities, such as the existence of rural communities, from which tribute was exacted, but he describes this as a transient survival of the tribute paid to the military aristocracy in patriarchal tribal societies.[8] The more important form of exploitation in these societies (because it represented a higher stage of historical development) was, according to Struve, the exploitation of slaves in the non-agricultural sector by the state (using the revenue collected from the rural communities for their upkeep). Hence of the two forms of exploitation present in the societies of the ancient East, the slave form provided the 'determining element' and the defining characteristic.[9]

Struve does not regard the distinction between private slave-

[7] *Short History of the C.P.S.U.*, Moscow, Foreign Languages Publishing House, 1939 p. 110.

[8] See Vassili Strouvé [Struve], 'Comment Marx définissait les premières sociétiés de classes', *Recherches internationales à la lumière du marxisme* No. 57–58 (Jan.-April 1967), pp. 93–94. This article, widely quoted by Soviet scholars, first appeared in *Sovetskaia etnografiia*, 1940, No. 3.

[9] *Ibid.*, p. 94.

owners employing slaves chiefly for the purposes of primary production in a largely commodity-based economy, and the state employing artisans and domestic slaves out of its tax revenue from rural communities in a predominantly natural economy, as an important distinction implying different modes of production. Furthermore Struve completely overlooks the point that Marx believed the character of a socio-economic formation to be determined by that mode of production found in it which produces the bulk of the social surplus. Because of the virtual disappearance of protagonists of the Asiatic mode, Struve's past polemics on the subject of the ancient Eastern civilisations were mainly directed against those who wished to extend the concept of feudalism to these societies on the basis of the 'attachment' of the peasants to the soil, thus neglecting, he argued, the necessary sequence 'slavery, feudalism' and replacing it with the sequence 'feudalism, slavery' as did the 'bourgeois historians of the imperialist epoch'.[10]

Such problems would clearly be avoided if one allowed the possibility of an alternative formation which encompassed both the attachment of the peasants to the soil, and state support of the non-agricultural sector. Struve, however, has been reluctant to concede the existence of such an alternative path of historical development, or indeed to concede any notion of historical plurality that might detract from the concept of a 'unitary world history'.[11]

The post-Stalinist textbook *Fundamentals of Marxism-Leninism* (1961) faithfully preserves the five-stage Stalinist schema, despite the assurance that:

... Historical materialism does not impose preconceived patterns on history and does not adapt the events of past and present to fit its own conclusions.[12]

The Kuusinen textbook outlines the four socio-economic formations

[10] *Ibid.*, p. 97. Other Soviet historians extended the scope of the concept of feudalism so far as to absorb completely the concept of a slave-based mode of production. For a recent example, see Iu.M. Kobishchanov who defines feudalism as the exploitation of petty producers in a natural economy by non-economic means (as opposed to the economic means employed in an exchange economy), and claims that slavery is merely a structure to be found within late-communal society, feudal society or even capitalist society. (Iu.M. Kobishchanov, 'Feodalizm, rabstvo i aziatskii sposob proizvodstva', in G.F. Kim, V.N. Nikiforov *et al.* ed., *Obshchee i osobennoe v istoricheskom razvitii stran Vostoka*, Moscow, Izd. 'Nauka', 1966, pp. 42–47.)

[11] Vassili Strouvé [Struve], 'Le concept de M.P.A.: légitimité et limites' (first published in *Narody Azii i Afriki*, 1965, No. 1), *Recherches internationales à la lumière du marxisme*, No. 57–58 (Jan.-April 1967), p. 238.

[12] O.W. Kuusinen ed., *Fundamentals of Marxism-Leninism*, Moscow, Foreign Languages Publishing House, 1961, p. 154.

[13] *Ibid.*, pp. 154–164.

which mankind passes through before achieving the transition stage to communism (i.e., socialism), and these exclude the Asiatic formation.[13]

Another method of dealing with the Asiatic mode of production in the context of the unilinear schema, more common since 1964, has been to dilute the concept of the Asiatic mode of production in such a way that it might appear to be plausible as an analysis of a primitive universal stage of development.

In 1964 the reopening of the discussion of the Asiatic mode of production in the Soviet Union was signalled by the publication of E. Varga's *Ocherki po problemam politekonomii kapitalizma* which contained an essay on the subject. Discussions were held in the (Academy of Sciences) Institute of Philosophy in December 1964, in the Institute of History on the 5th, 12th, and 16th March 1965, and in the Institute of the Peoples of Asia on the 27th and 28th of May, 1965.[14]

Meanwhile the French Marxists M. Godelier and J. Suret-Canale had prepared papers on the AMP for the Seventh International Congress of Anthropology and Ethnography held in Moscow, August 1964, and these papers, together with a reply from V. Struve, were published in the journal *Narody Azii i Afriki* at the beginning of 1965. Several academic journals such as *Vestnik drevnei istorii* and even *Voprosy filosofii* ran reports in 1965 on the work being published by the French Marxists in *La Pensée*. Soviet scholars interested in employing the concept of a distinct Asiatic formation were able to discover from Godelier and Suret-Canale a definition of such a formation which was compatible with the traditional unilinear framework of Soviet historiography.[15] Thus:

[14] For accounts of these various conferences see L.V. Danilova, 'Diskussiia po vazhnoi probleme', *Voprosy istorii*, 1965, No. 12, pp. 149–156; O.A. Afanas'ev, 'Obsuzhdenie v Institute Istorii AN SSSR problemy "Aziatskii sposob proizvodstva"', *Sovetskaia etnografiia*, 1965, No. 6, pp. 122–126; L.S. Vasil'ev, 'Obshchee i osobennoe v istoricheskom razvitii stran Vostoka', *Narody Azii i Afriki*, 1965, No. 6, pp. 96–100; Iu. M. Garushiants, 'Ob aziatskom sposobe proizvodstva', *Voprosy istorii*, 1966, No. 2, pp. 83- 100; S.E. Krapivensky, 'Osobaia formatsiia ili perekhodnoe sostoianie obshchestva?', *Narody Azii i Afriki*, 1966, No. 2, pp. 87–90; G.F. Kim and V.N. Nikiforov *et al*. ed., *Obshchee i osobennoe v istoricheskom razvitii stran Vostoka, op.cit.*

[15] The P.C.F. had taken the initiative in reviving the concept some years previously. As early as 1958 Suret-Canale, a member of the Central Committee, had stated that it was impossible to apply the categories feudal or slave-owning to the societies of tropical Africa, and had suggested the use of the concept of the Asiatic mode of production (*L'Afrique noire occidentale et centrale, géographie, civilisation, histoire*, Paris, Éditions sociales, 1958, p. 94. When the Central Committee set up the Centre d'études et de recherches marxistes (hereafter C.E.R.M.) in 1960, the question of the Asiatic mode was included in the programme of the Oriental section, on the suggestion of Charles Parain. This section held working sessions on the Asiatic mode in 1962–1963, and the results began emerging in roneoed and published form in 1964 (the papers prepared for Moscow summarised the work done by Godelier and Suret-Canale at the Centre). See Jean Chesneaux, 'Diskussiia o ranneklassovykh obshchest-

... The majority of the participants in the discussion, in its current stage, were of the opinion that by Marx's conception of the Asiatic mode of production one should understand not so much a specific particularity of the East (especially the particularity associated with the necessity for irrigation works) as those regularities (*zakonomernosti*) characteristic of nearly all early class societies, and which were retained over a prolonged period in many of the societies of Africa, Asia and pre-Columbian America.[16]

In the definition of the French Marxists and their Soviet followers, the Asiatic mode of production represented the original transition stage between classless and class society; the stage where the state had already come into being but private property did not yet exist. The stage was characterised by the existence of communal production and ownership at the village level, on the one hand, and by the appropriation of the surplus value by the state, and the existence of (state-directed) corvée labour on the other; economic classes did not yet exist, but there were elites associated with the state who performed religious, military and other public functions.

The broad definition of the Asiatic mode of production in general made it more or less a substitute for the somewhat problematic concept of 'military democracy'. (Depicted in *The Origin of the Family* ... as the universally occurring final phase of gentile society, illustrated for example by the Iroquois Confederation and Homeric Greece, a phase in which the institutions of public authority had taken on a certain complexity but class society based on private property and slavery had not yet come into its own.) The broad interpretation of Marx's concept of the Asiatic mode of production meant that it was shorn of its geographical connotations, and its connotations of highly developed entrepreneurial and/or bureaucratic activity on the part of the state. It thus became far more plausible as a universal stage of development to be found in the history of any given society.

The universalising of the concept of the Asiatic mode was exemplified in the work of Jean Chesneaux (with whom the Western pattern became more or less the exceptional case). Chesneaux wrote in 1964 that:

The Asiatic mode of production, for the very reason that it has been the most general form of evolution of primitive communist society, has established itself in very diverse regions, in societies on which both history and geography have

vakh na stranitsakh zhurnala "La Pensée"', *Voprosy istorii*, 1967, No. 9, p. 192ff; cf. L.V. Danilova: 'At the present time, on the initiative of a group of French Marxist historians, J. Suret-Canale, M. Godelier, J. Chesneaux, C. Parain, P. Boiteau *et al.*, the problem of the Asiatic mode of production has again become the subject of discussion'. 'Diskussiia po vazhnoi probleme', *loc.cit.*, p. 150.

[16] L.V. Danilova, 'Diskussiia po vazhnoi probleme', *loc.cit.*, p. 156.

imposed very different rhythms of development. Brutally destroyed in the Mediterranean by the Dorian invasion at the beginning of the first millenium BC, liquidated by the Spanish conquest in America in the sixteenth century, it nevertheless continued slowly to evolve in countries such as China, Egypt, India, and Black Africa.[17]

During the discussion at the Institute of the Peoples of Asia held on the 27th and 28th of May 1965, Iu.M. Garushiants and M.A. Vitkin in particular were to support the universalist definition of the Asiatic mode of production provided by the French Marxists, thus avoiding the multilinear implications of the definition given by the first generation of Soviet scholars working on the subject, such as E. Varga and L.I. Mad'iar. Vitkin argued that:

... the emphasis on the fundamental particularity of Asiatic history characteristic of nineteenth-century historiography underwent a sharp about-turn at the close of the century, so that the history of the East was assimilated to that of Europe. The particularity of the East was discovered to be only relative [...] because, as the latest information indicates, ancient Europe (Mycenae etc.) also experienced a stage similar to that which Marx described as characterising the ancient East. The acceptable meaning of the Asiatic mode of production seems to be that it is the last stage of the primitive communal formation, the transition stage to class society.[18]

Vitkin also differed from the first generation of Soviet scholars working on the problem, as did many of his colleagues, in the extreme caution he displayed in applying the term 'class' to those who expropriated the surplus product in the Asiatic mode of production (where private ownership was not yet significant).

Another departure from the views of those who supported the concept in 1925–1931 was that according to the new definition, the Asiatic formation had an internal *dynamic*, provided by the fact that its elites

[17] J. Chesneaux, 'Le mode de production asiatique: quelques perspectives de recherche', *La Pensée*, No. 114 (Jan.–Feb. 1964), p. 53. See also J. Suret-Canale. 'Problèmes théoriques de l'étude des premières sociétés de classes', *Recherches internationales à la lumière du marxisme*, No. 57–58 (Jan.–April 1967), p. 14. For the application of the AMP concept to the Minoan, Etruscan, Hittite and Mycenaean civilisations see Charles Parain. Parain drew a parallel between the way the 'barbarian' invasions brought about the fall of the Roman empire and cleared the way for the development of a new 'higher' mode of production, and the way in which the Dorian invasions brought about the fall of the Mediterranean empires and cleared the way for the development of the new, private slave-based mode of production. (Charles Parain, 'Protohistoire méditerranéenne et mode de production asiatique', *La Pensée*, No. 127 (May–June 1966), pp. 24–43.)

[18] M.A. Vitkin as reported by L.S. Vasil'ev, 'Obshchee i osobennoe v istoricheskom razvitii stran Vostoka', *Narody Azii i Afriki*, 1965, No. 6, p. 97. According to Vitkin, recognition of the existence of this universal stage had been delayed through the influence of Morgan on the Marxist analysis of primitive society (it was not present in Morgan's schema of development). See M.A. Vitkin, 'Podkhod k probleme aziatskogo sposoba proizvodstva', in G.F. Kim, V.N. Nikiforov *et al.* ed., *Obshchee i osobennoe v istoricheskom razvitii stran Vostoka, op.cit.*, p. 104.

would attempt to transform themselves into an economic class based on the private ownership of the means of production (e.g., ownership of slaves and land). The attribution of dynamic elements to the Asiatic formation was a necessary aspect of the attempt to fit it into a universal progression. However Marxists such as Parain, Chesneaux, Suret-Canale, Boiteau and Godelier in France were also, in eliminating the proposition concerning Asiatic stagnation, conscious of the need to make the hypothesis of an Asiatic mode of production acceptable to the national sensitivities of third world countries.[19] One Soviet Orientalist, who accepts the other elements of Marx's concept of the Asiatic mode of production has gone so far as to say that:

... it is difficult to imagine that dialecticians such as Marx and Engels might be parties to the possibility of absolute stagnation in societies of the type under consideration.[20]

However, the manner in which the French Marxists and those following their formulation denied the proposition of Asiatic stagnation was itself guided by criteria drawn from Western experience. Thus according to Suret-Canale the persistence of collective property did not necessarily mean that the Asiatic formations represented an impasse:

... their internal contradiction (collective property – class property) may be resolved by the dissolution of collective property and the appearance of private property.[21]

I.e., the French Marxists preserved Marx's viewpoint, formed under the influence of the British political economists that the emergence of private property was the key to progress whether in the West or East.

The broad interpretation of the Asiatic mode of production as the most primitive form of state exercised great appeal among French Marxists in that it enabled them to find a pigeon-hole for the pre-colonial societies of Black Africa which had resisted classification under any of the other Marxist categories (and similarly it appealed to those Marxists concerned with other problem areas, such as Pre-Columbian America and the Pacific).[22]

[19] See Jean Chesneaux, 'Diskussiia o ranneklassovykh obshchestvakh na stranitsakh zhurnala "La Pensée"', *loc.cit.*, p. 194.

[20] L.A. Sedov, 'La société angkorienne et le problème du mode de production asiatique', *La Pensée*, No. 138 (March–April 1968), p. 72.

[21] Jean Suret-Canale, 'Problèmes théoriques de l'étude des premières sociétés de classes', *loc.cit.*, p. 14.

[22] Apart from the bibliographical material published serially in *La Pensée* since 1964 by J. Chesneaux and M. Godelier, the bibliography attached to Iu. V. Kachanovsky; *Rabovladenie, feodalizm ili aziatskii sposob proizvodstva?*, Moscow, Izd. 'Nauka', 1971, provides a consolidated index to recent literature on the subject.

The extension of the concept to such diverse areas naturally required considerable modification of some of the characteristics which Marx attributed to Asiatic society: Godelier, for example, talked of two forms of the Asiatic mode, that with and that without 'great (public) works',[23] the latter form being found in tropical Africa, where the functions giving rise to the state related to the control of trade, the protection of markets, etc. In the early euphoria resulting from the rediscovery of the concept Godelier also believed that it might provide the solution to the categorisation of the nomadic pastoral societies[24] – i.e., the concept was on the way to becoming a portmanteau classification of all societies which had slipped through the net of the five-stage schema.

The elimination of the geographically-specific features of the Asiatic mode has been one method of giving the concept universal applicability and making it compatible with the unilinear schema of development. An interesting attempt to retain the geographical specificity of the Asiatic mode, and its status as an independent formation,[25] while also upholding the authority of the unilinear schema is to be found in the work of the Hungarian Sinologist Ferenc Tökei, who argued that the Asiatic mode was essentially determined by conditions of internal and external isolation, which had prevented the universal laws of development from operating as they had done in Europe. However, according to Tökei, the existence of the (static) Asiatic formation by no means disproved the unilinear theory of the five stages: on the contrary, it bore indirect witness to the operation of such a universal law. He asserted that despite the isolation of, for example, China, which had retarded its development, tendencies towards a slave stage had appe-

[23] M. Godelier, 'La notion de "mode de production asiatique" et les schémas marxistes d'évolution des sociétés' (first published in 1964), *Sur le 'mode de production asiatique'*, preface by Roger Garaudy, C.E.R.M., Paris, Éditions sociales, 1969, p. 88.

[24] *Ibid.*, p. 87. Chesneaux himself, although sympathetic towards extending the concept to Africa, America, etc., was to warn against such an enterprise; the problematic area of early Mongol society was no more susceptible to analysis by the Asiatic concept than by the old five-stage schema. (J. Chesneaux, 'Diskussiia o ranneklassovykh obshchestvakh na stranitsakh zhurnala "La Pensée"', *loc.cit.*, p. 194). Ernest Mandel has recently made a more far-reaching criticism of the tendency to extend the range of the concept beyond the agricultural societies of Asia and the Middle East. According to Mandel, 'By thus expanding the scope of the idea of the Asiatic mode of production (just as the 'dogmatic' Marxists who rejected this concept were forced to expand the scope of the idea of 'feudalism') these writers [Godelier, Chesneaux, Suret-Canale, Boiteau] risk losing altogether the specific meaning of the idea.' (E. Mandel, *The Formation of the Economic Thought of Karl Marx*, London, NLB, 1971, p. 125). Cf. also I. Sachs, 'Une nouvelle phase de la discussion sur les formations' (first published in *Nowe drogi*, March 1966), *Recherches internationales à la lumière du marxisme*, No. 57–58 (Jan.–April 1967), pp. 301–302.

[25] Tökei, like the French Marxists, conceptualised the Asiatic formation as a transition stage from tribal to class society, but as having sufficient distinctive features to be regarded as an independent historical formation.

ared in the era of antiquity, and tendencies towards feudalism had appeared in the middle ages. The fact that these tendencies manifested themselves (even in a weak form) in such an isolated society as China confirmed for Tökei the universal validity of the five-stage schema.[26]

The attempt to make the concept of the Asiatic mode of production compatible with the unilinear theory of history, and the tendency to over-extend the concept (to cover all societies which had resisted classification within the five-stage schema) are both typical of the initial phase of the de-Stalinisation of Marxist historiography. Marxist historians were eager to employ a concept, for which they now found there was ample authority in Marx, and which would serve to enrich the existing framework of Marxist historiography. But they were hesitant to explore the further implications of the concept, such as the implication that history was multilinear rather than unilinear, and that there existed other alternative modes of production not discussed by Marx because of his lack of information. Hence they loosened the concept of the Asiatic mode of production itself rather than loosening their approach to history in general, and attempted to 'save' non-Western societies from the grip of the five-stage schema by introducing a sixth category to accommodate all the exceptions.

THE HEGELIANISED VERSION OF THE UNILINEAR SCHEMA

The extreme difficulty of fitting every human society into the unilinear schema has given rise to yet another 'saving device' within the unilinear view, that of treating it in a Hegelian way. According to Hegel, world history evolved through a certain sequence of necessary stages, but each stage was primarily embodied in only one nation or group of nations.

One reason why it seemed plausible to assert that the centre of human progress shifted from area to area was primarily geographical – that different geographical factors became of decisive importance at different stages of socio-economic development. The employment of

---

[26] F. Tökei, *Sur le mode de production asiatique*, Budapest, Akadémiai Kiadó, 1966, p. 88. This line of argument may have been a ritualistic attempt by Tökei to come to terms with orthodoxy. It is inconsistent with much of the rest of his work which suggested a geographically determined multilinear pattern of development. For example, Tökei viewed the geographical configuration of the Japanese archipelago as serving the same function as the Germanic forests in inhibiting centralisation and giving rise to a feudal socio-economic formation. (*Ibid.*, pp. 85–86. Cf. K.A. Wittfogel, *Oriental Despotism*, New Haven, Yale U.P., p. 197).

this argument by Hegel, Mechnikov, Plekhanov and Wittfogel has been discussed in Chapter Three, pp. 122–124.

Another argument concerns the hypostatisation of a form of production in the society where it reaches its highest development. According to this argument, structures appropriate to a particular socio-economic formation, which also become associated with a period of national greatness, severely impede the development of structures appropriate to a later period.[27] Hence the next stage of human history tends to take place in a different arena, less cluttered with cherished institutional anachronisms.

A classic statement of this position is to be found in Maurice Cornforth's textbook on historical materialism:

Human society as a whole passes through the five stages we have listed, and the way is prepared for the appearance of a new system only as a result of the development of the previous system. But the new system does not necessarily appear first in that place where the old one has been most strongly entrenched and most fully developed. Indeed, in those communities where the old system has become most strongly entrenched it may be hardest to get rid of it, so that the breakthrough of the new system is effected in the first place elsewhere. As we know, this is what happened in the case of the first break-through of socialism, which was effected in Russia, 'the weakest link in the chain of imperialism', and not in the more advanced capitalist countries.[28]

The adoption of the 'Hegelian' version of the unilinear schema, whereby different societies represent the different epochs of human development, makes the concept of social laws governing the transition from one epoch to another even more difficult. There is a recurrence of the tension inherent in the Hegelian view of world history – i.e. world history consists in an organic process of development through various logically necessary stages, but within this process the leading role in some way passes from one society or group of societies to another.[29] The problem is to demonstrate the logical relationship between the stages when the subject of world history changes in such a manner. Nonetheless the concept of necessary laws governing the transition

[27] See A. Pannekoek, *Weltrevolution und Kommunistische Taktik* (Vienna, 1920) in *Pannekoek et les conseils ouvriers*, ed. S. Bricanier, Paris, EDI, 1969, p. 193. See also Antonio Gramsci on the comparative simplicity of making a socialist revolution in Russia, where capitalist civilisation and cultural hegemony was weakly developed.

[28] M. Cornforth, *Dialectical Materialism*, Vol. 2 (Historical Materialism), London, Lawrence and Wishart, 1953, p. 65.

[29] The need to discover the laws governing the development of universal history (i.e. the laws of transition from one stage to another) on the supra-societal level is stressed in V.N. Nikiforov, 'K voprosu ob istoricheskoi osnove literaturnoi periodizatsii', *Narody Azii i Afriki*, 1964, No. 3, pp. 86–90.

between epochs has remained a dogma within Soviet Marxism, even where the Hegelian notion of universal history has been most ardently embraced.[30]

One interesting attempt to grapple with the problem of the logical relationship between stages of history represented by different societies is to be found in the work of V. Gordon Childe. Childe was concerned with the logical relationship between the Asiatic and ancient formation, as progressive stages of universal history occurring in geographically distinct areas. He argued that the relationship between the Middle Eastern civilisations and Aegean civilisation was a symbiotic one, the surpluses accumulated by the despotic states supporting the emergence of craft specialisation in the West.[31] The secure Eastern markets meant that bronze-age civilisation in the Aegean was able to reach 'take-off' point without the despotic or centralised control of the surplus which had launched the Eastern civilisations. And precisely the fact that the emergence of civilisation in the Aegean had not depended on the leading economic role of the state meant that these societies had a greater potential for progress and change.

Childe's work has recently been utilised by the French Communist J. J. Goblot in a series of three articles presenting the case for a universal history in which objective laws of development govern the transformations from one stage to another. One socio-economic formation does not necessarily engender the next higher formation through the logic of its own internal development, but it *does* produce the technical prerequisites of the next stage. Thus the 'Asiatic' civilisations of the Near East and the Mediterranean provided the technical basis for the development of Greek antiquity (on Childe's evidence) and the Roman Empire provided the technical basis for Northern European feudalism. In both these cases the development for a new, higher mode of production depended on the fusion of a potentially more dynamic form of social organisation, evolved within tribal societies external to the old civilisation, with the technological achievements of the old civilisation.[32]

The Soviet attempt to modify in a Hegelian fashion the rigid

---

[30] See for example, Iu. V. Kachanovsky, *Rabovladenie, feodalizm ili aziatskii sposob proizvodstva?*, *op.cit.*, pp. 245–263. Kachanovsky's book represents the most systematic Soviet effort so far to relate the concept of the Asiatic mode of production to Marxist historiography, even though this is done from the negative standpoint that the concept is fundamentally incompatible with Marxist historiography.

[31] V. Gordon Childe, 'The Bronze Age', *Past and Present*, No. 12 (Nov. 1957), pp. 10–11.

[32] J.-J. Goblot, 'Pour une approche théorique des "faits de civilisation"', *La Pensée*, Nos. 133, 134, 136 (1967): see especially Part III, *La Pensée*, No. 136, pp. 78–88.

unilinear schema of history was officially promulgated by a Soviet spokesman at an international history conference in 1960. This modification did not extend to the overthrow of Stalin's five-stage schema which extruded the Asiatic formation. But according to the statement made in 1960, the Germanic and Slav peoples did not pass through an epoch of slavery, for the reason that at the period when they were forming themselves into states, the full contradictions of the slave-based mode of production had already emerged in the Roman and Byzantine empires respectively. The 'fact' that the Roman and Byzantine empires represented the full working-out of slavery as a mode of production meant that the Germanic and Slav peoples, on emerging from clan society, could move straight into an economic formation based on the comparatively more productive labour of dependent peasantry.[33]

In a similar vein, the statement observed that among the peoples incorporated in the Soviet Union were those who had been able to move straight from the feudal, or even the patriarchal stage of production, into the socialist one. This was due to the fact that the contradictions of world capitalism had already fully emerged and the socialist epoch had been ushered in by the time that these peoples emerged from their social isolation.[34]

The above forms of development may be summed up under the rubric of 'the advantages of backwardness' – i.e. societies that develop late, or whose tempo of development has been slowed down by geographical or historical factors, are able to benefit from the experience accumulated by other societies.

The development of societies on the periphery of the mainstream of history may also, however, be influenced by the *disadvantages* of

---

[33] Report made by E.M. Zhukov (Secretary to the Division of Historical Sciences of the Academy of Sciences, U.S.S.R.) to the Eleventh International Congress of Historical Sciences, Stockholm, 1960. 'O periodizatsii vsemirnoi istorii', *Voprosy istorii*, 1960, No. 8, p. 32. This line and its corollary, discussed below, has appeared widely among Soviet historians such as A.G. Prigozhin and B.D. Grekov since the thirties. The explanation of the absence of slavery among the Germans was elaborated by V.V. Struve in his article, 'Marksovo opredelenie ranneklassovogo obshchestva', *Sovetskaia etnografiia*, 1940, No. 3. B.D. Grekov drew out the parallels between the interaction of the Slavs with East Rome and the interaction of the Germans with Rome itself. (*Kiev Rus*, tr. from 1949 Russian edition by E. Sdobnikov, Moscow, Foreign Languages Publishing House, 1959, p. 37). Grekov summed up the Slavic case as follows: 'At the moment of their appearance the Slavs, and their eastern branch in particular, during the disintegration of their primitive communal system encountered a decaying slave-holding society. They were among the group of peoples who were able to regenerate moribund Europe with the aid of their community system. The new peoples possessed the potentialities of a more progressive system, the feudal system.' (*Ibid.*, pp. 144–145).
[34] E.M. Zhukov, *loc.cit.*, p. 31.

backwardness. Thus the social development of the nations in propinquity to the Greek and Roman empires was distorted by the systematic removal of manpower and its absorption into the slave-based imperial systems;[35] and likewise the development of the societies on the periphery of Western Europe was later distorted by the effects of 'colonialism'.

As we have seen, the 'Hegelian' version of the unilinear schema puts considerable stress on the relations between human societies, as compared with the schema previously discussed in which the inner logic of social development was the dominant factor.[36] So that this emphasis on external relations should not seem to enhance the role of contingency too far, considerable effort has been devoted to creating a 'universal periodisation' which would systematically present the dominant influence in international relations in any given epoch. As a recent Soviet publication has expressed it 'without calculating the leading line of a given epoch or, in other words, without calculating the influence of the leading formation, every concrete analysis loses its point – the description of the facts remains, but it becomes impossible to ascertain their laws of motion.'[37]

According to the kind of universal periodisation described, the capitalist epoch of world history dates from the beginning of the seventeenth century, and the socialist epoch from 1917. These dates are particularly important because the role of external influence becomes much more intense and generalised with the dawning of the capitalist era and the creation of the world market. Societies which are for the first time exposed systematically to external influence in these epochs are able to skip several stages of the five-stage schema. One aspect of Zhukov's periodisation which would meet with less favour today (1974) is his suggestion that the revolutionary transformation from slavery to feudalism first took place in ancient China.[38] A recent Soviet article has

[35] Iu.V. Kachanovsky, *Rabovladenie, feodalizm ili aziatskii sposob proizvodstva?, op.cit.,* p. 103.

[36] Marx himself appears to have considered such external (and contingent) relations to be of great importance. He lists the three possible results of conquest, for example, as: (a) the imposition of the mode of production of the conquering people; (b) the preservation of the old mode of production and the mere imposition of a tributary relation; (c) the synthesis of the two modes of production. Which of these results would follow from conquest could not be established by any scientific law, although as seen, all of the alternatives are related to the modes of production in existence in the two parties (a negative determinism). Conquest of one people by another could not in itself give rise to a new mode of production, as was argued by some theorists of feudalism, in particular. See the *Grundrisse*, Introduction, pp. 97–98.

[37] Iu.V. Kachanovsky, *Rabovladenie, feodalizm ili aziatskii sposob proizvodstva?, op.cit.,* p. 106.

[38] E.M. Zhukov, 'O periodizatsii vsemirnoi istorii', *loc.cit.*, p. 25.

strongly criticised Chinese historiography, particularly that appearing in the journal *Hung Ch'i*, for claiming that the Asiatic nations were in the vanguard of world history until the fifteenth century, and for implying that the retardation of the East was only occasioned by the Western colonial powers. The Soviet author argues that on the contrary:

> ... In the countries of the East, the Ch'in, Khazar, Mogul, Osmanli and other dynasties – supported by a centralised state apparatus – impeded the development of society; cultivated early feudal and pre-feudal forms of social relations; exhausted the strength of their peoples in predatory wars; destroyed the forces of production; and suppressed social thought. The feudal leadership of the absolute majority of Asiatic and African countries proved to be incapable of understanding the historical problems of the epoch – the preservation of the independence of their countries. They betrayed their peoples. It was not for no reason that the majority of Asiatic dynasties ended up as the marionettes of foreign capital.[39]

To sum up, the major disadvantage of transposing the sphere of operation of necessary laws of historical development from the societal to the supra-societal level is that there no longer exists any evidence external to that from which the theory is drawn, by which it might be tested. The theory of historical materialism becomes a description of a unique process, rather than a hypothesis based on the development of one society which might be tested by reference to the development of a society remote in space or time.

CHRONOLOGICAL AND LOGICAL PROBLEMS ASSOCIATED WITH THE PROGRESSIVE RANKING OF SOCIO-ECONOMIC FORMATIONS

As seen above, the Hegelian modification of the unilinear schema consists essentially in viewing the schema as the pattern of world history, rather than as the pattern inherent in the development of every society. Nonetheless the 'Hegelian' version retains the standpoint that the transitions between the stages are of a logically necessary character. A different approach to Marx's schema, which has been attempted recently, has been to view it as an analytic ranking of socio-economic formations, but not as a fixed chronological sequence in which the contradictions of one stage necessarily give rise to the next.

[39] F.B. Beleliubsky, 'Maoistskaia kontseptsiia vsemirnoi istorii i podlinnaia istoriia narodov Vostoka', *Narody Azii i Afriki*, 1972, No. 5, p. 64.

This approach has been attempted by Eric Hobsbawm. It is most obviously prompted by the fact that some societies (notably the Chinese) appear to have passed through several periods of feudal disintegration,[40] or again not to have passed through certain epochs at all.

The main problem involved in the interpretation of the unilinear schema as an analytic ranking consists in establishing the analytic criteria whereby socio-economic formations are to be graded as more progressive, or in 'crucial respects further removed from the primitive state of man'.[41]

Hobsbawm's main criterion consists in the degree of 'economic individualisation' which exists in the given formation. Thus the most primitive socio-economic formations are those which conserve to the greatest degree communal forms of property, while the most advanced are those which contain the most elements of free labour and capital.

However the difficulty of viewing Marx's schema as an analytic ranking according to this criterion is tacitly admitted by Hobsbawm himself when he states that:

... a reversion to feudalism from formations which, while *potentially* less progressive, are in actual fact more highly developed – as from the Roman Empire to the tribal Teutonic kingdoms – has always been allowed for.[42]

Here Hobsbawm is admitting that the 'ancient' formation is more highly developed than the feudal formation, as it probably must be regarded as being if one employs the most common Marxist indicators, such as the degree of division of labour, the level of commodity production and the productivity of labour in certain areas. Hobsbawm in the passage cited is claiming that feudalism should be ranked higher than 'ancient society' because it has more potential for progress. However this is *less* because the degree of economic individualisation is higher in the feudal formation (Hobsbawm's analytic criterion) than because of the appearance of a particular urban structure within Western feudalism. Hobsbawm elsewhere attempts to bridge these viewpoints by arguing that it was the degree of economic individualisation in the feudal countryside which made the system soluble, and enabled 'free labour' to be released to the cities, although even then he admits that this was only one of at least three important factors which

[40] For example, the 'refeudalisation' that took place in China between the collapse of the Han dynasty and the Sui reunification of 589 A.D.

[41] Introduction to Marx, *Pre-Capitalist Economic Formations*, ed. Eric Hobsbawm, London, Lawrence and Wishart, 1964, p. 38.

[42] *Ibid.*, p. 63.

contributed to the rise of the West European cities.[43] Hobsbawm's ranking of feudalism above slavery really rests on the argument that the slave stage contains contradictions which lead inevitably to its collapse and not to the generation of higher structures within itself. The feudal formation, while based on a fairly primitive economy does appear to Hobsbawm to have this potential, even if only in the unique circumstances of Western Europe.

Hobsbawm retreats from an argument that the socio-economic formations represent an analytic ranking, without logically necessary connections, to an argument that one formation (i.e. feudalism) is more progressive than another because chronologically, and to some extent logically, it has given rise to the stage of capitalism.

The problem of attempting to view the schema of Marx's preface as an analytic ranking of socio-economic formation is a general one which extends beyond the work of Western Marxists such as Hobsbawm. It has been easier for Western Marxists, including Hobsbawm, to view the schema fairly flexibly, and to argue that the pre-capitalist formations are not of the same universal nature as capitalism and socialism and hence are not governed by the same kind of universal laws of transition. The earlier formations may be seen as governed by specific historical and geographical circumstances, and technological advances made in one stage may in fact be lost in the succeeding stage owing to invasion or some other contingency such as the self-destroying tendencies of slave-based formations.[44]

Soviet Marxism has been far more committed to the line that Marx's schema represents both a chronological and an analytic summary of human progress, and that this progress is undirectional. The criteria developed by Soviet Marxists to demonstrate that the five stages represent analytically more progressive stages of the development of production have been various. There has been a tendency to drop the criterion of development of division of labour, and hence of economic complexity, because of the complications, already suggested, with

[43] *Ibid.*, pp. 46–47. The others were the development of urban crafts and the availability of money derived from usury and trade.

[44] Although Hobsbawm does adhere sufficiently closely to the traditional view of historical materialism to argue that development of the forces of production must always ultimately result in the development of an even higher stage of social relations. What he is arguing against is the view that the formations laid down in Marx's schema are logically connected and must always follow one from another. Hobsbawm does want to argue, however, that socialism develops logically out of capitalism, where one might well argue that the contradictions brought about by the development of productive forces within a capitalist system make the establishment of some new system of social relations necessary, but that only under very special circumstances will this result in a socialist system as Marx defined it.

regard to the slave formation and feudalism. Other criteria associated with the degree of development of production which have been suggested are the materials used in production (ranging from stone and bronze to polymers); the sources of energy used in production (ranging from man-power and animal power, through steam and electric power to nuclear and perhaps solar energy); and the forms taken by co-operation in labour, from the most simple forms resting on the simple aggregation of individual effort to the most articulated and complex forms of organisation.[45]

Kachanovsky, in the work cited above, takes the level of development of productive forces as the basic criterion of the progressiveness of a given epoch (i.e., in Marx's terms, the degree to which man has mastered the forces of nature, plus the productivity of human labour).[46] According to Kachanovsky, however, two other criteria are of relatively high importance. The first of these is the degree of juridical emancipation of the worker. This criterion correlates fairly closely with Hobsbawm's economic individualisation. The second is the role of class struggle in the economy. In the slave stage the role of class struggle in the economic process is posited as being insignificant, in the feudal stage much more important, and in the capitalist stage as being of preeminent importance in the realisation of economic laws and the determination of economic life. This criterion is particularly tendentious and based on an extremely simplistic view of the class structure of the ancient world.

The difficulty of Kachanovsky's major criterion, the development of productive forces, is firstly, as he himself admits, that it is extremely difficult to establish a comparative analysis of levels of productivity in different socio-economic formations. Secondly the criterion of the development of productive forces lends itself to any and every schema of history and not simply to the unilinear schema sometimes suggested by Marx. With Kachanovsky for example, it is used to justify the exclusion of the Asiatic socio-economic formation from Marxist historiography, because in Asiatic society the level of development of productive forces will correspond either to the level found in ancient society, or the level found in feudal society. The criterion of development of productive forces could, however, with equal justification be applied to some such schema as hunting/gathering, herding, sub-

[45] See E.C. Welskopf, Einleitung, *Jahrbuch für Wirtschaftsgeschichte*, Berlin, 1967, Part IV, cited in Kachanovsky, *Rabovladenie, feodalizm ili aziatskii sposob proizvodstva?, op.cit.*, p. 86.
[46] Kachanovsky, *Rabovladenie, feodalizm ili aziatskii sposob proizvodstva?, op.cit.*, pp. 84–89.

sistence farming, commodity production, industrial production and post-industrial production.

The judging of socio-economic formations in terms of labour productivity leaves out of account the factor which Marx described as central to the description of any socio-economic formation – i.e., the way in which the surplus is appropriated from the direct producers. The criterion of the way in which the surplus is appropriated would serve to distinguish sharply socio-economic formations which by the criterion of basic labour productivity would be classed together (i.e. the Asiatic and feudal modes, although co-operation results in much higher productivity in some areas in the former mode of production).

THE MULTILINEAR SCHEMA OF HISTORY AS FOUND IN MARX

Marx's multilinear perception of pre-capitalist society, as discovered in the *Grundrisse* has already been discussed in Chapter Three. The diagrammatic summary of Marx's *Grundrisse* schema is repeated below

THE MULTILINEAR SCHEMA

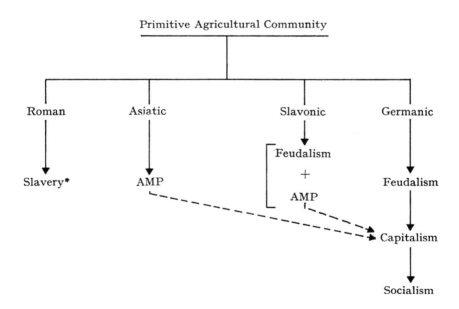

----- Non-progressive, but can develop into capitalism under pressure from pre-existing capitalist systems.
* Non-progressive and self-destructing.

for purposes of comparison with the other schemas of historical progress discussed in this Chapter.

As can be seen from the diagram, Marx believed that the multiplicity of forms of development which had existed in the pre-capitalist world would be brought to end by the universalising tendencies of capitalism. According to Marx the unifying force of the world market would ineluctably absorb all local particularities and prepare the way for the universal and uniform transition to socialism.

> ... It [the bourgeoisie] compels all nations, on pain of extinction, to adopt the bourgeois mode of production; it compels them to introduce what it calls civilisation into their midst, *i.e.*, to become bourgeois themselves. In one word, it creates a world after its own image.[47]

The transition from the multiplicity of forms in pre-capitalist society to the universal forms of capitalism and socialism is interpreted by the contemporary French Marxist Jean Suret-Canale as follows:

> ... With the appearance of class societies this diversity of forms which was due to geographical and historical circumstances etc., moves onto a different plane, thanks to *class relations*, expressable in a more abstract and generalisable form. It is only with capitalism, given the very nature of the productive forces on which it rests, and the nature of the social relations which it engenders, that forces of production and their corresponding relations of production become henceforth, in their essence, entirely independent of the peculiarities of the geographical and historical *milieu*. *By its very nature*, capitalism, as well as being one of the great stages of human progress, also assumes a universal value, destroying or reducing to the status of residual survivals, the previous modes of production. *A fortiore* such universality appertains to socialism. But one cannot project this universality of the last two stages of social development onto the history which precedes them.[48]

One is left with the question of whether Marx did not exaggerate the universalising force of capitalism, and whether there were not certain

---

[47] Marx and Engels, *The Communist Manifesto*, *MESW*, Vol. I, pp. 36–37. By 1858 Marx was more pessimistic about the rapidity with which the bourgeoisie would complete its universalising functions. He wrote that: 'The specific task of bourgeois society is the establishment of a world market, at least in outline, and of production based upon this world market. [...] The difficult question for us is this: on the Continent the revolution is imminent and will immediately assume a socialist character. Is it not bound to be crushed in this little corner, considering that in a far greater territory the movement of bourgeois society is still in the ascendant?' (Marx to Engels, 8 Oct. 1858, *MESC*, p. 111).

[48] Jean Suret-Canale, 'Problèmes théoriques de l'étude des premières sociétés de classes', *loc.cit.*, pp. 8–9. Cf. J.-J. Goblot on the factitiously homologous character ascribed to the five stages of the Stalinist schema. Goblot, however, while arguing that the pre-capitalist stages are of a less universal nature than the capitalist stage, holds to the unilinear view of history according to which there is one main thread of development rather than alternative forms. J.-J. Goblot, 'Pour une approche théorique des "faits de civilisation"', Part III, *La Pensée*, No. 136 (1967), p. 69.

socio-economic structures which, despite the impact of Western capital, were able to retain their homeostatic tendencies, and maintain their particularity into the new industrial era.

VARIATIONS OF THE MULTILINEAR SCHEMA AS APPLIED TO PRE-CAPITALIST SOCIETIES

Even among those Marxists accepting the equation of multilinear development with pre-capitalist society, and unilinear development with post-capitalist society,[49] many changes have been rung on the general theme. One such variation is that of Maurice Godelier, mentioned earlier in a slightly different context. Godelier combines the view that the Asiatic mode of production is an almost universally occurring transition stage (to class society) with the view that subsequent development is at least bilinear. As Godelier put it in 1964, given the specific circumstances, there might develop out of the Asiatic formation[50] *either* slave-owning and commodity production as in the Greco-Roman world, *or* feudalism and natural economy, as in China.[51] The kind of feudalism which developed directly out of the Asiatic formation, rather than out of the ruins of a slavery-based formation lacked the dynamic tendencies of Western feudalism, being still marked by many of the characteristics of the Asiatic epoch.[52] The following diagrams contrast the bilinear schema proposed by Godelier with the essentially bilinear schema suggested by Plekhanov and some of the participants in the first phase of the Soviet debate (1925–1931), such as Mad'iar and Lomakin. Whereas in the earlier schema the Asiatic mode of production was the *raison d'être* of the bilinearity, in Godelier's schema the existence of the Asiatic mode of production is incidental to it.

[49] At the discussion on the AMP at the Institute of Philosophy, Iu.A. Levada and others accepted this equation, rejecting the Stalinist viewpoint that there existed 'a single sequence (liniia) of socio-economic stages for all mankind' and arguing that 'the unity of man's historical development only comes into existence at a late stage.' (L.V. Danilova, 'Diskussiia po vazhnoi probleme', *loc.cit.*, p. 154).

[50] Defined, as previously noted as a transition stage where communal forms of property, still partly based on kinship relations, coexist with early forms of class exploitation; the latter expressed in terms of the appropriation by the state of surplus value and labour from the communities.

[51] M. Godelier, 'La notion de "mode de production asiatique" et les schémas marxistes d'évolution des sociétés', *loc.cit.*, pp. 90–92.

[52] *Ibid.*, p. 92.

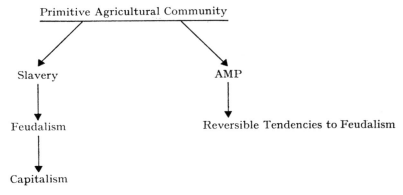

DIAGRAM I
(Plekhanov, Mad'iar, Lomakin *et al.*)

(Note that the primary division into slavery and the AMP corresponds to the two alternative accounts given in the *Anti-Dühring* of the genesis of state power.)

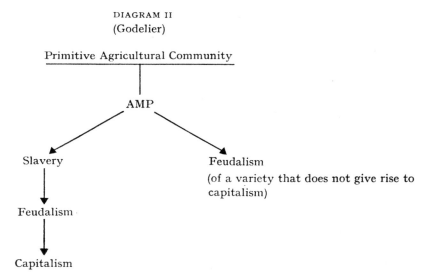

DIAGRAM II
(Godelier)

More recently Godelier has tended to go beyond his bilinear schema:

... Numerous commentators [...] hesitate to follow Marx when he uses the term 'mode of production' apropos the Celts, Slavs, etc. They have suggested that Marx was treating primarily forms of property and not modes of production, and that he was using the latter term with a certain carelessness. This is to forget that for Marx relations of ownership only had real existence in a definite process of production and that the older the forms of production, the more they assumed particular local forms, in contrast with the uniformity of the capitalist mode of production. There need be no constraint about multiplying the number of modes of production and even applying this notion to transitional forms between two distinct modes of production.[53]

In the same book Godelier writes that 'all discussion of the Asiatic mode of production hence leads *further*, towards the establishment of a multilinear theory of the evolution of societies'.[54] At the same time Godelier clings to his view that the Asiatic mode of production is a more or less universally occurring transition stage between classless and class societies.[55]

He also continues to argue that real progress does not occur in the Asiatic formation until it experiences the economic individuation achieved in Western societies.[56] Thus the Asiatic formation must be ranked logically below the classical and feudal formations. The Asiatic formation conserves the immediate unity of individual and community, at the village level, although historically the state supersedes the kinship community as the ultimate controller of the means of production. Within the Asiatic formation the direct producer is in a position of generalised dependence on the state and community, rather than in a position of personal dependence on slave owner or feudal lord.[57] However the position of the direct producer is not such that it can develop into the kind of personal freedom (but economic enslavement) represented by the free labour force of capitalism.

A more convincing attempt to reconcile the multilinear treatment of pre-capitalist society with the stadial conception of world history is to be found in a joint article by the Soviet historians L.S. Vasil'ev and I.A. Stuchevsky, entitled 'Tri modeli vozniknoveniia i evoliutsii dokapitalisticheskikh obshchestv'.[58] The burden of their argument is that the law of progressive development applies only to the following broad stages – primitive communal society (the primary formation of

---

[53] M. Godelier ed., *Sur les sociétés précapitalistes: textes choisis de Marx, Engels, Lénine*, C.E.R.M., Paris, Éditions sociales, 1970, Introduction, p. 61, fn. 1.

[54] *Ibid.*, p. 138.

[55] *Ibid.*, p. 134.

[56] *Ibid.*, p. 69.

[57] *Ibid.*, p. 75.

[58] L.S. Vasil'ev and I.A. Stuchevsky, 'Tri modeli vozniknoveniia i evoliutsii dokapitalisticheskikh obshchestv', *Voprosy istorii*, 1966, No. 5, pp. 77–90.

human history), pre-capitalist class society (the secondary formation), capitalist society, and socialism.[59] At a certain point of development each of these stages must be replaced by the next.[60] However the variety of forms found within the pre-capitalist stage, or secondary formation, of human history are not governed or related by the same law of progression. According to Vasil'ev and Stuchevsky, pre-capitalist development assumes three alternative forms, the slave-holding, the feudal, and the Asiatic – the Asiatic form representing a fusion of slave-holding and feudal elements.[61] Wherever the primitive communal constitution is in the process of disintegration, elements of either slavery or feudalism appear, but in the Asiatic formation these appear in conjunction with one another and hold each other in check. The lack of dynamism of the Asiatic formation is hence attributable to the 'fact' that within it neither the contradictions of slavery nor of feudal society are able to emerge in a pure form.[62]

Where the Vasil'ev and Stuchevsky article is weakest is in its attempt to portray the Asiatic formation as merely representing a mixture of Western forms of exploitation.[63] Vasil'ev, as we have seen in Chapter Two, has since gone some distance towards remedying this weakness.

He has now taken more account of Marx's view that in pre-capitalist society, where surplus labour is not yet expropriated by purely economic means (as through the 'free' but non-equivalent exchange of the capitalist market), there occurs either 'direct slavery, serfdom or political dependence',[64] i.e., that economic exploitation by the state, as in Asia, belongs to a different category than exploitation by private landowner or slaveholder and is not merely a fusion of the latter. Vasil'ev has, however, retained Marx's notion that stagnation was a structural characteristic of the Asiatic formation, and this marks his work off from that of those seriously concerned to develop the concept as the cornerstone of a new historiography liberated from 'European' bias.

[59] Cf. Marx to Zasulich, 8 March 1881, Third Draft: 'The secondary formation comprises, as you must understand, the series of societies based on slavery and serfdom.'
[60] L.S. Vasil'ev and I.A. Stuchevsky, 'Tri modeli...', *loc.cit.*, p. 89.
[61] *Ibid.*, p. 85.
[62] *Ibid.*, pp. 84–85.
[63] This view is shared by Iu.I. Semenov, who argues that the non-differentiation of these antagonistic relations of production in the Asiatic formation demonstrates its immaturity. See Iu.I. Semenov, 'Problema sotsial'no-ekonomicheskogo stroia drevnego Vostoka', *Narody Azii i Afriki*, 1965, No. 4, pp. 69–89; and also comments by Iu.A. Levada at the Institute of Philosophy discussion.
[64] Marx, *Theories of Surplus Value*, Part III, p. 400.

Where the Vasil'ev and Stuchevsky article does move in the direction of a new Marxist historiography is in its suggestion that the old Marxist historiography had overlooked for too long that Marx and Engels regarded slavery and feudalism as *parallel* forms of development. In consequence of this oversight, according to Vasil'ev and Stuchevsky, the development of feudalism among the Germans and Slavs was treated in an over-simplified fashion as the result of the preceding technical and productive advances of classical antiquity.[65] The productive forces of feudalism were not necessarily, however, of a higher level than those of slavery, though they had the potential for being so.[66] This potential existed within feudal relations of production not so much because the *tools* of production were of a more advanced nature, but because the direct producers had a higher stake in production, being semi-dependent rather than completely dependent.

The potential for development created by the use of semi-dependent labour did not depend on the contradictions of the slave-relationship having been revealed; the emergence of feudal relations of production was determined by the particular development of the primitive community under given historical and geographical circumstances.[67] Thus the question of whether the primitive community would develop into feudalism or slavery was not related to the chronological period in which the transition to class society took place, or to the pre-existing level of technological development, but to the nature of the prior development of the community.[68] This is an interesting rejection of the traditional Soviet view that societies which were isolated could not achieve feudalism without passing through a slave stage.

A different approach to the analysis of pre-capitalist societies, and one which opens up many of the problems associated with the new Marxist historiography of the non-Western world is to be found in the work of the Soviet historian L.A. Sedov. We have already looked at some of the views put forward by Sedov in 1965. Sedov has since developed an even more interesting framework for the analysis of

[65] L.S. Vasil'ev and I.A. Stuchevsky, 'Tri modeli...', *loc.cit.*, pp. 81–82. For an example of the kind of treatment the authors are criticising see Sid Douglas in *Marxism Today* (Vol. V, Dec. 1961, p. 381) arguing that China must have passed through a slave stage because: 'Primitive communism cannot accumulate enough wealth, even when it is affluent, to make a change to feudalism practicable.'

[66] I.A. Stuchevsky, 'O pervichnykh klassovykh formatsiiakh i aziatskom sposobe proizvodstva', in G.F. Kim, V.N. Nikiforov *et al.* ed., *Obshchee i osobennoe v istoricheskom razvitii stran Vostoka, op.cit.*, p. 124.

[67] L.S. Vasil'ev and I.A. Stuchevsky, 'Tri modeli...', *loc.cit.*, p. 83.

[68] *Ibid.*

'Asiatic' societies. He has taken as his starting point Marx's comment
that pre-capitalist economic formations are characterised by the appropriation of surplus value from the direct producers by means of
extra-economic pressures (as contrasted with the capitalist formation
where purely economic pressure is brought to bear).[69] He has then taken
over some of the apparatus of the American structural-functionalists.
He finds three different stages or moments of development to exist
within the Asiatic mode of production (which is distinguished from
European historical development by the dominant role of the state).[70]
Like the French Marxists mentioned earlier, he is concerned to eliminate
Marx's notion of the *semper idem* of the East from the concept of the
Asiatic mode of production. The first of the stages identified by Sedov
is that where the function of *integration* is dominant, i.e., the function
of integrating the dispersed rural communities into a social whole by
means of a state religion and associated theocratic structures. The
second stage, according to Sedov, is that where the function of *pattern
maintenance* [this phrase is rendered in English in the text] is dominant. Here the state is modelled on the family and assumes the
political form of the patriarchal bureaucratic monarchy. Sedov discusses in detail the existence of stages one and two in Cambodian
history of the Angkor and post Angkor periods. Cf. M. Godelier:
'To set forth a theory of the differentiated development of societies is
therefore at the same time to set forth a scientific theory of kinship,
of politics and of ideology. It means being ready to recognise that in
certain conditions kinship *is* the economy – or that religion can function
directly as the relations of production.'[71]

[69] Marx, *Theories of Surplus Value*, Part III, p. 400; *Capital* Vol. III, p. 791. Here Marx
cites only the role of force in the appropriation of surplus value in pre-capitalist formations,
but elsewhere he discusses the role of sacred authority.

[70] See L.A. Sedov, 'La société angkorienne et le problème du mode de production asiatique', *loc.cit.*, pp. 75–76. As Sedov wrote elsewhere: 'It is quite obvious that one cannot
compare these secondary class structures with feudalism of the European type, which in the
course of further development could give rise to capitalism.' The state retains its dominant
role in the exploitation of the people and the distribution of the surplus produce, in spite of the
appearance of private property and elements of slavery and feudalism. Status is still determined primarily by position in the service hierarchy. Hence 'the changes and progress which
took place in South-East Asia in the fourteenth and fifteenth centuries were only in the order
of evolution within the framework of the "Asiatic mode of production", seen as that type of
social structure within which stages can be distinguished distinct from the formations
observed in Europe.' (M.G. Kozlova, L.A. Sedov, V.A. Tiurin, 'Tipy ranneklassovykh
gosudarstv v Iugo-Vostochnoi Azii', *Problemy istorii dokapitalisticheskikh obshchestv*, Kniga
I, ed. L.V. Danilova *et al.*, Moscow, Izd. 'Nauka', 1968, p. 545.)

[71] Preface to *Sur les sociétés précapitalistes*, ed. M. Godelier, *op.cit.*, p. 141. Jürgen Habermas has also espoused this interpretation of historical materialism: only in modern societies,
especially capitalist ones, do the relations of production assume a purely economic form
instead of being constituted by kinship or political institutions. See Habermas, 'Historical
Materialism Reconsidered', *loc.cit.*, p. 73.

The third stage in Sedov's typology is that where the function of *mobilisation* is dominant, whether for military purposes, or to subserve ideological and economic competition with other states. In this stage the structures of the state are modelled on political or military organisation. The concept of a 'mobilisation' stage (a concept which derives from David Apter) within the framework of a characteristically 'Asiatic' political economy implicitly extends the chronological range of the Asiatic mode of production into the era of industrialisation. As we will see later this step has been explicitly taken by certain non-Soviet Marxists.

Overall, Sedov is making the point that in pre-capitalist or non-capitalist formations the organising principle of society may be the family, politics or religion. In these formations the economic sub-system is not separated out from the socio-political matrix in the distinctive fashion found in capitalism, and the priorities of social production do not stop short at 'purely economic' desiderata such as the maximisation of individual or social wealth.[72] The function of pattern maintenance, for example, may actively militate against the accumulation of wealth.

The idea of kinship structure as the organising principle of primitive society is to be found in the views expressed by Marx and Engels after they came under the influence of Morgan's anthropology. Marx and Engels adopted Morgan's proposition that the mode of production does not directly engender the forms of social organisation found in primitive society but rather that the structure of the family, or kinship structure, develops according to its own specific structural laws. These include the progressive development of incest taboos etc. Such independently evolving kinship structures played a dominant role in the organisation of social life. Thus Engels wrote to Marx in 1882 that the amazing similarity between the Germans described by Tacitus and the American Redskins, despite their completely different modes of production, the American Indians lacking animal husbandry or agriculture, 'just proves that at this stage the mode of production is less decisive than the degree to which the old blood bonds and the old mutual community of the sexes in the tribe have been dissolved'.[73]

---

[72] For a much older statement of this view see Georg Lukács: 'From the standpoint of an understanding of how the pre-capitalist societies were *really constituted* these quantitative gradations signify qualitative differences which are expressed epistemologically as the hegemony of completely different systems of categories and as the completely different functions of particular sectors within the framework of society as a whole.' (*History and Class Consciousness* (1923), tr. R. Livingstone, London, 1968).

[73] Engels to Marx, 8 Dec. 1882, *Werke*, Vol. 35, p. 125. Engels has been subjected to Marxist 'correction' on this point. He has been criticised for not consistently applying the

The emphasis on kinship structure to be found in contemporary Marxist anthropologists reflects the influence of Lévi-Strauss and recent structuralist theory. Lévi-Strauss has said that in primitive societies the rules of kinship and marriage 'have an operational value equal to that of economic phenomena in our own society'.[74]

However, while recent French structuralist theory incorporates the idea of the dominant role of kinship, it excludes other aspects of Morgan's anthropology which were accepted by Marx and Engels.[75] For example, there is a complete rejection of the kind of evolutionist anthropology found in Morgan, according to which social structures can be ranked on an evolutionary scale. The followers of Lévi-Strauss have concerned themselves with the way different societies have achieved the satisfactory communication of women, information and goods. Allowance is made for the fact that incompatibilities may arise between the sub-systems of society, which may cause the breakdown of the existing system, but this process is not described in an evolutionary manner. Nor is the economic sub-system seen as the most dynamic element in society, the element most likely to give rise to discontinuities in the rest of the system.

Most Marxists who have incorporated aspects of structuralist theory in their work would, however, argue that the development of the means of production does eventually assert its influence over the rest of society by giving rise to social tasks which cannot be fulfilled within the kinship structures.[76] New specialised structures then arise which express themselves as political relationships.

Marxists in general have also reserved the right to judge societies on an evolutionary scale in accordance with their capacity to control the external environment.[77] There are exceptions to this, for example

principles of historical materialism to the organisation of primitive society and for seeing the development of the family as an independently determining factor. 'In reality, however, the forms of the family were also always dependent on the conditions of production.' See I.Sellnow, 'Die Grundprinzipien einer Periodisierung der Urgeschichte', *Völkerforschung*, Berlin, Akademie-Verlag, 1954, p. 161.

[74] Claude Lévi-Strauss, interview in *Témoignage chrétien*, 8 April 1968, p. 18, quoted in Emmanuel Terray, *Marxism and 'Primitive Societies'*, tr. M. Klopper, N.Y., Monthly Review Press, 1972, p. 139. Some Marxist anthropologists would argue that in many primitive societies it is not so much kinship as the accumulation of support value (the 'big man' relationship) which is the dominating principle.

[75] One aspect of Morgan's anthropology which is now rejected by both Marxists and non-Marxists is the idea of a universal transition from matrifocal to patrifocal forms of social organisation.

[76] Preface to *Sur les sociétés précapitalistes*, ed. M. Godelier, *op.cit.*, p. 140.

[77] See E.J. Hobsbawm, 'Karl Marx's Contribution to Historiography', in *Ideology in Social Science*, ed. R. Blackburn, London, Fontana, 1972, pp. 275–277.

among those influenced by the ecological school. Such anthropologists analyse societies on the basis of their *adaptation* to a certain environment, rather than on the basis of their assumed 'mastery' over it, a mastery which is liable to give rise to imbalances in the ecological system.[78]

Certain problems connected with the incorporation of structuralist anthropology into Marxist theory remain unresolved. The most important of these is the relationship between the dominant role of kinship organisation and ultimate determination by the development of material production. If the priorities incorporated in kinship organisation (for example, the satisfactory regulation of the exchange of women) militate against investment in social production, that is, if other wealth is squandered but an orderly allocation of women, as the scarce resource, takes place, how can the demands of production be seen as the ultimately determining factor? Godelier's approach to this question is to seek the reason why a certain stage of economic development should dictate the dominance of kinship relations or politico-religious relations within society.[79]

The usual reason given for why kinship structures decay and are replaced by competing economic classes and a state structure is that an intensification of agriculture takes place, for population or other reasons.[80] This brings about an increase in economic inequalities and a solidifying of economic classes. The state structure becomes necessary to deal with the increased quantum of social conflict generated by the economic differentiation now established. In this case economic imperatives have come to exercise both an ultimately determining and a dominant role in the structuring of society.

However, where communal ownership or possession continues to exist side by side with a territorically-based state organisation, as in the different types of Asiatic formation discussed by Sedov, economic imperatives do not assume this distinct and dominant role. In these cases the (as yet un-class-divided) society requires a strong centralised body to conduct certain large-scale public works or to deal with certain military exigencies. (The need to control trade and safeguard a central market seems to be part of a specifically African model, rather than to be an aspect of a universal 'Asiatic' model *pace* the French Marxists.)

---

[78] See, for example, Marshall Sahlins, *Stone Age Economics*, Chicago, Aldine-Atherton, 1972.

[79] M. Godelier, *Rationality and Irrationality in Economics*, tr. Brian Pearce, London, NLB, 1972, p. ix.

[80] See my Note on the Population Factor, pp. 136–139.

In order to perform these tasks the state has to achieve the integration of the society under the umbrella of its common politico-religious authority. This authority assumes a dominant role in the society, and is the means by which the surplus is expropriated from the direct producers for redistribution to other sectors performing state functions. As mentioned earlier, the maximisation of social wealth through, for example, technical innovation and the emergence of entrepreneurial groups, may be actively discouraged in these societies, as in all pre-capitalist societies.

According to Sedov, the dominant pattern of state authority, and hence the structuring of all other social and economic relationships will depend on the particular crisis the society is going through in connection with its internal and external maintenance. Hence a multilinear pattern is manifested in the development of pre-capitalist societies.

THE DYNAMICS OF MODERNISATION IN THE NON-WESTERN WORLD: TOWARDS A NEW MARXIST HISTORIOGRAPHY

Although the multilinear perception of pre-capitalist society, strengthened in recent years by the new interest in Marx's *Grundrisse* (and developed creatively by a number of Marxists with the help of conceptual tools borrowed from the social sciences), provides a more satisfactory framework of analysis than the unilinear schema previously attributed to Marx, it is still tied to preconceptions and attitudes which anchor it in the nineteenth century. While the concept of the absolute stagnation of the Asiatic formation has been eliminated, Marx's central thesis that progress towards industrialisation is dependent on the dissolution of communal forms of economy in favour of private ownership has been retained. According to Marx's formulation in the *Grundrisse*, non-Western socio-economic formations were incapable of developing towards industrialisation without a fundamental structural change. On his view industrialisation, the prerequisite of socialism, was itself made possible only by the development of the forms of individual property found in the West; non-Western societies had to become Westernised, before they could progress in the direction of socialism. Thus the multiplicity of forms of development in the pre-capitalist era had to give way to a uniformity in the capitalist and post-capitalist epochs.

It has frequently been observed that for Marx industrialisation was synonymous with capitalism, and hence he tended to view history in terms of the creation of the preconditions of capitalism – i.e., increasing individuation. As Marx himself said: 'What is called historical evolution depends in general on the fact that the latest form regards earlier ones as stages in the development of itself and conceives them always in a one-sided manner [...]'[81]

Marx's own work, despite his implicit recognition of the existence of a multiplicity of historical paths, bore witness to the all-pervasive influence of the evolutionary paradigm in nineteenth-century social science. There was a tension in his work between the idea that different forms of social organisation represented real alternatives and the idea that different forms of social organisation merely represented different stages of a universal historical progression (stages through which Western Europe had already passed).

One limited revision of Marx's *Grundrisse* schema, which is in line with Lenin's so-called 'law of uneven development' is the argument that development may be multilinear up until the socialist stage rather than only up until the capitalist stage; that the world market may still not have dissolved certain pre-capitalist economic formations by the time that they come under the influence of socialist systems. These socialist systems will still themselves have depended on the prior development of capitalism in Europe, but they will to some extent take the place of capitalism as the vehicle of change and as the model for industrialisation and modernisation. Thus the multiplicity of historical forms of development is only transcended with the achievement of socialism.

A more drastic revision of Marx's *Grundrisse* schema consists in the argument that the existence of alternative forms of historical development in, for example, Europe and Asia gives rise to alternative forms of the development of socialism. According to this argument the traditional economic role of the state in the AMP lends itself to a state-initiated industrialisation process.[82] The traditional forms of village co-operation likewise present less obstacles to the development of a planned economy than the highly developed forms of private property found in Western Europe.

Thus the Asiatic formation may retain its distinctive structure and characteristics while undergoing the process of modernisation and

---

[81] Marx, *Contribution to the Critique of Political Economy, op.cit.*, p. 211.
[82] See for example B. McFarlane and S. Cooper, 'The Asiatic Mode of Production – An Economic Phoenix?', *The Australian Quarterly*, Vol. XXXVIII, No. 3 (Sept. 1966), pp. 27–43.

industrialisation. The village communities retain their economic autarky and continue to hand over their surplus value to the state. The state now uses part of this surplus value to subsidise industrialisation, and the structure of state functionaries is supplemented by the managerial and technical cadres associated with industrialisation. The symbolic attributes of the tutelary Asiatic state, embodied usually in a paternalistic 'head of state', provide continuity into the modern age and modify the disruption engendered by the industrialisation process.

According to the argument of Sencer Divitçioglu, whose economic model of the Asiatic mode of production will be reproduced below in a modified form, the basic dynamic of the Asiatic formation is provided by two classes, the state functionaries, and the people. The traditional state functionaries have a class interest in preventing the development of a capitalist class and a capitalist system in the process of industrialisation, as this would threaten their own position.[83] Nonetheless Divitçioglu points out that the 'Asiatic' form of industrialisation cannot give rise to popular socialism (i.e., the Marxist conception of socialism) as contrasted with tutelary socialism[84] until the class of functionaries is abolished and the state becomes identified with the people as a whole.

One should add that even were this egalitarian goal to be achieved the relationship between the individual and the collectivity is likely to differ from that in the West, where individualism has played a larger historical role. This point has been made again and again by Western (including Soviet) Marxists in relation to the Chinese version of socialism. One of the best-known proponents of the argument has been Roger Garaudy, who wrote in his *Le Problème chinois* that because the Chinese revolution arose not out of the internal contradictions of capitalism, but instead in a country dominated by feudal relations as well as survivals of the AMP, Chinese socialism lacked elements such as respect for the rights of the individual which were acquired in Western Europe during the liberal-democratic era. That is, because of its different historical experience, China's model of socialism could not but differ from those grounded in the Western European historical experience.[85]

To return to Divitçioglu's concept of the dynamics of development

---

[83] Sencer Divitçioglu, 'Essai de modèles économiques à partir du M.P.A.', *Recherches internationales à la lumière du marxisme*, No. 57–58 (Jan.-April 1967), pp. 288–289.

[84] Divitçioglu himself uses the expression 'tutelary state'.

[85] R. Garaudy, *Le Problème chinois*, Paris, Éditions Seghers, 1967.

we reproduce below his diagrams, firstly of the structure of the AMP in the pre-industrial phase, and secondly of the structure as modified during contact with industrial countries and during the industrialisation process.[86]

DIAGRAM I

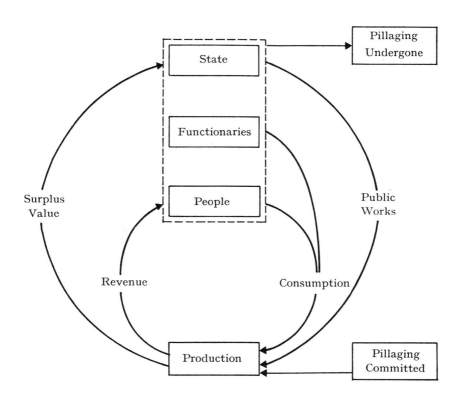

The idea illustrated in Divitçioglu's diagrams, that 'Asiatic' society may retain its basic structure while undergoing industrialisation, implies a complete rejection of Marx's thesis that the Asiatic form of political economy was incapable of generating anything approximating modern industrial development. According to Marx, the role of Western capital in *breaking down* the old structure of Asiatic society and providing the conditions for development in its own image was an essential element of the universal progress towards socialism. The notion that

[86] Sencer Divitçioglu, *sup.cit.*, pp. 279, 286.

DIAGRAM II

(Reflecting the existence of some private enterprise, not all the surplus value is absorbed by the state.)

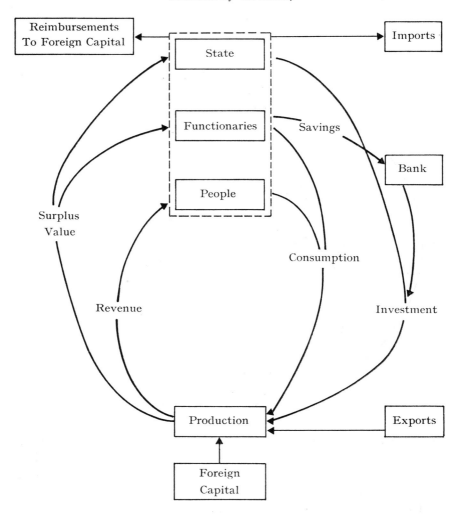

(contrary to Marx's beliefs) industrialisation and capitalism may be logically and historically separable has given rise to an interesting change of terminology in Marxist writing. One finds scholars such as Sedov discussing 'pre-industrial' societies rather than 'pre-capitalist' societies, implying that capitalism does not denote a universal stage of development whereas industrialisation does.[87]

To sum up then, Marx's perception of the dynamics of development in the non-Western world, together with some of the variations discussed in this essay, are illustrated in the diagrams below.

DIAGRAM I. THE STALINIST FIVE STAGE UNILINEAR SCHEMA

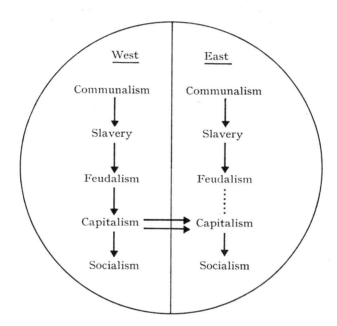

...... Buds or germs of capitalism which would have evolved independently into capitalism but for the impact of Western imperialism.

The first two diagrams are basically Europo-centric. Diagram I posits that the non-Western world would have developed capitalist and socialist stages independently, if it were not for the intervention of Western capitalism, which for some reason developed faster than Eastern capitalism. *But* all the categories employed in this diagram are basically derived from the study of European history. Nonetheless Asian communist parties such as the Chinese, through spokesmen such

---

[87] L.A. Sedov, 'O sotsial'no-ekonomicheskikh tipakh razvitiia', G.F. Kim, V.N. Nikiforov *et al.*, ed., *Obshchee i osobennoe v razvitii stran Vostoka, op.cit.*, pp. 49–50.

DIAGRAM II. MARX'S GRUNDRISSE MULTILINEAR SCHEMA

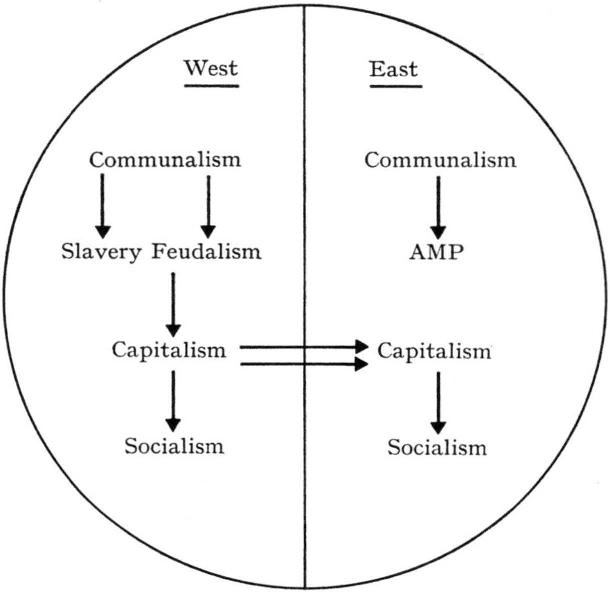

as Kuo Mo-jo, have been particularly anxious to validate Diagram I, by means of archeological commissions etc.

Diagram II is, if anything, more Europo-centric than Diagram I. It posits an alternative non-Western form of historical development but this lacks any dynamic element. Progress is brought to the East for the first time in the form of capitalism introduced from outside, and only capitalism leads, through its own contradictions, on to socialism.

Diagram III posits socialism as arriving first in the non-Western world, partly by reasons of the 'advantages of backwardness'. The fact that the preceding stages have reached their full flowering in the West means that the dialectical antithesis to capitalism tends to arise externally to the societies of Western Europe (i.e. the countries of the third world represent the internal contradiction of capitalism, they are 'proletarian countries'). This is the theory of the 'retarding lead'.

Diagram IV has the advantage of being less Europo-centric than Diagrams I and II, and on the other hand, not involving the logical problem of perceiving world history as a unitary organic process.

DIAGRAM III. THE HEGELIAN VERSION OF THE UNILINEAR MARXIST SCHEMA

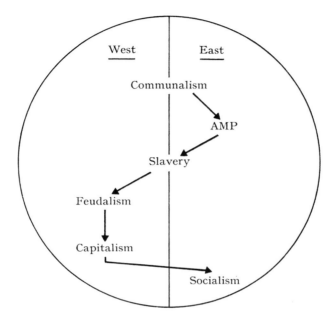

N.B. The geographical location of the centre of world history constantly shifts.

According to Diagram IV modernisation and industrialisation can take place with less dislocation and violent structural change than was necessary in the transition between feudalism and capitalism in the West, or between capitalism and socialism. Diagram IV, with its basic structural continuity between the AMP and tutelary socialism stages confirms Marx's belief that the structures of Asiatic society were extremely cohesive and resistant to change. On the other hand it contradicts Marx's notion that economic development or industrialisation could not take place within the structures of Asiatic society.

The argument that certain social structures (for example the Asiatic) are basically more resilient than others in the context of rapid economic development does not entail the view that modernisation would necessarily have been initiated in the 'Asiatic' societies without the impact of Western capitalism and Western industrialisation. Nor does it deny that the impact of Western capitalism on 'Asiatic' societies may have been so strong as to foreclose the possibility of the kind of structural continuity sketched above. The implications of the concept of

DIAGRAM IV. A NON-EUROPO-CENTRIC VERSION OF DIAGRAM II

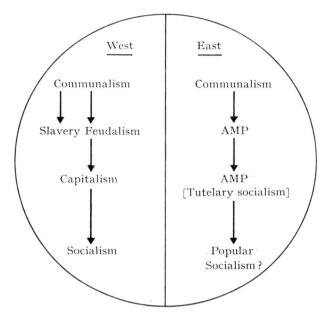

N.B. The Asiatic mode of production in this instance is conceived of as a dynamic structure capable o sustaining modernisation and industrialisation.

the Asiatic mode of production for contemporary Marxism lie in the realm of an enhanced understanding of the complexities of the historical process, rather than in the substantive content of the concept.

The functions of the model of an Asiatic mode of production in contemporary Marxist historiography have been to stimulate a new heuristic approach to Marxism as a theory of world history, and to strengthen the view that history is to be regarded as *prima facie* open, and not as a closed and unitary process governed by immutable general laws determining its movement towards a single goal.[88]

[88] The openness of history is in principle a separate point from whether all of history follows a European pattern, but the recognition of diverse patterns of historical development has in fact coincided with and to some extent given rise to the tendency to treat history as open. For one example see Guy Dhoquois in his *Pour l'histoire*, Paris, Éditions Anthropos, 1971. Dhoquois argues that the diverse patterns of pre-capitalist historical development tend to be brought to an end by the homogenising influence of the world market. However the movement from market capitalism into violent and unstable monopoly capitalism gives rise to a new era of diversity ranging from the proto-socialism emerging from anti-imperialist revolutions to the technocratic state-capitalism of the more advanced nations. This diversity is associated by Dhoquois with the possibility of developments either from proto-socialism

This does not mean a rejection of Marx's general view of social dynamics, the view that social structures appropriate to one level of economic development are liable to become a fetter on further development and subject to revolutionary change. It *does* mean a rejection of Marx's Western European perspective, and a recognition that non-European forms of historical development may have their own dynamics, which although overshadowed during the rapid industrial expansion of Western Europe in the nineteenth century are now re-asserting themselves in the form of self-proclaimed non-Western paths of development.

In the context of Europe itself, the stress on the openness of history is linked with the idea that although the development of productive forces will invariably affect the forms of social organisation, the achievement of the kind of socialist society which Marx foreshadowed will depend largely on subjective factors centring on social choice, social consciousness and social struggle. As these factors are deeply affected by the particular historical matrix in which they operate, the new approach assumes that the multiplicity of forms of social organisation which Marx attributed to the pre-capitalist era will continue into the future. The spread of industrial technology through the operation of the world market is no longer depicted as necessarily giving rise to the spread of a single form of social organisation. the assumption of unity has given way to an assumption of plurality, which expresses itself both in a more flexible historiography and in more flexible political and social policies.

into state-capitalism or from proto-socialism or state-capitalism into socialism, the direction taken depending on 'the power of human creativity'. For another example of the association of the multilinear conception of history with the conception of the openness of the future see Umberto Melotti, *Marx e il Terzo Mondo*, Milan, Centro Studi Terzo Mondo, 1971.

CHAPTER VI

EPILOGUE

Since the completion of this manuscript (in early 1974) there has been a great upsurge of debate in the English speaking world concerning the theoretical analysis of pre-capitalist modes of production. The stimulus for this upsurge has largely come from abroad – new theories of imperialism and underdevelopment on the one hand, and the methodological innovations of the Althusserian school of Marxism on the other. The former has given rise to the much-debated hypothesis of a 'colonial mode of production', in which production of commodities for a world-market is structurally tied to the continuance of a subsistence agriculture and pre-capitalist social relations within the colonial economy.[1] The methodological innovations have given rise, *inter alia*, to the two volumes published by Perry Anderson in 1974, *Passages from Antiquity to Feudalism* and *Lineages of the Absolutist State*, and the single volume *Pre-Capitalist Modes of Production* published by Barry Hindess and Paul Q. Hirst in 1975. It is the Anderson and Hindess and Hirst books which I wish to discuss here, as they have been the focus of much attention and both, though for very different stated reasons, deny the usefulness of the AMP concept.

Perry Anderson's two volumes, as the title suggest, are of monumental scope, and, what is even more gratifying, of corresponding depth of historical perceptions. The profusion of historical detail is controlled by a clear and self-conscious conceptual framework, a framework which owes much of its sophistication to recent French Marxism but which owes its solid relationship to factual material to a more Anglo-Saxon tradition. Anderson has adopted for his own work the Althusserian stress on the

---

[1] See for example, H. Alavi, 'India and the Colonial Mode of Production', *Socialist Register* 1975, pp. 160–197; J. Barbalet, 'Underdevelopment and the Colonial Economy, *Journal of Contemporary Asia* Vol. 6. No. 2, 1976, pp. 186–193.

relative autonomy of the practical and ideological 'levels' (in fact cognate with the despised Hegelian 'moments') of any given social formation. As noted in Chapter Five, the theoretical implications of this are particularly important in relation to precapitalist modes of production, where the political or ideological levels exert the dominant role according to the Althusserian scheme of analysis. The priority given to non-economic structures is justified by their centrality in the appropriation of social surplus where the labourer has not yet been separated from the means of valorising his labour. In pre-capitalist modes of production the economic level has neither the dominance nor the autonomy attributed to it in the capitalist mode of production, and appropriation cannot occur via the more purely economic mechanisms represented by the capitalist market.

In consequence, pre-capitalist modes of production cannot be defined *except* via their political, legal and juridical superstructures, since these are what determine the type of extra-economic coercion that specifies them. The precise forms of juridical dependence, property and sovereignty that characterize a pre-capitalist social formation, far from being merely accessory or contingent epiphenomena, compose on the contrary the central indices of the determinate mode of production dominant within it. A scrupulous and exact taxonomy of these legal and political configurations is thus a precondition of establishing any comprehensive typology of pre-capitalist modes of production.[2]

As can be seen from this passage, Anderson is drawing on the Althusserian propositions of the dominance of the ideological and political levels in pre-capitalist societies but at the same time moving beyond the restriction of the five orthodox modes of production (based on the differing combination of the five invariant factors) allowed by Althusser and Balibar. Anderson has his roots in the Anglo-Saxon historical tradition, despite the leavening of the pudding with the yeast of French conceptual inventiveness. He has nothing to do with the algebraical notions of ahistorical invariant factors (workers, means of production and non-labouring appropriators together with the appropriation relationship and the property relationship). Hence Anderson follows the more fruitful of the Althusserian school, such as Godelier, rather than the founder himself who combined a formal tribute to the dominance of political and ideological levels with an attempt to define modes of production via changes in the logical relationship of invariant economic categories, regardless of politico-juridical structures which subverted the significance of these categories

___

[2] P. Anderson, *Lineages of the Absolutist State*, London, NLB, 1974, p. 404.

themselves. As noted in Chapter Five above, Godelier found himself forced by the logic of the Althusserian argument *a*) – the dominance of the political and ideological levels – to suggest that an indefinite number of modes of production was possible within this scenario, corresponding to diverse political/juridical complexes. This leads to the rejection of the Althusserian argument *b*) – that the five orthodox modes of production and these only could be scientifically 'produced' through the differing combination of the five invariant factors. Both Godelier and Anderson also extended argument *a*) in ways unacceptable to the founders of this school of Marxism. That is, by arguing that in pre-capitalist modes of production not only do the political and ideological levels have a relative autonomy and dominant role in the structure of pre-capitalist societies, but that the economic level does not in fact exist in any easily demarcated way. This extension of argument *a*) does not satisfy the 'esprit de géometrie'[3] of the Althusserians who wish to regard all modes of production as determinate combinations and structures in dominance of invariant elements.

Anderson's work is dedicated to the investigation of why capitalism emerged only in Western Europe. His answers lie in the realm of the specific juridico-political heritage of the West. The institutional richness and complexity of Western feudalism combined with the juridical legacy of Rome rediscovered in the Renaissance produced the phenomenon of Western capitalism. Non-Western feudalism, such as the Japanese, was also receptive to capitalism because of its similar institutional constellation, but lacked the classical legacy (with its well-developed notions of private property and civil contract) which Anderson poses as essential for an indigenous development towards capitalism. Other non-Western pre-capitalist societies lacked both the specific genesis of Western feudalism and its institutional contours. Anderson quotes with approval Marx's comments on Kovalevsky, where Marx derides the conflation of Mughal India with Western European feudalism. Social formations lacking the parcellisation of sovereignty (both horizontal and vertical), the institutions of patrimonial justice and mutual obligation between protecting lord and producing peasant cannot on Anderson's account, earn the title 'feudal'.[4]

However, while approving Marx's discrimination in the use of the

---

[3] Mark Poster, 'Althusser on History Without Man', *Political Theory*, Vol. 2, No. 4 (Nov. 1974), p. 405.

[4] Western Europe supplies the mould and form of feudalism, for Anderson. Eastern Europe and Japan are also feudal, but the differing trajectories of their development are measured against the Western European model.

feudal category, Anderson rejects Marx's attempt to use the AMP concept to explain non-Western forms of development or non-development. Anderson's argument is an empirical one, that the AMP concept was derived from the great tradition rather than from any close analysis of non-Western social realities and that it is incompatible with contemporary knowledge of the areas to which Marx and Engels applied it. Marx and Engels chose to follow the great tradition in that they sought to define Europe in terms of what was not European, and enclosed the whole of this non-European experience within a single category. Anderson argues that this single category, the AMP, is in fact made up of elements which 'represented not so much *conjoint* as *alternative* principles of development.'[5] That is, on the one hand, the absence of private property in land, and on the other the provision by the state of major irrigation works (or transport canals). The first element Anderson sees as characterising the great Islamic empires, which however lacked large-scale public irrigation works (or where they inherited them allowed them to decay). The second Anderson finds to be important in imperical China, where however private property in land was firmly established from at least the Sung dynasty. Hence although Anderson agrees that in the Chinese and the Islamic empires there is a common absence of the highly developed civil law.[6] (which he finds to the enabling factor in the take-off of Western capitalism) he disagrees that a common concept can be employed to categorise them. Anderson's argument is that not only must one avoid inflating (and hence devaluing) the feudal concept by applying it to morphologically heterogeneous societies, but one must also avoid inflating any residual non-feudal category such as the AMP.

Hence Anderson accepts the basic lesson of the AMP concept for Marxist historiography – that concepts pertaining to Western European social formations should not lightly be extended to formations found outside the realm of Western European historical experience and juridico-political structures. As cited above this is because juridico-political structures are, in pre-capitalist societies, what specifies the mode of production; what enforces the particular kind of extra-economic coercion characteristic of the society. Anderson argues on empirical grounds that the AMP concept itself is unviable because it

---

[5] P. Anderson, *Lineages of the Absolutist State, op.cit.*, p. 491.

[6] And indeed of the highly developed concept of private agrarian property which emerged in Europe from the Renaissance. Anderson admits that while post-Tang China was much more highly developed in this area than the Islamic civilisations, it fell far short of Europe.

contains elements which have historically been mutually exclusive. He suggests that new and distinct concepts relating to the juridical-political complexes of the non-Western world must be drawn up to define the modes of production and social formations found there.

In his attempt to 'bury' the AMP concept Anderson is somewhat ungracious. His concentration on an empirical rejection of its validity deflects attention from the theoretical lesson already mentioned, which is utilised to such good effect in Anderson's own writing. Although Anderson can and has derived his theoretical standpoint on the dominance of non-economic levels in pre-capitalist societies from Althusserian premises, it was *only* with the rediscovery of the AMP concept in the 1960's that serious investigation of the possibility of further *alternative* pre-capitalist modes of production began. The rediscovery of the AMP concept legitimated the view that, given the centrality of non-economic factors in the appropriation of the surplus, pre-capitalist societies with widely divergent juridico-politico-religious complexions could not be said to share the same mode of production: hence even if the AMP concept is empirically false, it has had a much more profound effect on Marxist scholarship than Anderson here acknowledges.

Hindess and Hirst, in their book *Pre-Capitalist Modes of Production*, approach the problem of the AMP from a completely different, and much more orthodox Althusserian standpoint than does Anderson. Hindess and Hirst formally eschew the use of empirical argument, although in the chapter on the AMP it does indeed creep in the back door.[7] Their stated aim is to establish whether or not the AMP concept is theoretically compatible with the Marxist concept of a mode of production. In the words of the authors: 'The general concept of mode of production specifies the general conditions which must be satisfied by a concept of a determinate mode of production.'[8] The AMP concept does not satisfy these conditions, which demand that a mode of production must be characterised by a distinctive economic mechanism of the appropriation of surplus value, which corresponds to an 'articulated combination of relations and forces of production'.

According to Hindess and Hirst, the AMP appears initially to conform to the general Marxist concept of a mode of production, in that it

---

[7] E.g., B. Hindess, P. Hirst, *Pre-Capitalist Modes of Production*, London, Routledge & Kegan Paul, 1975, pp. 213–215.
[8] *Ibid.*, p. 9.

contains a distinctive economic mechanism for the appropriation of the surplus product – the 'tax/rent couple'. That is, the surplus is appropriated by means of tax, which assumes the function of rent in this mode of production. However, this economic mechanism of appropriation does not exist in a necessary relationship to one particular combination of relations and forces of production, as it is associated with both communal and peasant forms of production and conversely these forces of production may be associated with a different mechanism of appropriation.

Hindess and Hirst share with Anderson the general Althusserian position that in the pre-capitalist modes of production the dominant role is played by the political or ideological levels rather than the economic. However Hindess and Hirst then retreat from this position, in that, instead of awarding a logical primacy to politico-ideological institutions in the characterising of pre-capitalist formations, they attempt laboriously to separate the ideological and political conditions of appropriation from the economic form in which this appropriation takes place. It is this specific economic mechanism of appropriation (rent is the most coherent example given) that determines the necessary dominance of the ideological or political levels. This is truly standing the pre-capitalist world on its head. The most confused example of this is the Hindess and Hirst treatment of the ancient mode of production. The ancient mode of production is defined by the economic mechanism of appropriation by right of citizenship. It is this specific mode of appropriation which 'determines the necessary dominance of the political'.[9] However, as Hindess and Hirst admit in the Introduction, where they perform a self-criticism of their concept of appropriation by right of citizenship, an economic form of appropriation is here conflated with its political conditions of existence. In fact one might well argue, along with Anderson, that this conflation is essential, but one could not at the same time hold that this form of appropriation determines its own conditions of existence. Rather it is the dominance of the political level that determines that appropriation is by right of citizenship, or indeed that renders the latter intelligible.

The Hindess and Hirst position is summed up most clearly in a review by Hirst of Anderson. Hirst writes that:

---

[9] *Ibid.*, p. 79.

It is the economic form of exploitation and not the sanctions that support it that is the means of differentiation. Marx's position is that the social relations of production and the superstructure are not fused or equivalent. The political and ideological conditions of existence of exploitation are not exploitation itself, the legal forms of expression of property relations are not the actual economic relations of possession and control.[10]

The practical consequences of the Hindess and Hirst position are a return to the ubiquity of feudalism – whenever some form of rent, whether labour rent, rent in kind or money-rent is the dominant form of exploitation one has the feudal mode of production. This over-extension of the concept greatly reduces its explanatory power, and the differing histories of the societies included within its ambit can only be explained by factors external to their structure of exploitation and domination. This weakness is compatible with the anti-historical bias of Hindess and Hirst who claim that: 'Marxism as a theoretical and a political practice gains nothing from its association with historical writing and historical research. The study of history is not only scientifically but politically valueless.'[11] In their discarding of the historical parameters of political action Hindess and Hirst are even more thoroughgoing than Althusser, whom they criticise for clinging to the term 'science of history', even after having emptied this science of an historical content.

However, *pace* Hindess and Hirst, the political functions of historiography are so important that Marxists will never wholly abandon this area, or the attempt to improve their historical tools. Meanwhile, the attempts to increase the rigour of concepts such as mode of production or social formation (in which at least the remnants of more than one mode of production will be found in an articulated combination) should have a stimulating effect on Marxist history, once they filter down to practising historians.

The Anderson work, while also rejecting the AMP concept illustrates to a high degree a concern with the non-economic forms of appropriation and with the pluralism of pre-capitalist development; the kind of concern which the rediscovery of the AMP concept has served to legitimise. Hence while historians such as Anderson have thrown away the ladder, it has enabled them to scale new heights in the writing of Marxist history.

[10] P. Hirst, 'The Uniqueness of the West', *Economy and Society*, Vol. 4, No. 4, p. 464.
[11] B. Hindess and P. Hirst, *Pre-Capitalist Modes of Production, op.cit.*, p. 312.

SELECT BIBLIOGRAPHY

WORKS BY MARX AND ENGELS

ENGELS, FRIEDRICH, *Anti-Dühring*, tr. E. Burns, London, Lawrence and Wishart, n.d. (reprinted with minor revisions from the 1934 edition).

—, *The Dialectics of Nature*, tr. C.P. Dutt, London, Lawrence and Wishart, 1940.

—, *Principles of Communism*, tr. Paul M. Sweezy, London, Pluto, n.d.

MARX, KARL, *A Contribution to the Critique of Political Economy*, tr. S.W. Ryazanskaya, Moscow, Progress, 1970.

—, *Capital: A Critique of Political Economy*, 3 vols., N.Y., International Publishers, 1967.

—, *The Civil War in France*, Peking, Foreign Languages Press, 1966.

—, [Conspectus of M.M. Kovalevsky, *Obshchinnoe zemlevladenie, prichiny, khod i posledstviia ego razlozheniia* (Moscow, 1879)], first published serially in *Sovetskoe Vostokovedenie*, 1958, No. 3, pp. 3–13; No. 4, pp. 3–22; No. 5, pp. 3–33; *Problemy Vostokovedeniia*, 1959, No. 1, pp. 3–17. See also *Karl Marx über Formen vorkapitalistischer Produktion*, ed. H. -P. Harstick, Frankfurt, Campus Verslag, 1977.

—, *Early Writings*, ed. T.B. Bottomore, London, Watts, 1963.

—, *The Ethnological Notebooks of Karl Marx*, ed. Lawrence Krader, Assen, Van Gorcum, 1972.

—, *Grundrisse. Foundations of the Critique of Political Economy (Rough Draft)*, tr. Martin Nicolaus, Harmondsworth, Penguin, 1973.

—, *Karl Marx on Colonialism and Modernization*, ed. Shlomo Avineri, N.Y., Anchor Books, 1969.

—, *The Poverty of Philosophy*, N.Y., International Publishers, 1963.

—, *Pre-Capitalist Economic Formations*, ed. Eric Hobsbawm, London, Lawrence and Wishart, 1964.

—, *Revolution and Counter-Revolution*, ed. Eleanor Marx Aveling, London, Unwin, 1971.

—, *Secret Diplomatic History of the Eighteenth Century*, ed. L. Hutchinson, London, Lawrence and Wishart, 1969.

—, *Theories of Surplus Value*, 3 vols., London, Lawrence and Wishart, 1969.

MARX and ENGELS, *Ex Libris Marx und Engels; Schicksal und Verzeichnis einer Bibliothek*, ed. Bruno Kaiser, Berlin, Dietz, 1967.

—, *The German Ideology*, Moscow, Progress, 1968.

—, *On Colonialism*, Moscow, Foreign Languages Press, n.d.

—, *The Russian Menace to Europe*, ed. Paul W. Blackstock and Bert F. Hoselitz, London, Allen and Unwin, 1953.

—, *Selected Correspondence*, 2nd edn., Moscow, Progress, 1965.

—, *Selected Works*, 2 vols., Moscow, Foreign Languages Publishing House, 1951–55.

—, *Werke*, 39 vols., 2 supplementary vols., Berlin, Dietz, 1956–68.

OTHER WORKS CONSULTED

AFANAS'EV, O.A., 'Obsuzhdenie v Institute Istorii AN SSR problemy "Aziatskii sposob proizvodstva"', *Sovetskaia etnografiia*, 1965, No. 6, pp. 122–126.

ANDERSON, PERRY, *Passages from Antiquity to Feudalism*, London, NLB, 1974.

—, *Lineages of the Absolutist State*, London, NLB, 1974.

ANUCHIN, V.A., 'The problem of Synthesis in Geographic Science', in *Voprosy filosofii*, 1964, No. 2, tr. in *Soviet Geography*, Vol. V (1964), No. 4, pp. 34–46.

—, 'A Sad Tale about Geography', in *Literaturnaia Gazeta*, 18 Feb. 1965, tr. in *Soviet Geography*, Vol. VI (1965), No. 7, pp. 27–31.

—, 'O sushchnosti geograficheskoi sredy i proiavlenii indeterminizma v sovetskoi geografii', *Voprosy geografii*, 1957, No. 41, pp. 47–64.

—, *Teoreticheskie problemy geografii*, Moscow, Gos. izd. geog. lit., 1960.

ARISTOTLE, *Politica*, tr. Benjamin Jowett in Vol. X of *The Works of Aristotle*, Oxford, Clarendon Press, 1921, reprinted 1946.

ATKINSON, GEOFFROY, *The Extraordinary Voyage in French Literature*, 2 vols., Vol. I, 'Before 1700', N.Y., Burt Franklin, 1965.

BAKUNIN, MICHAEL, Letter to Sergei Nechaev, 2 June 1870, *Encounter*, July 1972, pp. 89–90.

BARON, SAMUEL H., *Plekhanov: The Father of Russian Marxism*, London, Routledge and Kegan Paul, 1963.

BAYLE, PIERRE, *Oeuvres Diverses*, Vol. 3, Hildesheim, Georg Olms, 1966.

BELELIUBSKY, F.B., 'Maoistskaia kontseptsiia vsemirnoi istorii i podlinnaia istoriia narodov Vostoka', *Narody Azii i Afriki*, 1972, No. 5, pp. 61–71.

BENTHAM, JEREMY, *Traités de législation civile et pénale*, ed. Et. Dumont, 3 vols, 2nd edn, Paris, 1920.

BERNIER, FRANÇOIS, *Travels in the Mogul Empire, A.D. 1656–1668*, London, Constable, 1891.

BLACKBURN, R., ed., *Ideology in Social Science*, London, Fontana, 1972.

BODIN, JEAN, *Les six livres de la République* (facsimile of Paris, 1583 edition), Aalen, Scientia, 1961.

—, *Six Books of the Commonwealth*, tr. M.J. Tooley, Oxford, Blackwell, n.d.

BOSERUP, ESTER, *The Conditions of Agricultural Growth*, Chicago, Aldine, 1965.

BOULANGER, NICOLAS ANTOINE, *Oeuvres de Boullanger* (sic), 8 vols., Paris, Jean Servieres and Jean-François Bastien, 1792-1793.

BUCKLE, HENRY THOMAS, *History of Civilisation in England*, Vol. I, 2nd edn, London, Parker, 1858.

BUKHARIN, NIKOLAI, *Historical Materialism*, N.Y., International Publishers, 1925.

CAMPBELL, GEORGE, *Modern India: A Sketch of the System of Government*, London, Murray, 1852.

CARNEIRO, ROBERT L., 'From Autonomous Villages to the State, A Numerical Investigation', in Brian Spooner ed., *Population Growth: Anthropological Implications*, MIT Press, 1972.

CATHERINE THE GREAT, *Documents of Catherine the Great*, ed. W.F. Reddaway, Cambridge U.P., 1931.

CHESNEAUX, JEAN, 'Diskussiia o ranneklassovykh obshchestvakh na stranitsakh zhurnala "La Pensée"', *Voprosy istorii*, No. 9 (Sept. 1967), pp. 192-200.

—, 'Le mode de production asiatique: quelques perspectives de recherche', *La Pensée*, No. 114 (Jan.–Feb. 1964), pp. 33-55.

—, 'Où en est la discussion sur le "mode de production asiatique"?'. *La Pensée*, No. 122 (Aug. 1965), pp. 40-59; No. 129 (Oct. 1966), pp. 33-46; No. 138 (April 1968), pp. 47-55.

Chetvertyi (ob"edinitel'nyi) s"ezd RSDRP: Protokoly, Moscow, Gos. izd. pol. lit., 1969.

CHICHERIN, B.N., *Opyty po istorii russkogo prava*, Moscow, 1858.

CHILDE, V., Gordon, 'The Bronze Age', *Past and Present*, No. 12 (Nov. 1957), pp. 2-15.

—, *Man Makes Himself*, London, Watts, 1948.

—, *What Happened in History*, London, Max Parrish, 1960.

CORDIER, HENRI, *Bibliotheca Sinica*, 2nd edn, Paris, E. Guilmoto, 5 vols., 1904-1924.

CORNFORTH, M., *Dialectical Materialism*, Vol. 2 (Historical Materialism), London, Lawrence and Wishart, 1953.

CUSTINE, Astolphe, Marquis de, *Russia*, abridged edn, London, Longmans, 1855.

DALIN, S. A., [Review of L. Mad'iar, *Ekonomika sel'skogo khoziaistva v Kitae* (Moscow, 1928)], *Izvestiia*, 4 Oct. 1928.

—, *Taipiny* [Sbornik statei], Moscow, 1928.

DANILOVA, L.V., 'Diskussiia po vazhnoi probleme', *Voprosy istorii*, 1965, No. 12, pp. 149–156.

DANILOVA, L.V., *et al.*, eds., *Problemy istorii dokapitalisticheskikh obshchestv*, Kniga I, Moscow, Izd. 'Nauka', 1968.

DHOQUOIS, G., *Pour l'histoire*, Paris, Éditions Anthropos, 1971.

'Diskussiia o sotsial'no-ekonomicheskikh formatsiiakh', *Istorik-Marksist*, Vol. 16 (1930), pp. 104–161.

Diskussiia ob aziatskom sposobe proizvodstva. Po dokladu M. Godesa, Moscow, Gos. sots.-ekon. izd., 1931.

DIVITÇIOGLU, Sencer, 'Essai de modèles économiques à partir du M.P.A.', *Recherches internationales à la lumière du marxisme*, No. 57–58 (Jan.–April 1967), pp. 277–293.

DOSKACH, A.G., *et al.*, 'The Problem of Interaction of Nature and Society and Present-Day Geography', *Voprosy filosofii*, 1965, No. 4, pp. 104–115.

DUBROVSKY, S.M., *K voprosu o sushchnosti 'aziatskogo' sposoba proizvodstva, feodalizma, krepostnichestva i torgovogo kapitala*, Moscow, 1929.

DULOV, A.V., 'Literatura o roli geograficheskoi sredy v istorii obshchestva' *Voprosy istorii*, 1973, No. 8, pp. 142–148.

DUTT, RAJANI PALME, *India Today*, 2nd rev. Indian edition, Bombay, People's Publishing House, 1949.

FLETCHER, G., *Of the Russe Commonwealth*, London, Hakluyt Society, 1856 (First Series, No. XX).

FOX, PAUL, 'Vzgliady Marksa i Engel'sa na aziatskii sposob proizvodstva i ikh istochniki', *Letopisi marksizma*, Vol. III (XIII), 1930, pp. 3–29.

GARUSHIANTS, IU.M., 'Ob aziatskom sposobe proizvodstva', *Voprosy istorii*, 1966, No. 2, pp. 83–100.

GAZGANOV, EM., 'Istoricheskie vzgliady G.V. Plekhanova', *Istorik-Marksist*, Vol. 7, 1928, pp. 69–110.

GERSCHENKRON, A., *Europe in the Russian Mirror*, Four Lectures in Economic History, Cambridge U.P., 1970.

GETZLER, I., *Martov*, Melbourne U.P., 1967.

GLEZERMAN, G. and KURSANOV, G., *Historical Materialism*, Moscow, Progress, 1968.

GOBLOT, JEAN-JACQUES, 'Pour une approche théorique de "faits de civilisation"', *La Pensée*, No. 133, pp. 3–24; No. 134, pp. 3–34; No. 136, pp. 65–88 (1967).

GODELIER, M., 'La notion de "mode de production asiatique" et les schémas marxistes d'évolution des sociétés', *Sur le "mode de production asiatique"*, C.E.R.M., Paris, Éditions sociales, 1969, pp. 47–100.

—, *Rationality and Irrationality in Economics*, tr. Brian Pearce, London, NLB, 1972.

—, ed., *Sur les sociétés précapitalistes: textes choisis de Marx, Engels, Lénine*, C.E.R.M., Paris, Éditions sociales, 1970.

GODES, M.S., *Spornye voprosy metodologii istorii. Diskussiia ob obshchestvennykh formatsiiakh*, Kharkov, 1930.

GREKOV, B.D., *Kiev Rus*, tr. E. Sdobnikov, Moscow, Foreign Languages Publishing House, 1959.

GUY, BASIL, 'The French image of China before and after Voltaire', *Studies on Voltaire and the Eighteenth Century*, Vol. 21 (1963), pp. 1–468.

HALDE, JEAN-BAPTISTE DU, *History of China*, London, Watts, 1841.

HAXTHAUSEN, VON, *The Russian Empire, its People, Institutions and Resources*, 2 vols., London, Chapman Hall, 1856, reprinted Frank Cass, 1968.

HEGEL, GEORG WILHELM FRIEDRICH, *The Philosophy of History*, tr. J. Sibree, London, Bell, 1905.

—, *The Philosophy of Right*, tr. T.M. Knox, Oxford, Clarendon Press, 1942.

—, *Science of Logic*, tr. W.H. Johnston and L.G. Struthers, 2 vols., London, Allen and Unwin, 1929.

HELVÉTIUS, CLAUDE ADRIEN, *Oeuvres*, Paris, Briand, 1794.

—, *A treatise on man*, 2 vols., tr. W. Hooper, N.Y., Franklin, 1969.

HERBERSTEIN, FREIHERR SIGMUND VON, [Sigismund von Herberstein], *Notes Upon Russia*, 2 vols., Hakluyt Society, 1851, (First Series, No. X), reprinted Burt Franklin, N.Y., n.d.

HERDER, JOHANN GOTTFRIED VON, *Outlines of a Philosophy of the History of Man*, tr. by T. Churchill, London, 1800, reprinted N.Y., Bergman, n.d.

HINDESS, BARRY and HIRST, PAUL Q., *Pre-Capitalist Modes of Production*, London, Routledge & Kegan Paul, 1975.

History of the Communist Party of the Soviet Union, Short Course, London, Cobbett, 1943.

ILICHEV, L.F., 'L.F. Ilichev's Remarks about a Unified Geography', tr. in *Soviet Geography*, Vol. V, 1964, No. 4, pp. 32–33.

JONES, RICHARD, *Essay on the Distribution of Wealth*, London, 1831, reprinted N.Y., Kelley and Millman, 1956.

JONES, RICHARD, *Political Economy*, ed. W. Whewell, London, Murray, 1859.

KACHANOVSKY, IU.V., *Rabovladenie, feodalizm ili aziatskii sposob proizvodstva?*, Moscow, Izd. 'Nauka', 1971.

KALESNIK, S.V., 'Some Results of the New Discussion about a "Unified" Geography', *Izvestiia Vsesoiuznogo Geograficheskogo Obshchestva*, 1965, No. 3, tr. in *Soviet Geography*, Vol. VI (1965), No. 7, pp. 11–26.

KANTOROVICH, A.IA., 'Sistema obshchestvennykh otnoshenii v Kitae dokapitalisticheskoi epokhi', *Novyi Vostok*, No. 15 (1926), pp. 67–93.

KAUTSKY, KARL, *Der Weg zur Macht*, Berlin, Buchhandlung Vorwärts, 1909.

KEEP, JOHN, 'The Current Scene in Soviet Historiography', *Survey*, Winter, 1973, pp. 3–26.

—, 'The Rehabilitation of M.N. Pokrovsky', in Alexander and Janet Rabinowitch *et al.* ed., *Revolution and Politics in Russia*, Bloomington, Indiana U.P., 1972.

KIM, G.F., NIKIFOROV, V.N., *et al.*, ed, *Obshchee i osobennoe v istoricheskom razvitii stran Vostoka*, Moscow, Izd. 'Nauka', 1966.

KIZILOV, IU.A., 'Predposylki perekhoda vostochnogo slavianstva k feodalizmu', *Voprosy istorii*, 1969, No. 3, pp. 90–104.

KLIUCHEVSKY, V.O., *A History of Russia*, 5 vols., N.Y. Russell & Russell, 1960.

KOEBNER, RICHARD, 'Despot and Despotism: Vicissitudes of a Political Term', *Journal of the Warburg and Courtauld Institutes*, Vol. XIV (1951), pp. 275–302.

KOROSTOVTSEV, M.A., 'On the Concept "The Ancient East",' in *Vestnik drevnei istorii*, 1970, No. 1, tr. in *Soviet Studies in History*, Vol. IX, No. 2 (Fall, 1970), pp. 107–132.

KOVALEVSKY, M.M., *Obshchinnoe zemlevladenie, prichiny, khod i posledstviia ego razlozheniia*, Frankfurt, Campus Verslag, 1977. (Reprint).

KOZLOVA, M.G., SEDOV, L.A., and TIURIN, V.A., 'Tipy ranneklassovykh gosudarstv v Iugo-Vostochnoi Azii', *Problemy istorii dokapitalisticheskikh obshchestv*, Kniga 1, ed. L.V. Danilova *et al.*, Moscow, Izd. 'Nauka', 1968.

KRADER, LAWRENCE, *The Asiatic Mode of Production*, Assen, Van Gorcum, 1975.

—, *The Ethnological Notebooks of Karl Marx*, Assen, Van Gorcum, 1972.

KRAPIVENSKY, S.E., 'Osobaia formatsiia ili perekhodnoe sostoianie obshchestva?', *Narody Azii i Afriki*, 1966, No. 2, pp. 87–90.

KUUSINEN, O.W., ed., *Fundamentals of Marxism-Leninism*, Moscow, Foreign Languages Publishing House, 1961.

LABRIOLA, ANTONIO, *Essays on the Materialist Conception of History*, tr. Charles Kerr, reprinted N.Y., Monthly Review Press, 1966.

LACH, DONALD, *Asia in the Making of Europe*, Vol. I (The century of discovery), University of Chicago Press, 1965.

LE CLERC, NICOLAS-GABRIEL, *Yu le Grand et Confucius*, 4 vols., Soissons, 1769.

LENIN, V.I., *Collected Works*, London, Lawrence and Wishart, 1960, (Vol. 40 appeared in 1968).

—, *Selected Works*, 2 vols., Moscow, Foreign Languages Publishing House, 1950–52.

LETICHE, JOHN M., ed. *A History of Russian Economic Thought: Ninth through Eighteenth Centuries*, University of California Press, 1964.

LICHTHEIM, GEORGE, *The Concept of Ideology*, N.Y., Random House, 1967.

LINGUET, SIMON NICOLAS, *Théorie des lois civiles, ou Principes fondamentaux de la société*, 2 vols., London, 1767.

LOBANOV-ROSTOVSKY, A., *Russia and Asia*, Michigan, Wahr, 1965.

LOMINADZE, B., 'Novyi etap kitaiskoi revoliutsii i zadachi kitaiskikh kommunistov', *Bol'shevik*, 1928, No. 3–4, pp. 86–107.

LOUIS XIV, *Mémoires... pour l'instruction du Dauphin*, ed. C. Dreyss, 2 vols., Paris, 1860.

LOWE, DONALD M., *The Function of 'China' in Marx, Lenin, and Mao*, University of California Press, 1966.

LUCAS, ERHARD, 'Marx's Studien zur Frühgeschichte und Ethnologie 1880–82', *Saeculum*, Vol. 15 (1964), pp. 327–343.

LUKÁCS, GEORG, 'Entretien avec Georg Lukács', *L'Homme et la Société*, No. 20 (April–June 1971), pp. 3–12.

—, *History and Class Consciousness*, tr. R. Livingstone, London, Merlin, 1968.

LUXEMBURG, ROSA, 'Organisationsfragen der russischen Sozialdemokratie', *Die Neue Zeit*, Jg. XXII, ii (1904), pp. 484–492.

McFARLANE, B. and COOPER, S., 'The Asiatic Mode of Production – An Economic Phoenix?', *The Australian Quarterly*, Vol. XXXVIII, No. 3 (Sept. 1966), pp. 27–43

MACHIAVELLI, NICCOLÒ, *The Prince*, tr. George Bull, Harmondsworth, Penguin, 1971.

MACKINNON, W.A., *History of Civilisation and Public Opinion*, 2 vols., 3rd edn., London, Henry Colburn, 1849.

MAD'IAR, L., 'Dve agrarnye programmy v kitaiskoi revoliutsii', *Problemy Kitaia*, 1930, No. 4–5, pp. 60–83.

—, *Ekonomika sel'skogo khoziaistva Kitaia*, Moscow, Gos. Izd., 1928.

—, 'Ob izuchenii agrarnogo voprosa v Kitae', *Revoliutsionnyi Vostok*, 1928, No. 4–5, pp. 77–99.

—, *Ocherki po ekonomike Kitaia*, Moscow, Izd. Kom. Akad., 1930.

MANDEL, E., *The Formation of the Economic Thought of Karl Marx*, London, NLB, 1971.

MARSILIUS OF PADUA, *Defensor Pacis*, ed. C.W. Previté-Orton, Cambridge U.P., 1928.

MASPERO, G., *The Dawn of Civilization*, 4th edn, London, Society for Promoting Christian Knowledge, 1901.

MATLEY, IAN M., 'The Marxist Approach to the Geographical Environment', *Annals of the Association of American Geographers*, Vol. 56 (1966), pp. 97–111.

MAVERICK, LEWIS A., *China: A model for Europe*, San Antonio, Texas, P. Anderson, 1946. (Two vols. bound together, Vol. Two comprising a translation of François Quesnay's *Le despotisme de la Chine*.)

MECHNIKOV, LEV ILICH [LÉON METCHNIKOFF], *La civilisation et les grands fleuves historiques* (avec une préface de Élisée Reclus) Paris, Hachette, 1889.

MELOTTI, UMBERTO, 'Marx e il Terzo Mondo', *Il Terzo Mondo*, Vol. 3, No. 11 (1970–1971), pp. 7–32.

—, *Marx e il Terzo Mondo. Per una schema multilineare della concezione marxiana delle sviluppo storico*, Milan, Centro Studi Terzo Mondo, 1971.

MILIUKOV, P., *Ocherki po istorii russkoi kul'tury*, 5th edn., 3 vols., St. Petersburg, Mir Bozhii, 1902–1904.

MILL, JAMES, *The History of British India*, 9 vols., ed. and with commentaries by H.H. Wilson, London, J. Madden, 1840–1848.

MILL, JOHN STUART, 'Mr Maine on Village Communities', *Fortnightly Review*, Vol. IX, New Series (May 1871), pp. 543–556.

—, *Principles of Political Economy*, ed. Ashley, London, Longmans, 1873.

MIRABEAU, *Essai sur le despotisme*, 2nd edn, London, 1776.

MONTESQUIEU, CHARLES LOUIS DE SECONDAT, BARON DE LA BRÈDE ET DE, *The Spirit of Laws*, tr. Thomas Nugent, 2 vols., London, Colonial Press, 1900.

MOORE, BARRINGTON, *Social Origins of Dictatorship and Democracy*, London, A. Lane, Penguin Press, 1967.

MORGAN, LEWIS H., *Ancient Society*, Bellknap Press of Harvard U.P., 1964.

NEEDHAM, JOSEPH, [Review of K.A. Wittfogel's *Oriental Despotism*], *Science and Society*, Vol. 23 (1959), pp. 58–65.

NETTING, ROBERT McC., 'Sacred Power and Centralization: Aspects of Political Adaptation in Africa', in Brian Spooner ed., *Population Growth: Anthropological Implications*, MIT Press, 1972.

NIKIFOROV, V.N., 'Diskussiia sovetskikh istorikov ob obshchestvenno-ekonomicheskom stroe Kitaia (1925–1931)', *Narody Azii i Afriki*, 1965, No. 5, pp. 75–91.

—, 'K voprosu ob istoricheskoi osnove literaturnoi periodizatsii', *Narody Azii i Afriki*, 1964, No. 3, pp. 86–90.

—, *Sovestskie istoriki o problemakh Kitaia*, Moscow, Izd. 'Nauka', 1970.

—, 'Zakliuchitel'noe slovo po dokladu', *Obshchee i osobennoe v istoricheskom razvitii stran Vostoka*, Moscow, Izd. 'Nauka', 1966, tr. in *Recherches internationales à la lumière du marxisme*, No. 57–58 (Jan.–April 1967), pp. 240–250.

OCCAM, WILLIAM OF, *Dialogus de imperio et pontificia potestate* (facsimile of the 1495–96 edition of Occam's works), London, Gregg Press, 1962.

PALGRAVE, SIR FRANCIS, *The Rise and Progress of the English Commonwealth*, The Anglo-Saxon Period, Part I, new edn, Cambridge U.P., 1921.

PANNEKOEK, A., *Weltrevolution und kommunistische Taktik*, in *Pannekoek et les conseils ouvriers*, ed. S. Bricianer, Paris, EDI, 1969, pp. 163–201.

PARAIN, CHARLES, 'Protohistoire méditerranéenne et mode de production asiatique', *La Pensée*, No. 127 (May–June 1966), pp. 24–43.

PARVUS, *Rossiia i revoliutsiia*, St. Petersburg, izd. N. Glagoleva, 1906.

PAVLOV-SIL'VANSKY, N.P., *Feodalizm v drevnei Rusi*, St. Petersburg, Brockhaus-Efron', 1907.

PEČIRKA, J., 'Discussions soviétiques', *Recherches internationales à la lumière du marxisme*, No. 57–58 (Jan.–April 1967), pp. 59–78.

Piatnadtsatyi s"ezd VKP/b: Protokoly, 2 vols., Moscow, Gos. izd. pol. lit., 1961–62.

PLEKHANOV, G.V., *Essays in Historical Materialism*, N.Y., International Publishers, 1940.

—, *Essays in the History of Materialism*, tr. Ralph Fox, reprinted N.Y., H. Fertig, 1967.

—, *Fundamental Problems of Marxism*, tr. J. Katzer, Moscow, Foreign Languages Publishing House, n.d.

—, *In Defence of Materialism. The Development of the Monist View of History*, tr. Andrew Rothstein, London, Lawrence and Wishart, 1947.

—, *The Materialist Conception of History* (review of A. Labriola) tr. A. Fineberg, Moscow, Foreign Languages Publishing House, 1946.

—, 'O knige L.I. Mechnikova', *Sochineniia*, Vol. VII, pp. 15–28.

—, 'Rabochii klass i sotsial-demokraticheskaia intelligentsiia', *Iskra*, No. 70 (25 July 1904), No. 71 (1 Aug. 1904).

—, *Selected Philosophical Works*, one vol. to date, London, Lawrence and Wishart, 1961.

—, *Sochineniia*, 2nd edn., 24 vols., ed. D. Riazanov, Moscow, 1923–1927.

POCOCK, J.G.A., *The Ancient Constitution and the Feudal Law*, Cambridge U.P., 1957.

POKROVSKY, M.N., *A Brief History of Russia*, 10th edn, 2 vols., tr. D.S. Mirsky, London, Martin Lawrence, 1933.

—, 'G.V. Plekhanov kak istorik Rossii', *Pod znamenem marksizma*, 1923, No. 6–7, pp. 5–18.

PRIGOZHIN, A.G., *Karl Marks i problemy istorii dokapitalisticheskikh formatsii*, Moscow, 1934.

—, *Karl Marks i problemy sotsio-ekonomicheskikh formatsii*, Moscow, 1933.

—, 'O nekotorykh svoeobraziiakh russkogo feodalizma', *Izvestiia Gosudarstvennoi Akademii Istorii Material'noi Kultury*, No. 72 (1934).

—, 'Problema obshchestvennykh formatsii', *Pod znamenem marksizma*, 1930, No. 7–8, pp. 159–193.

RABINOWITCH, ALEXANDER and JANET, *et al.*, ed., *Revolution and Politics in Russia*, Bloomington, Indiana U.P., 1972.

RAFFLES, SIR THOMAS STAMFORD, *The History of Java*, 2 vols., London, Black, Parbury and Allen, 1817.

RATZEL, FRIEDRICH, *Anthropo-Geographie; oder Grundzüge der Aufwendung der Erdkunde auf die Geschichte*, Stuttgart, 1882.

RIAZANOV, DAVID, 'Karl Marx et la Chine', *La Correspondance Internationale* (Vienna), Yr. 5, No. 68 (8 July 1925), pp. 563–564.

RIVIÈRE, LE MERCIER DE LA, *L'Ordre naturel et essentiel des sociétés politiques*, London and Paris, 1767, facsimile ed., Paris, P. Geuthner, 1910.

ROSE, E., 'China as a Symbol of Reaction in Germany 1830–1880', *Comparative Literature*, Vol. III (1951–1952), pp. 57–76.

RUBEL, MAXIMILIEN, *Bibliographie des Oeuvres de Karl Marx*, Paris, Marcel Rivière, 1956; Supplément, 1960.

—, 'Les cahiers de lecture de Karl Marx: 1840–1853', *International Review of Social History*, New Series, 2, 1957, pp. 392–420.

—, ed., *Marx/Engels: Die russische Kommune*, Munich, Carl Hanser Verlag, 1972.

RYBAKOV, B.A., *Remeslo drevnei Rusi*, Moscow, 1948.

RZHIGA, V.F., *I.S. Peresvetov, publitsist XVI veka*, 2 vols., Moscow, 1908.

SACHS, IGNACY, 'Une nouvelle phase de la discussion sur les formations', *Recherches internationales à la lumière du marxisme*, No. 57–58 (Jan.–April 1967), pp. 294–307.

SAHLINS, MARSHALL, *Stone Age Economics*, Chicago, Aldine-Atherton, 1972.

SAKHAROV, A.M., *Goroda Severo-Vostochnoi Rusi XIV-XV Vekov*, Moscow, 1959.

—, 'Problema obrazovaniia russkogo tsentralizovannogo gosudarstva v sovetskoi istoriografii', *Voprosy istorii*, 1961, No. 9, pp. 70–88.

SAUSHKIN, IU.G., 'Concerning a Certain Controversy', *Vestnik Moskovskogo Universiteta, Seriia geografii*, No. 6 (1965), tr. in *Soviet Geography*, Vol. VII (1966), No. 2, pp. 9–14.

—, 'The Interaction of Nature and Society', in *Geografiia v shkole*, 1964, No. 4, tr. in *Soviet Geography*, Vol. V (1964), No. 10, pp. 34–45.

—, 'Methodological Problems of Soviet Geography as Interpreted by some Foreign Geographers', *Vestnik Moskovskogo Universiteta*, 1964, No. 4, tr. in *Soviet Geography*, Vol. V (1964), No. 8, pp. 50–65.

SCHMIDT, ALFRED, *Der Begriff der Natur in der Lehre von Marx*, Frankfurt a.M., Europäische Verlagsanstalt, 1962.

SEDOV, L.A., 'La société angkorienne et le problème du mode de production asiatique', *La Pensée*, No. 138 (March–April 1968), pp. 71–84.

SELLNOW, I., 'Die Grundprinzipien einer Periodisierung der Urgeschichte', *Völkerforschung*, Berlin, Akademie-Verlag, 1954, pp. 138–173.

SEMENOV, IU.I., 'Problema sotsial'no-ekonomicheskogo stroia drevnego Vostoka', *Narody Azii i Afriki*, 1965, No. 4, pp. 69–89.

SEMPLE, ELLEN CHURCHILL, *Influences of Geographic Environment: On the Basis of Ratzel's System of Anthropo-Geography*, N.Y., Henry Holt, 1911.

Short History of the C.P.S.U., Moscow, Foreign Languages Publishing House, 1939.

SHTEPPA, K.F., *Russian Historians and the Soviet State*, New Brunswick, Rutgers U.P., 1962.

SMITH, ADAM, *Lectures on Justice, Policy, Revenue and Arms*, ed. Edwin Cannan, first published 1896, reprinted N.Y., Kelley & Millman, 1956.

—, *The Wealth of Nations*, London, Routledge, 1898.

SOFRI, GIANNI, *Il modo di produzione asiatico. Storia di una controversia marxista*, Turin, Einaudi, 1969.

SOLOV'EV, S.M., *Istoriia Rossii s drevneishikh vremen*, 15 vols., Moscow, Izd. sots.-ekon. lit., 1960–1966.

—, *Nachalo russkoi zemli*, Sb. gos. znanii, T. IV, St. Petersburg, 1877.

STELLING-MICHAUD, SVEN, 'Le mythe du despotisme oriental', *Schweizer Beiträge zur allgemeinen Geschichte*, 1960–1961, pp. 328–346.

STEPNIAK (S.M. KRAVCHINSKY), *Russia under the Tzars*, tr. W. Westall, first published 1885, new edn, London, Downey, n.d.

STOKES, ERIC, *The English Utilitarians and India*, Oxford U.P., 1959.

STRUVE, V. (VASSILI STROUVÉ), 'Comment Marx définissait les premières sociétés de classes' (first published in *Sovetskaia etnografiia*, 1940, No. 3), *Recherches internationales à la lumière du marxisme*, No. 57–58 (Jan.–April 1967), pp. 79–97.

—, 'Le concept de M.P.A.: légitimité et limites' (first published in *Narody Azii i Afriki*, 1965 No. 1), *Recherches internationales à la lumière du marxisme*, No. 57–58 (Jan.–April 1967), pp. 232–239.

Sur le 'mode de production asiatique', Preface by Roger Garaudy, C.E.R.M., Paris, Éditions sociales, 1969.

SURET-CANALE, JEAN, *Afrique noire occidentale et centrale, géographie, civilisation, histoire*, Paris, Éditions sociales, 1958, 2nd edn., 1961.

—, 'Problèmes théoriques de l'étude des premières sociétés de classes', *Recherches internationales à la lumière du marxisme*, No 57–58 (Jan.–April 1967), pp. 5–16.

TAVERNIER, JEAN BAPTISTE, (BARON D'AUBONNE), *Travels in India*, tr. from original edition of 1676 (Les six voyages), 2 vols., London, Macmillan, 1889.

TER-AKOPIAN, N.B., 'Aziatskii sposob proizvodstva', *Bol'shaia Sovetskaia Entsiklopediia*, 3rd edn.

—, 'Razvitie vzgliadov Marksa i Engel'sa na aziatskii sposob proizvodstva i zemledel'cheskuiu obshchinu', *Narody Azii i Afriki*, 1965, No. 2, pp. 74–88; No. 3, pp. 70–87.

TERRAY, EMMANUEL, *Marxism and 'Primitive Societies'*, tr. M. Klopper. N.Y., Monthly Review Press, 1972.

THORNER, DANIEL, 'Marx on India', *Contributions to Indian Sociology*, Dec. 1966, pp. 33–66.

TIKHOMIROV, M.N., *Drevnerusskie goroda*, Moscow, Gos. izd. pol. lit., 1956.

TÖKEI, F., *Sur le mode de production asiatique*, Budapest, Akadémiai Kiadó, 1966.

TROTSKY, LEON (N. TROTSKY), *Do deviatogo ianvaria*, Geneva, R.S.D.L.P., 1905.

TROTSKY, LEON, *The History of the Russian Revolution*, tr. Max Eastman, 3 vols., London, Gollancz, 1932–1933.

—, *Karl Marx*, 3rd edn, London, Cassell, 1946.

—, *1905*, tr. Anya Bostok, London, Allen Lane, 1972.

—, *The Permanent Revolution and Results and Prospects*, N.Y., Pioneer Publishers, 1965.

— (LEON TROTSKI), *Stalin*, tr. and ed. Charles Malamuth, London, Hollis and Carter, 1947.

VARGA, E., 'Ekonomicheskie problemy revoliutsii v Kitae', *Planovoe Khoziaistvo*, 1925, No. 12, pp. 165–183.

—, 'Osnovnye problemy kitaiskoi revoliutsii', *Bol'shevik*, 1928, No. 8, pp. 17–40.

— (Y. VARGA), *Politico-Economic Problems of Capitalism*, Moscow, Progress, 1968.

—, 'Les problèmes fondamentaux de la révolution chinoise', *La Correspondance Internationale*, Yr. 8 (1928), Nos. 56, 60, 61, 62, 63.

VASIL'EV, L.S., 'Sotsial'naia struktura i dinamika drevnekitaiskogo obshchestva', in L.V. Danilova (*et al.*), ed., *Problemy istorii dokapitalisticheskikh obshchestv*, pp. 455–515.

—, 'Obshchee i osobennoe v istoricheskom razvitii stran Vostoka', *Narody Azii i Afriki*, 1965, No. 6, pp. 96–100.

VASIL'EV, L.S. and STUCHEVSKY, I.A., 'Tri modeli vozniknoveniia i evoliutsii dokapitalisticheskikh obschestv', *Voprosy istorii*, 1966, No. 5, pp. 77–90.

VENTURI, FRANCO, 'Oriental Despotism', *Journal of the History of Ideas*, Vol. 24 (Jan.–March 1963), pp. 133–142.

VERNADSKY, GEORGE, *A History of Russia*, 3rd. rev. edn, New Haven, Yale U.P., 1951.

VOGEL, ULRICH, *Zur Theorie der chinesischen Revolution: Die asiatische Produktionsweise und ihre Zersetzung durch den Imperialismus*, Frankfurt a.M., Athenäum, 1973.

VOLTAIRE, *The Philosophy of History*, London, Vision Press, 1965.

WALICKI, ANDRZEJ, *The Controversy over Capitalism*, Oxford, Clarendon Press, 1969.

WALLACE, SIR DONALD MACKENZIE, *Russia*, 2 vols., London, Cassell., 1905.

WEBER, MAX, *Economy and Society*, 3 vols., N.Y., Bedminster Press, 1968.

WILKS, MARK, *Historical Sketches of the South of India*, 3 vols., London, Longman, 1810–1817.

WITTFOGEL, K.A., *Das erwachende China*, Vienna, Agis-Verlag, 1926.

—, 'Geopolitika, geograficheskii materializm i marksizm', *Pod znamenem marksizma*, 1929, No. 2–3 (Feb.–March), pp. 16–42; No. 6 (June), pp. 1–29, No. 7–8 (July–Aug.), pp. 1–28.

—, 'The Marxist View of Russian Society and Revolution', *World Politics*, Vol. 12 (1959–1960), pp. 487–508.

—, Die natürlichen Ursachen der Wirtschaftsgeschichte', *Archiv für Sozialwissenschaft und Sozialpolitik*, Vol. 67 (1932), Part I, pp. 460–492; Part II, pp. 579–604; Part III, pp. 711–731.

—, *Oriental Despotism*, New Haven, Yale U.P., 1957.

—, 'Results and Problems of the Study of Oriental Despotism', *The Journal of Asian Studies*, Vol. XXVIII, No. 2 (Feb. 1969), pp. 357–365.

ZHUKOV, E.M., 'O periodizatsii vsemirnoi istorii', *Voprosy istorii*, 1960, No. 8, pp. 22–33.

INDEX

Kantorovich, A.Ia., 82, 91
Katzer, J., 73n, 89n, 118n, 167n
Kautsky, Karl, 62n, 125, 130, 141n, 142n, 187, 190n
Keep, John L. H., 152n, 154n
Keltuiala, V.A., 166n
Kerr, Charles, 120
Khrushchev, Nikita S., 133
Kim, G.F., 135n, 192n, 193n, 195n, 213n, 223n
Kireevsky, Ivan, 157
Kizilov, Iu.A., 136n
Kliuchevsky, V.O., 146, 148–150, 159, 164n, 171, 181
Klopper, M., 216n
Knox, T.M., 42n, 122n
Kobishchanov, Iu.M., 192n
Koebner, Richard, 6n
Kokin, M.D., 90n, 93n, 94, 95, 98
Kolokol, 182
Kommunist, 92n
Kommunisticheskii Internatsional, 84n
Korostovtsev, M.A., 109n, 123n, 134n
Kovalevsky, Maksim M., 65, 78n, 79, 80n, 87, 89, 151n, 230
Kozlova, M.G., 214n
Krader, Lawrence, 45n, 66n
Krapivensky, S.E., 193n
Krasnaia Nov', 186n
Kravchinsky, Sergei M., 63n
Kuo Mo-jo, 224
Kurbsky, Andrei Mikhailovich, Prince, 170
Kursanov, G., 106n, 135n
Kuusinen, Otto W., 106n, 128n, 192

Labriola, Antonio, 120, 121n
Lach, D., 9n
Lafargue, Laura, 142n
Lafargue, Paul, 142n
Lenin, Vladimir I., 71n, 75, 83, 85, 87n, 89, 91, 92, 106n, 116, 129n, 175–177, 188n, 191, 219
Leske, C.W., 69n
Letiche, John M., 169n
Letopisi marksizma, 94n
Levada, Iu.A., 209n, 212n
Lévi-Strauss, Claude, 216
Lichtheim, George, 64n
Linguet, Simon Nicolas, 22, 23, 42n
Literaturnaia Gazeta, 130n, 134
Livingstone, R., 215n
Livshin, Ia.I., 152n
Lobanov-Rostovsky, A., 147n
Lomakin, A.I., 88n, 90n, 91, 97, 209
Lominadze, V.V., 84, 85
Longuet, Jenny, 141n
Louis XIV, 10, 12, 37
Lowe, Donald M., 46–49
Lucas, Erhard, 66n
Lukács, Georg, 76n, 125, 130, 215n

Machiavelli, Niccolò, 7, 11
Mackinnon, W.A., 42n
Mad'iar, L., see Magyar, Lajos I.
Magyar, Lajos I., 84n, 86–90, 93–95, 97, 101, 195, 209
Maine, Sir Henry Sumner, 66, 69n
Malamuth, Charles, 182n
Malthus, T.R., 31, 37
Mandel, Ernest, 158n, 197n
Marsilius of Padua, 6
Martov, Iu.O., 175, 178
Martynov, A., 175–177
Marx-Aveling, Eleanor, 127n
Marxism Today, 213n
Maslov, P.P., 176
Maspero, G., 122
Matley, Ian M., 129n, 131n
Maurer, Georg Ludwig von, 73n
Maverick, Lewis A., 21n
Mazarin, Jules, 12, 37
McFarlane, B., 219n
Mechnikov, Lev Il'ich, 60, 61, 118, 121–123, 199
Melotti, Umberto, 157, 227n
Mercier de la Rivière, P.P.F.J.H., Le, 20
Mif, P.A., 85
Mileikovsky, A., 103n
Miliukov, Paul, 150, 151n
Mill, James, 22n, 30–32, 37n, 39
Mill, John Stuart, 33–34, 37, 39
Mirabeau, Honoré Gabriel Riqueti, Comte de, 18n
Mirsky, Dmitri S., 108n, 148n
Montesquieu, Charles Louis de Secondat, baron de la Brède et de, 1, 13–19, 22, 23, 25, 27, 37, 38, 42, 104, 107, 108n, 118, 147
Moore, Barrington, 53
Morgan, Lewis Henry, 72–74, 89, 90, 189, 195n, 215, 216
Morozov, N.V., 132n

Narody Azii i Afriki, 81n, 88n, 102n, 134n, 192n, 193, 195n, 199n, 203n, 212n
Navarrete, Fernandez, 21n, 22n
Nechaev, Sergei G., 67n
Nechkina, M.V., 84n
Needham, Joseph, 17n
Netting, Robert McC., 139
Neue Rheinische Zeitung, Die, 174n
Neue Zeit, 60n
New York Daily Tribune (N.Y.D.T.), 24n, 26n, 34n, 36n, 41, 42n, 43, 44n, 48n, 62n, 64n, 141n, 143n, 145n
Nicolaus, Martin, 49n, 90n
Nikiforov, V.N., 77n, 81n, 86n, 94n, 135n, 192n, 193n, 195n, 199n, 213n, 223n
Nikolai-on, see Danielson, N.F.
Novoe Slovo, 53n, 116, 120n
Novoe Vremia, 90
Novyi Vostok, 82n, 97n